Two Dragon Heads

Two Dragon Heads

Contrasting Development Paths for Beijing and Shanghai

Shahid Yusuf
Kaoru Nabeshima

THE WORLD BANK
Washington, D.C.

© 2010 The International Bank for Reconstruction and Development / The World Bank
1818 H Street NW
Washington DC 20433
Telephone: 202-473-1000
Internet: www.worldbank.org
E-mail: feedback@worldbank.org

1 2 3 4 12 11 10 09

This volume is a product of the staff of the International Bank for Reconstruction and Development / The World Bank. The findings, interpretations, and conclusions expressed in this volume do not necessarily reflect the views of the Executive Directors of The World Bank or the governments they represent.

The World Bank does not guarantee the accuracy of the data included in this work. The boundaries, colors, denominations, and other information shown on any map in this work do not imply any judgement on the part of The World Bank concerning the legal status of any territory or the endorsement or acceptance of such boundaries.

ISBN: 978-0-8213-8048-2
eISBN: 978-0-8213-8128-1
DOI: 10.1596/978-0-8213-8048-2

Library of Congress Cataloging in Publication Data

Yusuf, Shahid, 1949–
   Two dragon heads : contrasting development paths for Beijing and Shanghai / Shahid Yusuf and Kaoru Nabeshima.
       p. cm.
   Includes bibliographical references and index.
   ISBN 978-0-8213-8048-2—ISBN 978-0-8213-8128-1 (electronic)
   1. Economic development—China—Beijing. 2. Economic development—China—Shanghai. 3. Beijing (China)—Economic policy. 4. Shanghai (China)—Economic policy. I. Nabeshima, Kaoru. II. World Bank. III. Title.

   HC428.B4Y87 2009
   338.951'132—dc22

                                                                              2009036023

Cover design by Drew Fasick, Serif Design Group.

Contents

Acknowledgments

This volume is one of a series of publications emerging from a project on East Asia's Prospects cosponsored by the government of Japan. It was written in close collaboration with the Finance and Private Sector Unit of the East Asia and Pacific Regional Office in the World Bank, the Shanghai Municipal Administration of Finance and Taxation, and the Shanghai Academy of Social Sciences. Chunlin Zhang and Tunc Tahsin Uyanik invited us to embark on this study. They and Professor Zuo Xuejin were a source of much needed and most welcome encouragement, support, and guidance throughout the gestation of this book. We owe special thanks to Professor Zuo and to Liu Hanyong for their warm hospitality during our visits to Shanghai and for enabling us to gather a wealth of first-hand information. Suggestions from Mark Dutz and Itzak Goldberg at the inception of the study helped us in defining the scope.

The early draft benefitted greatly from the many suggestions and comments we received from participants of two seminars hosted by the Shanghai Academy of Social Sciences. In particular we would like to thank Liu Hanyong and Zhang Hailin (Shanghai Municipal Administration of Finance & Taxation); Tu Qiyu, Quan Heng, and Wang Hongxia (Shanghai Academy of Social Sciences); Chen Shoumian and Tao Jinlong (Shanghai IC R&D Center); Zeng Gang (East China Normal University); Zhang Naigen (Fudan University); Hua Yuda (Shanghai Ventures Co., Ltd.); Wang Pingao (Shanghai Venture Capital Corporation); Yu Ningni (Shanghai Pharma Engine Co., Ltd.); Ji Long (Shanghai Zhangjiang Functional District Administration Committee); Jui Shang-Ling (SAP Labs China); Hu Ping (MicroPort Medical [Shanghai] Co., Ltd.); Deng Wei (Shanghai Univ. of Finance & Economics Science Park); and Shen Bing and Yu Mingwei (J.Z.M.C. Data Technologies Co., Ltd.). Additional and most welcome feedback was provided by Professor Xue Lan at Tsinghua University and the participants of the seminar that he hosted.

When the study was initiated, both authors were a part of the Development Economics Research Group of the World Bank. During its later stages, we moved to the World Bank Institute. We thank Martin Ravallion and Raj Nallari for giving us the time and the freedom to write unencumbered by other responsibilities. We thank Lopamudra Chakraborti and Xiaoqing Yu for their excellent research support.

Paulina Sintim-Aboagye and Rory Birmingham together did a fine job of producing the manuscript, for which we are immensely grateful. Patricia Katayama, Cindy A. Fisher, and Andrés Meneses at the World Bank Office of the Publisher shepherded the publication process with their customary efficiency, and the editors at Publications Professionals sharpened and polished the manuscript once again. They made the process of transforming a manuscript into a book as painless as it can ever be—almost fun.

About the Authors

Shahid Yusuf is economic adviser in the World Bank Institute and currently manages a major project on East Asia's prospects. He was the director for *World Development Report 1999/2000: Entering the 21st Century* and has held positions in the Bank's regional and research departments. He received his BA in economics from Cambridge University and his PhD in economics from Harvard University.

He has written extensively on development issues, with a special focus on East Asia. His most recent publications include *Postindustrial East Asian Cities*, coauthored with Kaoru Nabeshima (2006); *Dancing with Giants*, coedited with L. Alan Winters (2007); *How Universities Promote Economic Growth*, coedited with Kaoru Nabeshima (2007); *China Urbanizes*, coedited with Tony Saich (2008); *Growing Industrial Clusters in Asia*, coedited with Kaoru Nabeshima and Shoichi Yamashita (2008); *Accelerating Catch-Up: Tertiary Education and Growth in Africa*, coauthored with William Saint and Kaoru Nabeshima (2008); *Development Economics through the Decades* (2009); and *Tiger Economies Under Threat*, coauthored with Kaoru Nabeshima (2009).

Kaoru Nabeshima is a consultant for the World Bank Institute and previously served as an economist in the Bank's Development Research Group. He received his BA in economics from Ohio Wesleyan University. He holds a PhD in economics from the University of California, Davis.

His recent publications include *Postindustrial East Asian Cities*, coauthored with Shahid Yusuf (2006); *How Universities Promote Economic Growth*, coedited with Shahid Yusuf (2007); *Growing Industrial Clusters in Asia*, coedited with Shahid Yusuf and Shoichi Yamashita (2008); *Accelerating Catch-Up: Tertiary Education and Growth in Africa*, coauthored with Shahid Yusuf and William Saint (2008); and *Tiger Economies Under Threat*, coauthored with Shahid Yusuf (2009).

Abbreviations

ATP	Advanced Technology Program (United States)
CAS	Chinese Academy of Sciences
CAT	computed axial tomography
ERSO	Electronic Research and Service Organization
FDI	foreign direct investment
FIRE	finance, insurance, and real estate
FY	fiscal year
GDP	gross domestic product
GE	General Electric
GVIO	gross value of industrial output
HTIZ	high-tech industrial zone
IBM	International Business Machines
IC	integrated circuit
ICT	information and communication technology
I-O	input-output
IP	intellectual property
IT	information technology
JV	joint venture
LMEs	large and medium-size enterprises
MNC	multinational corporation
MRI	magnetic resonance imaging
NASDAQ	National Association of Securities Dealers Automated Quotations
NSBPIB	National Shanghai Biotechnology and Pharmaceutical Industry Base
OECD	Organisation for Economic Co-operation and Development
PC	personal computer
R&D	research and development
RCA	revealed comparative advantage
SAIC	Shanghai Automotive Industry Corporation

SEMATECH	Semiconductor Manufacturing Technology
SJTU	Shanghai Jiao Tong University
SOE	state-owned enterprise
SSE	Shanghai Stock Exchange
STEM	science, technology, engineering, and mathematics
TFP	total factor productivity
UC	University of California
VAT	value added tax
ZJHP	Zhangjian Hi-Tech Park

1

Introduction and Overview

In broad terms, the sources of economic growth are well understood, but relatively few countries have succeeded in effectively harnessing this knowledge for policy purposes so as to sustain high rates of growth over an extended period of time (Commission on Growth and Development 2008; Yusuf 2009a).[1] Among the ones that have done so, China stands out. Its gross domestic product (GDP) growth rate, which averaged almost 10 percent between 1978 and 2008, is unmatched. Even more remarkable is the performance of China's three leading industrial regions: the Bohai region, the Pearl River Delta,[2] and the Yangtze River (Changjiang) Delta area. These regions have averaged growth rates well above 11 percent since 1985. Shanghai is the urban axis of the Yangtze River Delta's thriving economy;[3] Beijing is the hinge of the Bohai region. Their performance and that of a handful of other urban regions will determine China's economic fortunes and innovativeness in the coming decades.[4]

Can Beijing and Shanghai, China's premier megacities, sustain their momentum over the medium term with the help of investment in infrastructure, real

---

[1]Easterly and others (1993) showed that for most countries periods of fast or slow growth have tended to be temporary, with countries reverting to a global mean rate after a brief period. The correlation in rates of growth between successive periods is close to zero (Durlauf, Johnson, and Temple 2005).

[2]The Pearl River Delta covers an area exceeding 40,000 square kilometers and has a population of 41 million (Yusuf 2007). Two-thirds of the Pearl River Delta's GDP comes from just four cities: Foshan, Dongguan, Guangzhou, and Shenzhen (World Bank 2009b).

[3]See Yao and Ning (2008) and P. Hu (2007) for an analysis of the changing composition and spatial distribution of industry in the Yangtze River Delta.

[4]Urban regions in eastern China accounted for almost three-fourths of the total number of scientists and engineers. Most were located in Beijing, Guangdong, Tianjin, and the Yangtze River Delta area (Simon and Cao 2009).

estate, and industry? Are growth rates in the 8 to 10 percent range feasible given the stage of urban development they are at and the likelihood that foreign trade might be a less reliable source of future growth?[5] Would an accelerated expansion of the services sector be a desirable step, and could the export of services to other countries and to the rest of China partially offset declining growth of commodity trade? Could a systematic effort to deepen innovation capacity significantly improve the growth prospects of China's key urban regions? And if so, what measures and what circumstances are likely to yield growth-promoting outcomes? These are some of the questions that are uppermost in the minds of policy makers in China's megacities and in the central government as they come to terms with the maturing industrial economies of the major cities along the eastern seaboard and the knowledge that cost-efficiency will be only one factor contributing to future competiveness and dynamism.

Each of the two Chinese megacities has followed a distinctive historical trajectory, which is imprinted on its physical and economic characteristics. The cities are also differentiated by geographic location, and Beijing's economy, architecture, and spatial characteristics are influenced by the presence of the vast administrative apparatus of the central government. The cities also share some common features having to do with size, level of per capita GDP, human capital resources, quality of physical infrastructure, and access to financing. Their longer-term economic objectives are also similar in certain respects. Both are intent on maintaining relatively high growth rates, and the municipal authorities in the two cities are of the view that the services sector should contribute a significantly larger share of future growth. Moreover, the local governments are eager to develop local innovation capacity, which would increase the competitiveness and productivity of existing manufacturing and services industries and, in addition, stimulate the emergence of new industries offering products that can profitably command global markets. With that objective in the forefront, municipal governments are emphasizing the role of tertiary institutions and of research and development (R&D).

To realize their longer-run growth objectives, the two cities will need to pursue strategies that fully reflect their acquired comparative advantages and their current industrial mix as well as the opportunities for growth, local employment, and trade offered by the various activities that either city could develop. Although an overlap between the activities conducive to rapid growth is inevitable, the trajectories followed by Beijing and Shanghai to date and the economic composition of

---

[5]World trade grew by 12 percent per year during 2001 to 2007 but by only 7.2 percent per year during 1980 to 2000. A return to earlier rates—or even lower ones—would depress GDP growth in China and East Asia. Furthermore, the rise in oil prices resulting from the difficulties in finding and extracting oil from new deepwater fields and the cost of squeezing it out of shale and tar sands would dampen the growth of global trade or even partially reverse the recent globalization (Rubin 2009).

the two cities also recommend a differentiation of future strategies and, necessarily, a differentiation of objectives. For Shanghai, this book argues for a strategy that puts more stress on manufacturing industries producing complex capital goods and high-tech components.[6] The urge to rely on business and especially financial services as the principal drivers of growth should be tempered, without minimizing the contribution that a more developed financial industry in Shanghai could make to the economic performance of the Shanghai urban region and the Yangtze Delta region as a whole.

For Beijing, which has a large government sector, a burgeoning information technology sector, and a vast research infrastructure, this book proposes a strategy that focuses on the high-tech[7] and creative industries, on supporting business services, and on those activities that constitute the government sector and complement the functioning of government agencies. In one respect, such a strategy is riskier, because high-tech industries, for all their glamour, can fail to deliver growth, profits, and employment while simultaneously absorbing large amounts of financing. Likewise, the creative industries may add questionable amounts of value and generate only a modest number of well-paid jobs. Counterbalancing these risks is the government sector, which is easily the most reliable source of demand and an ideal balance wheel for an economy that is attempting to grow a high-tech sector. The economy of the Washington, D.C., region for example, has demonstrated resilience in the face of shocks because of the steady demand from the federal government, while the presence of federal research entities has stimulated industrial diversification.

Success at innovating appeals to all parties because it promises to introduce new products and services, the profitability of which increases with globalization; it offers ways of enhancing productivity; and it would increase consumer welfare by widening choices and providing better value. Moreover, national market integration and globalization have both increased the returns to innovation. If innovation could be systematized and effectively harnessed by manufacturers and service providers alike, then it would complement and appreciably extend the gains from investment and from progressive improvements in the quality of the urban workforce.

An innovative urban economy is a highly attractive objective, and international experience offers some clues as to how it might be achieved. But the current state of knowledge offers only a number of broad policy directions that collectively can contribute to making an economy innovative. There is no shortcut: ideas

---

[6]Redesigning and engineering these industries so as to reduce carbon coefficients, increase the use of biodegradable material, and facilitate recycling would contribute to the future competitiveness.

[7]See Yusuf and Nabeshima (2006b) for a detailed account of the development of the information technology industry in Beijing.

conducive to innovation of all kinds are likely to flourish in urban environments that have elastic supplies of skilled workers, that furnish certain kinds of institutions and amenities, and that host economic activities with a better than average potential for technological change (Glaeser 2009). There are no tested recipes for creating such an environment; however, research is providing some guidance. The biggest challenge is to embed a culture of innovation that both nourishes existing growth industries and stimulates desirable creative destruction by inducing new activities that could be tomorrow's leading sectors.

To sustain growth close to recent trend rates over the next decade and more, and to make a transition to economies that derive their impetus from innovation, the megacities will need strategies that build on their strengths and, through these strategies, develop tradable activities with the greatest potential for innovation capable of generating attractive returns. Growth that derives from gains in productivity and myriad advances in knowledge impinging on a host of activities is a function not only of urbanization but also of the industrial competitiveness of cities. Sustaining competitiveness is the key, and cities need to rely on policies and resource mobilization to strengthen their comparative advantage for business purposes while managing change so as to preserve the quality of the environment (see Begg 1999; Devas and Rakodi 1993). Identifying the cities' advantages in this regard, examining the innovation potential of candidate activities, and indicating how the cities can realize their potential are the purposes of this volume.

The strengths of the megacities derive from their size and industrial diversity, which are a source of scale and urbanization economies; from the competitiveness of several manufacturing subsectors; from the emergence of business services; from the expanding technological capabilities arising from a deepening pool of human capital, increased R&D, foreign direct investment in high-tech activities, and increased openness to the rest of the world; and from a growing middle class, which is likely to feed a nascent demand for innovation. Manuel Castells (1998: 1–2) aptly ascribes the importance of megacities to their "new, distinctive spatial form," interconnectedness, and internal coherence. "They constitute a complex unit of production, a single labor market, and a specific system of power. . . . Mega cities are . . . the centers for technological innovation, the senders of symbolic messages . . . , the producers of producer services, the collective factories of the new manufacturing, as well as depositories of the remnants of traditional manufacturing. Mega cities are the nerve centers of our interconnected global system."

Beijing and Shanghai are pursuing strategies that are attempting to raise the salience of finance and business services in GDP.[8] Both the Beijing and the Shanghai municipal governments have designated a part of the city as a financial district and have strongly championed the development of the financial sector

---

[8]The Shanghai authorities started giving priority to the services sector with the Eighth Five-Year Plan (1985–90).

and its affiliated services because each sees these steps as necessary to acquiring the status of a global city.[9] In Shanghai, this district is the part of Pudong across from the Bund, and in Beijing, the Financial Street is in the Fuxingmen and Fuchengmen areas. These and other actions have helped to create financial districts in the heart of both cities and have set in motion a pattern of land use that is modeled on the central business districts of other global cities, even though these models might be of questionable relevance in the future. In fact, the concentration of banks and securities and brokerage houses on New York's Wall Street has been thinning for some time,[10] to be replaced by residential accommodations and retail outlets that offer a balanced mix of uses, possibly more appropriate for a modern city. Undoubtedly services tend to agglomerate more than industry, but with the advances in information technology, the degree of urban proximity that gave rise to a Wall Street, that carved out central business districts, that entrenched a form of commuting, and that led to a particular form of land use might be well worth reconsidering. As later chapters will discuss, privileging the financial sector could be an expensive choice for a megacity over the longer term.

The two Chinese megacities are also putting their bets on a number of the currently most favored high-tech activities viewed as having the greatest potential for innovation. These activities are the life sciences, advanced materials, non–fossil energy sources, and nanotech-based activities. In addition, Shanghai is actively pursuing the synergies between transport, finance, and manufacturing that a multimodal hub can generate.

This study maintains, however, that a high-growth strategy that places technology upgrading and innovation at the forefront might warrant a different approach from the one currently adopted by either city. This thinking is based on the experience of global cities such as London and New York and the empirical research on industrial performance and on innovation in industrial economies. This research has yielded four significant findings. First, monosectoral, service-based economies grow slowly because they benefit less from increases in productivity and from innovation within the sector. Second, manufacturing industries producing complex capital goods, electronic equipment, and sophisticated

---

[9]The plan to make Shanghai a financial hub is not new. As early as 1991, Deng Xiaoping wanted Shanghai to develop its financial sector so as to stimulate the growth of the Yangtze River Delta. In terms of official policy, the State Council promulgated the Proposals for Promoting Modern Services and Advanced Manufacturing Industries and Building International Financial and Shipping Centers in Shanghai on April 29, 2009. Shanghai leads other cities in financial development. The value added of the financial industry in 2008 was Y 144.3 billion, a 15 percent increase from 2007. Shanghai also has the largest number of financial institutions: 124 banks, 291 insurance companies, and 94 security companies (Lan 2009).

[10]Financial entities have forsaken the prestige of a Wall Street address for less pricey accommodation elsewhere in Manhattan or across the river in New Jersey.

components are more R&D intensive, generate many more innovations, are more export oriented, have a solid track record of rising productivity, and—having achieved competitiveness—are in a better position to sustain it because the entry barriers to these industries tend to be higher. By giving rise to dense backward and forward links, these industries can serve as the nuclei of urban clusters and maximize employment generation. Third, industrial cities create many more jobs for a middle class and tend to have a more equal distribution of income than do cities that are dominated by services. Fourth, and finally, cities with a world-class tertiary education and research infrastructure that is linked to industry are more innovative and are better able to reinvent their economies (Glaeser 2005a, 2009).

Strategies for Beijing and Shanghai

These findings and others motivate four broad strategic directions, which will be discussed by drawing on international experience and elaborated with reference to each of the two cities:

• Both cities—but particularly Shanghai—should aim for a balanced economic structure with manufacturing activities continuing to account for a significant share of GDP. The growth of business services will be important for the performance of both cities, although more so in the case of Beijing, where the share of services is already large and is growing. Shanghai's objective should be to maintain a substantial presence of key manufacturing sectors in the periphery of the core metro area and to promote their competitiveness. The focus should be on complex capital goods and associated components whose productivity, profitability, and competitiveness are more durable. Both Shanghai and Beijing should encourage the life sciences, new materials, and electronics while recognizing that these areas are subject to long gestation lags and might not generate significant profits or employment and, therefore, might contribute modestly to growth in the medium term. A multisectoral strategy is more likely to lead to sustainable growth with equity and to attract a diverse urban population. Such a strategy would call for a rationalizing and recalibrating of incentive policies for industry, thereby affecting land use, the cost of inputs, and tax obligations, so as to avoid a narrowing of the incentives for industry relative to services or other activities.

• An innovative economy will be a function of what kind of industry flourishes in the city; the competition strategies of the leading firms (many of which are currently state-owned enterprises), because innovation is industry specific and large firms conduct the bulk of the research; and the flow of new entrants into high-tech industries. There is only a limited correlation between innovations and spending on R&D by firms; hence, incentives for R&D are subject to diminishing returns. An innovative economy will also depend on the quality of the leading universities and the ways they contribute to the intellectual culture of the city. Aside from aiming to attract the best talent, universities must view teaching and basic research as their primary missions. In so doing, they can most effectively serve the knowledge economy and enhance the demand for innovation. Downstream research that could have commercial applications should be—as it is in the advanced countries—a secondary and, for the majority of universities, a relatively minor objective.

• In both cities, education and medical services can be the basis of two important research-cum-industrial high-tech clusters. As the experience of Boston and San Francisco has shown, tertiary education and health services, if they are world class, can be immensely profitable sectors that generate demand for other business services, can become leading exporters, can give rise to significant idea spillovers, and can induce the entry of new firms. Other creative industries can also contribute to a significant degree.

• The innovativeness of the megacities will depend in part on their openness to ideas and people and on livability,[11] which together help to attract and retain highly skilled, entrepreneurial, and mobile knowledge workers. It will also be influenced by the city emerging as an intellectual leader among the global centers, with its own distinctive vision and strategic initiatives. The current real estate–driven development is leading to sprawl, automobility, multiplication of residential towers with limited recreational amenities, and gated communities, all of which threaten the cultural, aesthetic, and environmental attributes of the cities, not to mention their social capital. Other world cities that have gone down this road are now having to reinvent themselves and redefine livability and cultural capital, emphasize compactness and dynamic mixed-use neighborhoods, put a premium on amenities, and minimize their environmental footprints.[12]

---

[11]The *Financial Times*'s ranking of cities is determined by easily measurable statistics such as average earnings, school performance, and health care costs as well as more subjective issues such as physical and technological connectivity, tolerance, the strength of local media and culture, and culinary and entertainment options. Most of the highly livable cities in Asia based on this ranking are in Japan. Singapore was ranked 18th (Brule 2009). There are other rankings, such as those of Mercer and the Economist Intelligence Unit, that rank cities on the basis of similar yet different sets of attributes.

[12]Urban environmental adjustments are exceedingly difficult in the United States, for example, because of opposition from the community to structural changes and the absence of sufficiently broad political support for measures to raise environmental quality and contain carbon emissions. In some cases, this situation permits cities only enough leeway to make small changes. However, such small changes do not affect the physical attributes and the feel of the city in a fundamental way. Daniel Burnham, the principal author of the 1909 plan to rebuild Chicago after the Great Chicago Fire, said it aptly: "Make no little plans: They have no power to stir men's blood" (Ford 2008: 239).

Rethinking Urban Development

The financial crisis and the global slowdown that started in 2008 have brought the world economy to a crucial juncture. There is need to interpret afresh, for the purposes of policy making, the past trends, stylized facts, and lessons from the developed world, as well as the direction, pace, and characteristics of urban development in China. Now is a time for global economic consolidation and a rethinking of urban strategies that factors in the longer-term implications of global warming. Views—and past findings—regarding the roles of industry and services and of policies to "rebalance" the economy could usefully be reconsidered. In the years ahead, the opportunities for China might be different and greater if it exercises strategic foresight in fully harnessing its economic potential and advantages. The major economies of the world are in for an industrial shakeout. Many firms will close their doors, and industrial capacity will be redistributed throughout the world. This outcome—which will be painful—represents a great opportunity for China to strengthen its economic base. No other major industrializing country has the nascent urban centers, the savings, the low indebtedness, the accumulated industrial capabilities, the elastic supply of human capital, and the momentum that China has to discover growth opportunities in these challenging times.

A new medium-term development strategy should include three additional short-term objectives. First, because its current and future comparative advantage lies, among others, in complex capital goods and high-tech components, Shanghai needs to ensure that these sectors survive and emerge stronger and better positioned to compete and to expand their shares of the global market.[13] This objective requires that such firms have access to the resources to outlast the downturn, to sustain capability-enhancing investments, and to add to their technological capacities. Certain capital goods sectors are likely to benefit from the investment in physical infrastructure, which has strong policy support in China and the world. Second, now might be a time to very selectively acquire production, research, and intellectual property–related assets from foreign companies that are going out of business, as well as critical tacit knowledge and brand names. Third, now is also the time to move faster with the transition out of those industrial subsectors in which the comparative advantage of the megacities is vanishing and to channel the resources from these sectors to others with better prospects, as well as to redouble the efforts to retrain and equip the human assets released by these subsectors so that they can be absorbed into other activities as recovery gathers steam. Such a transfer of resources will provide a welcome boost to productivity and reduce the overhang of excess capacity in light industries.

---

[13]The midterm evaluation of the 11th Five-Year Plan (2006–10) reveals that though the growth of high-tech industry has been impressive, it falls short of expectations. The target was for high-tech industry to account for 10 percent of the value added. However, by 2006, its share was 5 percent, and a doubling in four years is unlikely (World Bank 2008b).

The balance of this volume is divided into five chapters. Chapter 2 encapsulates the sources of China's growth and the current and future role of urban regions in China. The case for the continuing substantial presence of manufacturing industry for growth and innovation in the two urban centers is made in chapter 3. Chapter 4 briefly examines the economic transformation of four global cities and distills stylized trends that can inform future development in Beijing and Shanghai. Chapter 5 describes the industrial structure of the two cities, identifies promising industrial areas, and analyzes the resource base that would underpin growth fueled by innovation. Finally, chapter 6 suggests how strategy could be reoriented on the basis of the lessons delineated in chapter 4 and the economic capabilities presented in chapter 5.

2

China's Development and Its Megacities

China's growth experience from 1979, when the reform and opening of the economy began, has been exhaustively analyzed (see, for instance, Brandt and Rawski 2008; Holz 2008; Lin, Cai, and Li 2003; Naughton 2007; Yusuf, Nabeshima, and Perkins 2005); hence, it suffices at the outset to briefly identify the principal determinants over the past three decades and to indicate which of them are most likely to influence the economic prospects of China's urban regions.[1] Although agriculture played an important role in the first half of the 1980s,[2] much of the impetus since has derived from the intersectoral transfer of resources and the continuous double-digit growth of industry supported by domestic and foreign demand.

Rapid institutional evolution of the economy, triggered by reforms and the technological catching-up of manufacturing, coupled with expanding exports of sophisticated industrial products, has been largely responsible for China's industrial performance to date (Holz 2008; Schott 2006). Manufacturing activities are likely to remain the engine of China's urban growth through 2020 and possibly longer (see figures 2.1 and 2.2). Other countries have attempted to achieve high growth rates

---

[1]Allen Scott (2001a, 2001b: 813) extends the concept of a global city, "as a cosmopolitan metropolis, a command post for the operations of [multinational corporations], a center of advanced services and information processing activities, and a deeply segmented space marked by extremes of poverty and wealth, to incorporate the notion of a wider (urban) region as an emerging political economic unit with increasing autonomy of action on the national and world stages."

[2]Rural reforms, which spearheaded China's reforms and were responsible for the growth spurt (7.7 percent annually) from 1979 to 1984, are described by Carter, Zhong, and Cai (1996); J. Huang, Otsuka, and Rozelle (2008); and Perkins and Yusuf (1984).

Figure 2.1 GDP Composition of China, 1979–2006

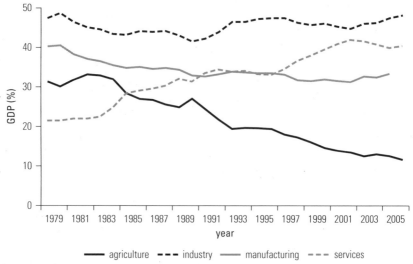

Source: World Bank World Development Indicators database.

Figure 2.2 Share of Exports in GDP and Growth of Exports in China, 1979–2007

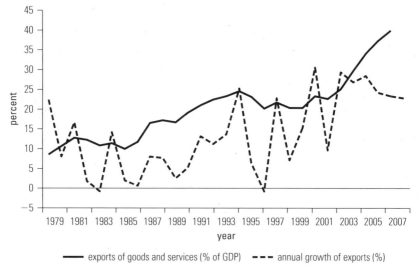

Source: World Bank World Development Indicators database.

through industrialization; however, few have equaled China's performance. Thus, the question frequently asked is, why has China done so much better than most other developing nations? Seven reasons may explain China's success.

Seven Factors of Chinese Success

First, China's Big Push to industrialize,[3] starting in the 1950s, helped lay the foundations of manufacturing capacity, created a broad base of expertise in both light and heavy manufacturing in several parts of the country, and brought into existence an urban industrial labor force of managers, technicians, and factory workers. When China's reforms began in 1979, a large industrial sector, accounting for more than half of China's gross domestic product (GDP), already existed and was able to exploit the opportunities inherent in the wide technological and productivity gaps between China and the industrially advanced countries. Few, if any, other developing countries had an industrial establishment as large as China's in the 1980s or earlier.

Second, this accumulated industrial capacity was vital in leveraging the gains from opening to trade and foreign direct investment (FDI) starting in 1979 and accelerating after 1994 (see figure 2.3).[4] In the initial postreform years, FDI channeled capital into export-oriented light industries and stimulated the growth of this important sector.[5] Since then, domestic capital and FDI have flowed into high-tech manufacturing industries, services, and real estate as well. Trade and FDI have served as vehicles for technology transfer embodied in plant and equipment as well as knowledge transfer on plant operations, management, business organization, workplace practices, logistics, and other areas.[6] These transfers have substantially augmented productivity in firms with foreign investment and,

---

[3]For a brief history of the term *Big Push*, coined by Paul Rosenstein-Rodan in 1943 and elaborated by Murphy, Shleifer, and Vishny in 1989, see Easterly (2006) and Yusuf (2009a).

[4]The extensive involvement of foreign firms in China's export-oriented industrialization was neither planned nor anticipated when reforms were initiated. It evolved over time.

[5]Kleinberg (1990) describes China's opening up, and S.-J. Wei (1993) estimates the positive effects of trade on industrial production in cities. Initially, the opening aroused opposition within the country; however, following Deng Xiaoping's intervention in 1984 and the creation of 14 open cities, the process acquired new momentum (Lai 2006). See also Comin and Hobijn (2004) on the positive effect of increased trade and human capital on technology adoption.

[6]Trade is one of the conduits for technology transfer, especially of technologies embedded in capital goods (D. Coe and Helpman 1995; D. Coe, Helpman, and Hoffmaister 1997; Eaton and Kortum 1999, 2001).

through knowledge spillovers, in domestic enterprises.[7] FDI has partially amelio-rated the distortions in China's financial markets and made more capital available to small and medium enterprises producing tradable goods (Y. Huang 2005).[8] FDI has accelerated the integration of China's manufacturing sector with the global

---

[7]FDI inflow is another important avenue of technology transfer. However, the empirical findings to date present a mixed picture (Aitken, Hanson, and Harrison 1997; Aitken and Harrison 1999; Blomström and Sjöholm 1999; Haddad and Harrison 1993). For a survey of technology transfer via FDI, see Saggi (2006). The literature mainly focuses on the flow of spillovers from multinational corporations (MNCs) to local firms. However, spillovers can also proceed from local firms to MNCs. See Y. Wei, Liu, and Wang (2008) on the case of China. A number of different avenues for technology spillovers have been identified: demonstration effects, vertical links, circulation of workers, and managerial capabilities (Smeets 2008). Demonstration effects are often measured as the change in productivity of firms in the same sector (horizontal spillovers). Castellani and Zanfei (2003); Griffith, Redding, and Simpson (2002); Griffith, Redding, and Van Reenen (2004); and Peri and Urban (2006) note that increased FDI positively affects the productivity of the local firms (relative to the best performance within the same industrial category). Using design patents as the measure, Cheung and Lin (2004) found evidence of increased FDI leading to a rise in the number of design patents that can be most easily copied. On balance, vertical spillovers seem to be a more prevalent mode. Javorcik (2004) finds evidence of positive effects through backward links only, whereas Javorcik and Spatareanu's (2008) research identifies vertical (interindustry) spillovers through increased demand for intermediate inputs under the condition of joint ownership, while the horizontal (intraindustry) impact was negative. Bwalya (2006), Kugler (2006), and Schoors and van der Tol (2002) also find evidence of positive backward links. However, Blalock and Gertler (2008) and Javorcik and Spatareanu (2005) point out that local firm productivity increases might be a consequence of inten-tional technology transfers rather than spillovers. Circulation of workers between foreign and domestic firms seems to be broadly productivity enhancing, although such positive spillovers occur only when workers are moving within a single industry or related indus-tries (Görg and Strobl 2001). Knowledge spillovers are confined in rather small areas and therefore proximity is an important factor (Barrios, Bertinelli, and Strobl 2006; Girma and Wakelin 2007; Nicolini and Resmini 2007). Moreover, even if many MNCs are willing to assist local firms through backward links and these firms are located close to each other, local firms need to have a certain level of absorptive capacity (as noted by Cohen and Levinthal 1990). Girma (2005) and Girma and Görg (2007) show that the mediating effect of knowledge spillover is maximized at intermediate levels of absorptive capacity. Smeets (2008) concludes by pointing out that the positive spillover effect of FDI depends on spillover channels, mediating factors, and heterogeneities in industry, MNCs, and condi-tions in the host country, which coexist and interact in determining the extent of knowledge spillovers. According to Liang (2008) and Y. Wei and Liu (2006), theoretical and empirical research should therefore try to address these aspects simultaneously.

[8]Y. Huang (2008) nevertheless argues that private firms continue to suffer from a scarcity of financing, which is evident from the dearth of new starts.

Figure 2.3 Foreign Direct Investment Inflow to China, 1990–2007

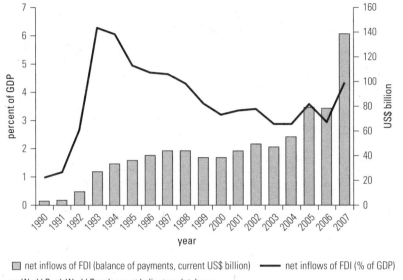

□ net inflows of FDI (balance of payments, current US$ billion) ▬▬ net inflows of FDI (% of GDP)

Source: World Bank World Development Indicators database.

economy. This process, assisted by the overseas Chinese diaspora, is enabling Chinese producers to tighten their links with international production networks and consolidate their entry into foreign retail markets (Bair 2009; Rauch and Trindade 2002; Yusuf and others 2003).[9] Trade and FDI will continue to promote technological change in Beijing and Shanghai during the medium term, though to a lesser degree as technological capacity in those cities increases.

Third, the large volume of domestic investment in production capacity and in physical infrastructure has complemented FDI and conferred several significant benefits. It has rapidly increased capital-to-labor ratios and introduced new technologies embodied in capital equipment that confer productivity and quality advantages and contribute to China's industrial competitiveness. By enabling Chinese producers to quickly ramp up capacity, the outlay on production facilities has accelerated learning and made the production scale required by foreign buyers

---

[9]Access to the markets of developed countries frequently depends on entry into the global value chains of core firms from industrial economies (Nolan, Zhang, and Liu 2008). See P. Li and Lin (2006) and Fung, Fung, and Wind (2008) on the mutually reinforcing inter-action between global value chains, the increasing logistical sophistication of producers, and effective assimilation of information technology; the science and art of networked logistics; and the flexibility of manufacturing in East Asia.

Table 2.1 Productivity Growth in China, 1978–2005

	Bosworth and Collins (2007)			He and Kuijs (2007)	
	1978–2004 (%)	1978–93 (%)	1993–2004 (%)	1978–93 (%)	1993–2005 (%)
Output growth	9.3	8.9	9.7	9.7	9.6
Employment	2.0	2.5	1.2	2.5	1.1
Output per worker	7.3	6.4	8.5	7.0	8.4
Physical capital	3.2	2.5	4.2	3.2	5.3
Land	0.0	−0.1	0.0	—	—
Education	0.2	0.2	0.2	0.5	0.2
Factor productivity	3.8	3.6	4.0	3.3	2.8
Factor productivity attributable to reallocation of labor between sectors	—	—	—	1.3	1.1

Sources: Bosworth and Collins 2007; He and Kuijs 2007.
Note: — not available.

easier to achieve.[10] Moreover, investment spending generates domestic demand, and alongside exports and growth, such demand has been a consistent source of growth.

Fourth, by drastically reducing the share of state-owned enterprises and increasing competition, the reform of the state sector initiated in the early 1980s and accelerated after the mid-1990s has channeled resources to more efficient users and thereby raised industrial productivity. Total factor productivity (TFP), which is the main source of differences in per capita GDP among countries, rose by 3 to 4 percent between 1993 and 2005 (see table 2.1).[11]

Investment in physical capital and reform of state-owned enterprises are two strands of China's growth story. Human capital, increasingly abundant in the large urban centers such as Beijing and Shanghai,[12] is an equally important part

---

[10]The ability to quickly and flexibly service large orders from foreign buyers is a big advantage for Chinese suppliers over competitors in India—although that gap may now be closing in certain industries as Indian firms enlarge capacity (Luthra, Mangaleswaran, and Padhi 2005). This surge in capacity and the willingness of Chinese producers to price aggressively have a downside, which is unevenness in the quality of Chinese products (see Midler 2009).

[11]See Comin and Hobijn (2004); Comin, Hobijn, and Rovito (2008); and R. Hall and Jones (1999) on lags in technology adoption and their implications for TFP.

[12]Shanghai was the door through which modern technology was introduced into China during the first three decades of the 20th century. It acquired tall, Western-style office buildings and the longest bar in the world. It became the center of finance, commerce, industry, and fashion. And it took the first steps in bringing Western-style higher education to China (H. Lu 1999).

Table 2.2   Gross Enrollment Rates in China, 1991, 2001, and 2006

Education level	1991	2001	2006
Primary	125.9	117.4	111.2
Secondary	49.1	65.0	75.5
Tertiary	3.0	9.9	21.6

Source: World Bank World Development Indicators database.

and a fifth reason for China's unusually brisk economic performance. Achieving universal literacy and a high level of primary enrollment was China's objective from the late 1950s (MacFarquhar and Fairbank 1987).[13] This education equipped the Chinese workforce with the basic skills needed for the earlier stages of industrialization in the late 1970s and early 1980s. A redoubling of efforts at raising educational levels after 1980 has paid handsome dividends. Domestically, China has vastly expanded secondary and tertiary education[14] and vocational training (see table 2.2). It has sent hundreds of thousands of its nationals for training abroad as well.[15] Beijing and Shanghai are among the most successful cities in attracting some of these knowledge workers back. These efforts are expanding the supplies of skilled, technical, and professional workers, who are needed to assimilate advanced technologies from overseas in manufacturing and services, to manage China's increasingly complex economy, and to initiate home-grown innovations in a variety of fields (Yusuf, Nabeshima, and Perkins 2007). With technology absorption and innovation now viewed as the most potent sources of economic dynamism and of gains in productivity, the supply and quality of human capital might eventually overtake physical capital as the principal driver of growth through gains in TFP.[16] As shown by Comin, Hobijn, and Rovito (2008),

---

[13]Of China's total population, 4.6 percent of those between the ages of 25 and 64 years hold a college degree, 85 million are illiterate, 120 million are unemployable because they suffer from a debilitating disease or a disability, and—according to the metric used by the Chinese authorities—some 30 million people fall below the poverty line (C. Li 2004).

[14]For more on tertiary education, see M. Gallagher and others (2009). In 1981, the number of college graduates was 139,000. By 2009, the number of graduates had risen to 6.1 million. However, because of a serious graduate unemployment problem, the central government introduced a measure to hire freshly graduated students as short-term teachers with initial contracts of three years (Y. Wang 2009). In Guangdong province, only 7 percent of the class of 2009 had secured job offers by March. Nationwide, the demand for college graduates was down 20 percent in 2009 compared to 2008, although the number of graduates has increased by 15 percent ("Most College Students" 2009).

[15]Approximately 800,000 Chinese have gone abroad to study, and of these, about 30 percent have returned, although the percentage is on the rise.

[16]Chi (2008) finds that the effect of fixed capital on growth is insignificant. Instead, the stock of human capital, especially tertiary-level skills, determines the accumulation of physical capital and has the strongest influence on growth.

closing intercountry disparities in TFP is in large part a function of lags in the adoption of new technologies and the intensity of usage. Human and intellectual capital can reduce both.

Sixth, the renewed priority given to education starting in the 1980s[17] was followed later in the decade by increasing attention to research and development (R&D) with the launching of a number of programs, such as the Spark and Torch programs (table 2.3 lists various national innovation programs; see also Sigurdson 2005). The priority given to education is building technological capacity and laying the groundwork for a culture of innovation, most notably in the leading urban regions. The early emphasis given to R&D means that China is accumulating research capital faster, which expedites technology transfer and technology absorption.[18] Gao and Jefferson (2007) introduce the notion of a science and technology take-off, which refers to the scientific productivity of a country. They suggest that such a take-off, which is likely to precede a surge in innovation, is associated with the doubling of research expenditures over a period of a decade or less. They show that the United States, several European countries, and a few East Asian economies were able to achieve this take-off, and some are now demonstrating their innovation capabilities. By this yardstick, China—and even more notably its two leading megacities—have achieved take-off. How rapidly this translates into a steady flow of innovations that are reflected in new products, exports, and GDP growth remains to be seen.

From the early 1980s, China's industrial capacity grew most rapidly in a few densely populated urban regions centered on cities such as Guangzhou, Shanghai,[19] and Shenzhen, which are gaining agglomeration economies (Yusuf 2007).[20] This process accelerated between 1998 and 2005, although relative to more advanced countries, China is still low on the scale of industrial agglomeration (J. Lu and Tao 2009).[21] Size and the agglomeration of activities translate into advantages of scale, of industrial diversity, of deep labor markets, and of a strong service economy. Together, these advantages have led to productivity gains for firms and have created an environment more conducive to technological advancement, which is universally an urban phenomenon (Yusuf and others 2003).[22] In other words, agglomeration

---

[17]The first loan by the World Bank to China in 1981 was for higher education.

[18]In 2008, China joined the list of countries with the 10 fastest computers in the world. The fastest computer in China is produced by Dawning, a domestic server manufacturer established in 1995 through the "863" program (http://www.dawning.com.cn/en/aboutus. asp). The computer is housed in the Shanghai Super Computer Center. China now has 15 of the world's 500 fastest computers (Vance 2008).

[19]In Shanghai, 1.27 percent of China's population lives in 0.06 percent of the country's land area.

[20]Ge (2009) finds that export orientation and FDI have contributed to the agglomeration of industries in China.

[21]One constraint on further agglomeration is local protectionism (J. Lu and Tao 2009).

[22]From the 19th century onward, innovation has flourished in cities and diffused most readily in the urban environment (Bairoch 1991: chap. 20).

Table 2.3 Major National Science and Technology Programs in China

Program	Agency	Year begun	Key focus
Spark	Ministry of Science and Technology	1985	To improve agricultural technology and develop agroindustrial clusters
Torch	Ministry of Science and Technology	1998	To develop high-tech industries and development zones and provide laboratories and equipment
863 (national high-tech R&D program)	Ministry of Science and Technology	March 1986	To enhance international competitiveness and improve overall capability of R&D in high technology (with 19 priorities)
National Key Technologies R&D Program	Ministry of Science and Technology	1982	To support applied R&D to meet critical technological needs in key sectors
R&D Infrastructure and Facility Development	Ministry of Science and Technology	1984	To support the National Key Laboratories Development Program, National Key Science Projects Program, and National Engineering Technology Research Centers Development Program
National Natural Science Foundation	National Natural Science Foundation	1986	To promote and finance basic research and some applied research
211	Ministry of Education	1995	To improve overall institutional capacity and develop key disciplinary areas in selected universities; to develop a public service system of higher education (3 networks)
973 (national basic research program)	Ministry of Science and Technology	June 1997 (combined with "Climbing" program, initiated in 1992)	To strengthen basic research in line with national strategic targets (primarily in agriculture, energy, information, resources and the environment, population and health, and materials)
985	Ministry of Education	1998 (first phase); 2004 (second phase)	To turn China's top 150 universities into world-class research institutions
Outline of the Medium- and Long-Term National Plan for Science and Technology Development, 2006–20		2006	To make China an innovation-driven economy by 2020 by increasing investment in science and technology, shifting focus to basic and frontier research; granting preferential tax treatment to stimulate R&D; increasing government procurement; indigenizing foreign technologies; strengthening intellectual property protection; and developing human capital (R&D-to-GDP ratio should be at least 2.5%, and China should rank among top 5 in patents granted and papers published by 2020)

Sources: Rongping and Wan 2008; Sigurdson 2005; Wu 2007.

economies have reinforced the six factors already referred to. Urbanization has thus interacted most fruitfully with other factors in promoting growth.

These seven elements highlight the role of industrialization: an early start at building industrial capacity; FDI that initiated the growth of exports; the high level of investment in plant, equipment, and infrastructure; reform of the state enterprise sector; rapid accumulation of human capital on a broad front; the attention given to R&D; and the geographically concentrated urbanization. Together they are responsible for stimulating and sustaining China's growth to date. Each contributing element depended on a succession of policy initiatives that, after experimentation and validation, defined and progressively elaborated China's unique development strategy.[23] In other words, policies that gave primacy to or accommodated these seven elements were ultimately responsible for the huge economic strides taken by the country during the past three decades.

Outlook for the Future

Starting in the 1980s, China's industrial efforts were assisted by the global industrial product cycle[24] and by the strategies of multinational corporations (MNCs) and of major retailers in the United States. Rising costs of production in their home countries and the emerging capacity to manage dispersed operations with the help of information technology persuaded the MNCs to transfer the manufacture of mature standardized commodities (whose production technologies had stabilized and become codified) to East Asia. The big retail chains in the United States found sourcing from overseas expedient and cost-effective (Bair 2009).[25]

---

[23]Vividly depicted as "crossing the river by feeling the stones," this strategy combined varied countrywide experimentation with the rapid diffusion of selected models. However, in determining which models to adopt, the authorities have tended to eschew rigorous assessment and instead favored a qualitative evaluation based on early outcomes.

[24]This cycle refers to the transfer of production from advanced to industrializing countries as products mature and the product itself becomes a commodity (see Vernon 1979).

[25]Japanese trading companies and "lean retailers" in the United States were responsible for production networks spanning the Pacific. Their interest and involvement stimulated entrepreneurship in the Republic of Korea and Taiwan, China, thereby giving rise to a highly efficient base of small suppliers in Taiwan, China, that produced a variety of light consumer items and to a comparable production base in Korea created by conglomerates called *chaebol*. The remarkable celerity with which the business communities in these two economies grasped the opportunities largely explains the subsequent expansion of the production networks and their contribution to the growth of intraregional and cross-Pacific trade (Feenstra and Hamilton 2006). For a recent survey on global production networks, see N. Coe, Dicken, and Hess (2008) and Sturgeon, Van Biesebroeck, and Gereffi (2008) on the automotive industry and Pietrobelli and Saliola (2008) on the role of lead MNCs in creating global production networks and developing local suppliers.

Table 2.4   China's Exports as a Share of World Exports, 2006

Commodities	Share (%)
Outerwear, knitted or crocheted, not elastic nor rubberized	36.1
Baby carriages, toys, games, and sporting goods	31.2
Articles of apparel, clothing accessories, nontextile, headgear	29.8
Undergarments of textile fabrics, not knitted or crocheted	29.3
Men's and boys' outerwear, textile fabrics, not knitted or crocheted	28.5
Clothing accessories, of textile fabrics, not elsewhere specified	26.8
Women's, girls', and infants outerwear, textile fabrics, not knitted or crocheted	26.7
Undergarments, knitted or crocheted	25.9
Furniture and parts thereof	17.0
Manufactures of leather or of composition leather, not elsewhere specified	14.7
Leather	6.8

Source: Authors' calculations.

As transport costs fell, the cost advantage enjoyed by East Asian producers grew (Hummels, Ishii, and Yi 2001).[26] Starting in the 1980s and at an accelerating rate in the second half of the 1990s, China was able to seize the opportunities as they emerged by building production capacity, thereby acquiring the manufacturing capability and scale demanded by foreign buyers at an astonishing speed. Moreover, Chinese producers offered prices that firms in other countries were unable to match.[27] According to Hamilton and Gereffi (2008), the speed with which Chinese and other East Asian manufacturers adapted to the needs of contract manufacturing combined with cost competitiveness explains why they were able to beat the competition. Furthermore, as China's technological know-how improved, it diversified into medium- and high-tech products at a faster rate than did other countries and established a commanding lead in markets for a wide range of manufactures. Table 2.4 shows that China currently dominates the export market for various types of garments, toys, furniture, and leather goods.

That was the past. What of the future? China is now the world's largest exporter and second-largest manufacturer. Maintaining the recent trend rates of growth of the existing mix of products in the unfolding world environment will be

---

[26]Glaeser and Kohlhase (2003) estimate that transport costs declined by 95 percent during the 20th century.

[27]On the "China price," see Harney (2008).

difficult—perhaps impossible.[28] Market saturation for some manufactured exports, rising domestic costs of production, growing concerns regarding the quality and safety standards of Chinese products, natural resource scarcities, and trade frictions[29] are some of the factors arguing for a growth and export strategy that more fully harnesses technology assimilation from abroad, domestic innovation, productivity growth, industrial deepening, and the potential residing in tradable business services (still a relatively underdeveloped sector in China). The "low-cost" model and industrial widening will continue to deliver growth, but to a lesser degree. Thus, if gains in productivity; backward integration to increase value added; and innovation to generate new goods and services, better processes, and better business models are the means of sustaining rapid growth in the medium to long term, then strengthening technological and innovation capabilities promises the highest payoff.[30] By building, tuning, and coordinating technological capabilities and by creating a functioning innovation system, the economy will be more productive, less resource and energy intensive, and better able to generate goods and services enjoying wider profit margins.[31]

Many empirical findings and lessons from more advanced countries can help make China's industrial economy more innovative, and among these lessons, one stands out. Whether in manufacturing or in services, innovation needs to be rooted in a few major urban centers. Successful centers combine significant agglomeration economies with intellectual and business cultures that encourage innovation and an urban environment high on the scale of quality. How agglomeration and the

---

[28]Being a very large economy, China is better positioned than smaller export-oriented economies to weather global financial crises, but it is not immune from such crises. China has relied on exports for between 2 and 3 percent of its growth. When exports stagnate, growth slackens (Dyer 2008). Before the crisis of 2008 to 2009, the Chinese authorities tightened credit to avoid inflation. As a result, domestic consumption and investment also slowed. The estimated growth for 2008 was 9.0 percent, the first single-digit growth since 2001.

[29]A lengthy period of slower growth could lead to a reappearance of trade barriers, as happened in the earlier decades of the 20th century, thereby diluting some of the major gains from globalization. Recognizing this danger, several economists have proposed ways of avoiding such an outcome (see Baldwin and Evenett 2008; Hufbauer and Stephenson 2009), although so-called murky protectionism has begun spreading since 2008.

[30]For an assessment of the science and technology system in China, see A. Hu and Jefferson (2008); see Sigurdson (2005) for a general overview; see Zhang and others (2009) for analysis of innovation by small and medium enterprises and of other issues such as the role of venture capital. On East European experience with developing a competitive, knowledge-based economy, see Goldberg and others (2008) and the papers in Runiewicz-Wardyn (2008).

[31]Although China exported 4,898 products of 5,041 products traded globally in 2004, compared with 4,932 by Germany, Japanese unit values for similar products were 2.9 times higher, and those of the United States were 2.4 times higher (Fontagne, Gaulier, and Zignago 2008).

concentration of skills can interact is evident from the experience of the United States since 1970. At that time, people with a college degree were relatively evenly dispersed across metropolitan regions—ranging from 9 to 13 percent of the metro populations as against a national average of 11 percent. By 2004, the distribution had become far more skewed even as the national average rose to 27 percent. In San Francisco, 45 percent of the adult population had a college degree, and similar concentrations existed in Washington, D.C., and San Jose. However, the share of the population with tertiary-level qualifications was 11 percent in Detroit and just 4 percent in Cleveland. This skewness is also reflected in the performance of these cities (Florida 2009). Research by Glaeser and Resseger (2009) indicates that urban agglomeration effects interact with human capital. In other words, the presence of more knowledge workers in large cities increases learning spillovers and speeds up technological changes. "Together both effects create the interaction between city size and population across skilled metropolitan areas" (Glaeser and Resseger 2009: 17). China's technological capacity is already highly concentrated, and very likely a relatively small number of cities will drive knowledge-intensive growth. Thus, the ongoing efforts in megacities such as Shanghai and Beijing to raise the skill and knowledge quotient should lead to a virtuous spiral of learning through interaction that stimulates technology development and growth.

Although the past is one guide to future development, past patterns should not be seen as binding. In fact, they could mislead. Hence, this study draws selectively and critically on the relevant global and Chinese experience of megacities in proposing strategies for Beijing and Shanghai that could deliver moderately high rates of growth over the course of the next decade.

3

Manufacturing Industry: Locomotive for Innovation and Growth

Twenty years ago, Dertouzos, Lester, and Solow (1989) recognized the importance of the manufacturing industry for the U.S. economy. In *Made in America*, they stressed that

> the United States . . . has no choice but to continue competing in the world market for manufactures . . . . [T]he best way for Americans to share in rising world prosperity is to retain on American soil those industries that have high and rapidly rising productivity. Manufacturing, and high-technology manufacturing in particular, belongs in this category. (Dertouzos, Lester, and Solow 1989: 40)

Their argument is based on the innovation intensity of manufacturing industry:

> A related fact is that manufacturing firms account for virtually all of the research and development done by American industry. They thus generate most of the technological innovations adopted both inside and outside their own industry. High-technology manufacturing industries account for three-quarters of all funding for research and development and the other manufacturing industries account for most of the rest. The roots of much of the technological progress responsible for long-term economic growth can ultimately be traced to the nation's manufacturing base. (Dertouzos, Lester, and Solow 1989: 40–41)

Since then, the significance of manufacturing for the advanced economies has been periodically debated even as the share of manufacturing in gross domestic product (GDP) has gone on shrinking quite rapidly in the United Kingdom and the United States and less steeply in Germany and Japan.

When one looks at the experience of members of the Organisation for Economic Co-operation and Development (OECD), an inverted U-shaped relationship seems to exist between the share of manufacturing and the level of income (see figure 3.1). At the initial stage, as countries increase their share of manufacturing, the income is rising. When their income reaches a certain level, the share of

Figure 3.1 Relationship between the Share of Manufacturing and Per Capita Income, 1960–2007

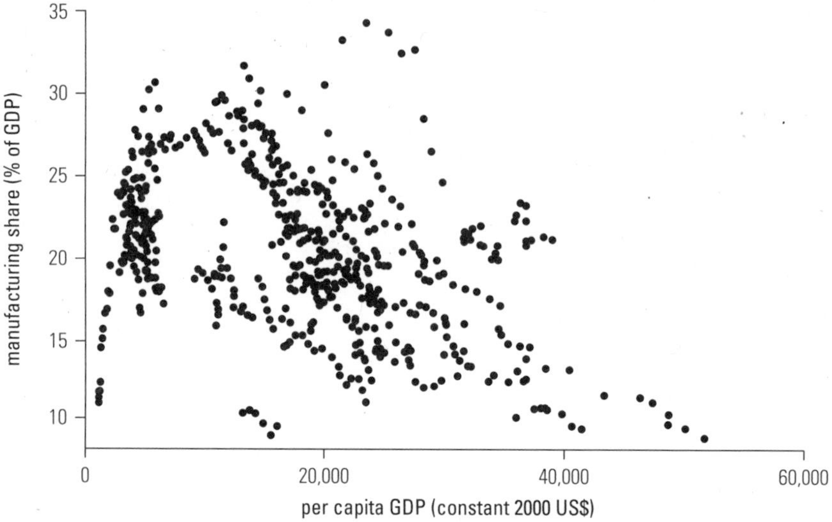

Source: Authors' calculations based on data from the World Bank World Development Indicators database.

Note: Data include all current OECD members (30 countries) between 1960 and 2007 for which data were available.

services starts to expand.[1] The relationship between the share of manufacturing and the growth of income is revealing. A slight positive correlation exists between the share of manufacturing and growth for OECD countries and also for East Asian economies (figures 3.2 and 3.3). This relationship may account in part for the slower growth of higher-income countries and the continuing importance of the manufacturing industry for growth.[2]

Even though the manufacturing industry now employs just 10 percent of the workforce and produces less than one-fifth of GDP in the United States (its share is somewhat higher in Germany and Japan), the financial crisis that began in 2008 has focused attention on the longer-term role of the manufacturing industry in restoring growth and enabling the United States and other countries that have outsourced and offshored a large part of their manufacturing to narrow trade gaps.[3] Interestingly, this debate coincides with a parallel debate on the drawbacks

---

[1] The rising share of services in GDP relates more to the trends in relative prices, which favor services, than to a decline in the goods intensity of final demand.

[2] A simple, fixed-effect panel regression also suggests that the share of manufacturing is an important and sizable contributor to growth.

[3] Dertouzos, Lester, and Solow (1989) were also of the opinion that sustaining trade deficits was impossible and that the increase in service exports had not and would not be able to finance the imports of manufactured goods.

**Figure 3.2   Relationship between the Share of Manufacturing and Growth
for OECD Countries, 1961–2007**

manufacturing share (% of GDP)

• per capita GDP   —— trend line

Source: Authors' calculations based on data from the World Bank World Development Indicators database.
Note: Data include all current OECD members (30 countries) between 1960 and 2007 for which data were available.

**Figure 3.3   Relationship between the Share of Manufacturing and Growth for
East Asian Economies, 1961–2007**

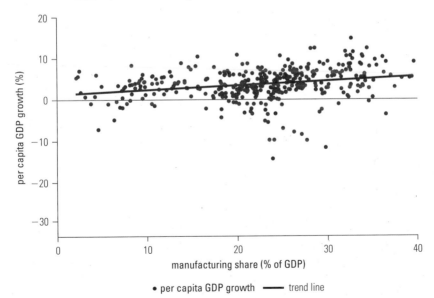

manufacturing share (% of GDP)

• per capita GDP growth   —— trend line

Source: Authors' calculations based on data from the World Bank World Development Indicators database.
Note: Data are for China; Hong Kong, China; Indonesia; Japan; the Republic of Korea; Malaysia; the Philippines;
Singapore; Taiwan, China; and Thailand between 1961 and 2007.

of growth reliant on the export of manufactures, which was precipitated by the steep reduction in commodity trade resulting from the global recession of 2008 and 2009 (see Eichengreen and O'Rourke 2009; Freund 2009).

Why a Broad Manufacturing Base Matters

Problems associated with global recession notwithstanding, cities that are able to sustain manufacturing activities should be able to capitalize on gains in industrial productivity and the scope for innovation.[4] However, the longer-term implications of the global economic slowdown caused by the financial crisis of 2008 and 2009 could jeopardize the growth prospects of segments of industry that depend heavily on exports. World trade grew by just 4 percent in real terms during 2008 and is forecast to decline by 9 percent in 2009 (WTO 2009). The adjustments required of countries such as the United States to correct their external and internal resource imbalances could also presage a period of slower growth in global trade in manufactures and the persistence of excess capacity in a number of industries over the near term. During 2009 and 2010, exports are likely to contribute less to the growth of Beijing and Shanghai, for example, than in the past. Foreign direct investment (FDI) will diminish,[5] and less technology transfer will occur through the medium of imports. Some of the remaining low-tech and labor-intensive industries in the two cities are likely to suffer rapid erosion in competitiveness and to either close down or relocate elsewhere.[6] Some shrinkage of the manufacturing sector seems unavoidable in the near term. However, an expansion of the tradable services in China's megacities—even if it is feasible in the face of weaker domestic and foreign demand—is unlikely to restore growth and employment in the short run and, if it increasingly displaces manufacturing, would be detrimental to growth over the longer term.

If the objective of China's megacities is to achieve rising incomes increasingly through gains arising from a productively networked and innovative economy, a sizable manufacturing sector must remain a vital component of the urban economy. However, the future of a diversified and growing industrial base will depend on measures taken to bolster the competitiveness of mature industries with considerable potential in domestic as well as global markets. It will also be a

---

[4]This observation does not mean that factories would locate in the core downtown area. A city wanting to maintain a solid manufacturing base must develop edge industrial centers and be well integrated into them to form a polycentric urban region. To a certain extent, Shanghai has a plan in place to achieve this goal. The plan calls for "one core, three circular belts, six development corridors, and eight medium-sized cities" (Han 2000: 2102). The core will be the central business and commercial area. Three belts and six development corridors will concentrate on specific industries, such as petrochemical, electronic machinery, and automotives. These areas are all linked by major highways, subways, a bridge, and an additional airport (Han 2000).

[5]FDI in China declined in each month from October 2008 through May 2009, and in the first five months of 2009, it was a fifth lower than in the same period a year earlier.

[6]Not just low-tech but also other industries are likely to be squeezed.

function of the entry of manufacturing firms into both mature and emerging industrial subsectors because such firms are frequently the source of new and disruptive technologies.[7] Such entry will depend on a variety of policies and institutions, including spatial development policies in urban and suburban areas. Industrial hollowing is not inevitable, but once it gathers momentum, it is difficult to reverse.

Manufacturing offers the densest backward and forward links among the various economic activities. The input-output table for the United States shows that the manufacturing industry consumes about 30 percent of all the intermediate inputs (see table 3.1). The manufacturing industry is the largest consumer of the products of the agriculture, mining, utilities, and manufacturing sectors; of services provided by the transportation, warehousing, wholesale, and retail sectors; and of services offered by professional and business services providers.[8] Finance, insurance, and real estate (FIRE) consumes about 14 percent of the intermediate inputs, the second-largest overall consumer after the manufacturing sector. However, FIRE consumes only 2.4 percent of manufacturing output for intermediate use.[9] Construction represents the bulk of intermediate inputs consumed by FIRE, of which real estate is the largest consumer of the output of the construction industry, of FIRE itself, of arts and entertainment, and of other services. As in the United States, the manufacturing industry is China's largest user of other intermediate inputs, consuming 44 percent of all the intermediate inputs (see table 3.2). Unlike the U.S. sectors, China's banking and insurance sectors are major consumers of manufacturing outputs such as computers, office equipment, and furnishings.

The Case for Complex Capital Goods

As industrial cities ascend the income ladder, the attractiveness of certain types of manufacturing industries increases. One set of activities are those whose profitability rests on the slow accumulation of learning, tacit knowledge, and specialized

---

[7]Entry barriers to firms are a function, among other things, of the efficacy of competition laws. China's antimonopoly law (promulgated on August 30, 2007) finally came into force on August 1, 2008 (Subler 2008). Whether this law will be effective is too early to judge. Much of the concern over its effectiveness stems from the lack of an independent judiciary and a mature legal system. In addition to the weaknesses of the legal infrastructure, another issue is how this law would handle state-imposed monopolies, often at the province and local levels, a legacy from the socialist past (Mehra and Meng 2008).

[8]It is also the largest consumer of scrap metal.

[9]The information sector (financial services, other producer services, and advanced consumer services) consumed very little of the manufacturing output in 1972 and in 1996. The share of outputs sold by the information sector to the goods production and distribution sector between 1972 and 1996 dropped significantly, from 44.0 percent to 18.7 percent. This decrease suggests that the goods-producing sector is becoming a less important customer for the information-producing industry (Drennan 2002).

Table 3.1 Share of Intermediate Input Use in the United States, 2002

Industry	Manufacturing (%)	Wholesale trade (%)	Retail trade (%)	Transportation and warehousing (%)	Information (%)	Finance, insurance, real estate, rental, and leasing (%)	Professional and business services (%)
Agriculture, forestry, fishing, and hunting	63.0	0.1	0.8	0.0	0.0	0.6	0.3
Mining	60.5	0.0	0.0	0.5	0.1	0.6	0.2
Utilities	32.4	2.5	6.6	1.9	2.3	9.6	4.3
Construction	8.0	0.7	2.0	2.9	3.5	36.4	3.3
Manufacturing	55.5	1.7	2.6	2.7	2.3	2.4	2.9
Wholesale trade	50.3	7.4	3.9	2.2	1.8	3.4	2.3
Retail trade	11.2	1.0	3.0	2.9	0.2	10.8	1.2
Transportation and warehousing	23.5	7.5	7.7	18.3	3.2	3.6	6.3
Information	8.4	2.3	3.0	1.7	34.6	7.7	14.1
Finance, insurance, real estate, rental, and leasing	5.8	2.8	6.0	3.1	3.3	42.3	9.5
Professional and business services	20.5	5.5	4.9	3.1	6.1	11.2	15.3
Educational services, health care, and social assistance	0.2	0.9	4.5	0.1	0.9	0.2	1.1
Arts, entertainment, recreation, accommodation, and food services	9.0	2.4	3.0	2.8	10.3	12.9	22.2
Other services, except government	11.9	4.0	4.5	3.5	4.7	16.3	13.0
Government	3.2	9.9	9.4	17.7	5.1	8.9	8.5
Scrap, used, and secondhand goods	75.1	0.0	3.8	6.6	0.5	−5.0	3.2
Other inputs	16.8	7.3	0.5	15.9	11.1	21.1	8.4
Total intermediate inputs	30.2	3.4	4.1	3.6	5.0	13.6	8.1

Source: U.S. Bureau of Economic Analysis (http://www.bea.gov/industry/xls/2002summary_makeuse_sector.xls).

Note: For the distribution of commodities consumed by an industry, read the column for that industry. For the distribution of industries consuming a commodity, read the row for that commodity. For space considerations, 10 columns were omitted: "Agriculture, forestry, fishing, and hunting"; "Mining"; "Utilities"; "Construction"; "Educational services, health care, and social assistance"; "Arts, entertainment, recreation, accommodation, and food services"; "Other services, except government"; "Government"; "Scrap, used, and secondhand goods"; and "Other inputs."

Table 3.2 Share of Intermediate Input Use in China, 2002

Industry	Manufacturing (%)	Transportation, postal, and telecommunication services (%)	Wholesale and retail trades, hotels, and catering services (%)	Real estate, leasing, and business services (%)	Banking and insurance (%)	Other services (%)
Agriculture	48.0	0.8	7.8	0.1	0.0	0.7
Production and supply of electricity	51.7	2.8	6.5	3.2	1.1	8.0
Coking, gas, and petroleum refining	30.4	28.7	4.6	0.8	0.4	4.5
Mining and quarrying	37.4	0.7	0.5	0.4	0.0	1.9
Construction	3.8	10.7	12.5	20.1	6.1	41.0
Manufacturing	1.4	0.5	13.4	2.4	13.7	37.0
Transportation, postal, and telecommunication services	39.1	14.9	6.1	2.2	1.9	9.2
Wholesale and retail trades, hotels, and catering services	46.7	3.0	9.2	4.6	2.0	12.7
Real estate, leasing, and business services	30.6	3.0	14.3	7.9	7.8	17.2
Banking and insurance	24.6	11.5	17.8	12.0	7.9	8.2
Other services	27.3	3.1	11.1	5.5	2.7	26.1
Total input	43.8	4.7	7.8	5.5	2.3	9.8

Source: National Bureau of Statistics of China 2007.

Note: For the distribution of commodities consumed by an industry, read the column for that industry. For the distribution of industries consuming a commodity, read the row for that commodity. For space considerations, five columns were omitted: "Agriculture"; "Production and supply of electricity"; "Coking, gas, and petroleum refining"; "Mining and quarrying"; and "Construction."

skills. This type of industry produces customized, complex capital goods or engages in small-batch production of customized high-value items. Industries producing complex capital goods (for example, plant equipment, power-generating equipment, and transport equipment) have significant backward links and involve a host of specialized suppliers that frequently cluster near the main assemblers and collaborate in conducting research and development (R&D) programs to meet specific needs of end users and in producing new generations of equipment.[10] With respect to innovation in the capital goods and components industries, Cooke and others (2007: 57) note that these are characterized by a *synthetic knowledge base.* In such settings, the application of existing knowledge or the new combination of available knowledge may lead to innovations. This often occurs in the need to solve actual problems on the shop floor or in interaction with key customers or users and suppliers. Research and development are generally less important . . . University-industry links are less frequent . . . Accordingly, knowledge is created . . . through . . . an inductive process of testing, experimentation, or through practical work."

The revealed comparative advantage (RCA)[11] of Germany, Japan, and the Republic of Korea still lies in these industries.[12] Such industries also derive substantial

---

[10]This collaborative activity between assemblers and their suppliers, most notably in the transport sector, is well known and associated with the embracing of just-in-time delivery practices. Subcontractors have taken on the responsibility for major modules (see Smitka 1991). Collaboration and proximity might be taken a step further if Toyota, for example, realizes its ambition to further minimize the movement of parts (Stewart and Raman 2007).

[11]Revealed comparative advantage is often used to measure the export competitiveness of a commodity (or an industry) of a country. It is a ratio of two shares: (a) the share of a commodity's export in the overall exports of a country and (b) the share of the same commodity in global exports, as follows:

$$RCA = \frac{Export_{ij} / \sum_i Export_{ij}}{\sum_j Export_{ij} / \sum_i \sum_j Export_{ij}}.$$

In this equation, i denotes the commodity and j denotes countries (over the set of commodities, $i = 1 \ldots I$, and over the set of countries, $j = 1 \ldots J$). An RCA greater than 1 means that the country has a revealed comparative advantage in that commodity, assuming that the numerator and the denominator are increasing. If that is not the case, greater care is needed in interpreting the results. Rearranging the equation, one can obtain the following:

$$RCA = \frac{Export_{ij} / \sum_j Export_{ij}}{\sum_i Export_{ij} / \sum_i \sum_j Export_{ij}}.$$

The numerator is now country j's market share of commodity i in the world export market, and the denominator is country j's share of exports in overall world exports. Thus, even if country j is losing market share, if overall exports from country j relative to world exports are shrinking faster, the RCA will be greater than 1 (Sanjaya Lall, Weiss, and Zhang 2006).

[12]Manufactures constitute 83 percent of Germany's exports: transport and automotive equipment are the leading exports.

Table 3.3 RCA in Engineering and Electronics Goods, 2006

Country	RCA
Germany	1.1
Japan	1.4
United States	1.1

Source: United Nations Commodity Trade Statistics Database (UN Comtrade).

Table 3.4 Selected Japanese Exports with High RCA, 2006

Standard International Trade Classification	Short description	RCA	Technology class
7851	Motorcycles, autocycles; sidecars of all kinds, and so on	6.5189	MT1
7126	Steam power units (mobile engines but not steam tractors, and so on)	6.5187	HT2
8841	Lenses and other optical elements of any material	4.7949	MT3
7133	Internal combustion piston engines, marine propulsion	4.6160	MT3

Source: UN Comtrade.
Note: Technology classification is based on Sanjaya Lall (2000): MT1 = automotive, MT3 = engineering, and HT2 = other high-technology.

revenues from after-sales services by maintaining, upgrading, refurbishing, or rebuilding existing equipment (for example, aircraft, earthmoving equipment, engines, and locomotives) and by supplying spare parts for long-lived capital goods, including automobiles. Global suppliers of complex goods can sustain a flotilla of affiliated firms that provide well-paid jobs in an urban environment. In line with this reasoning, the 11th Five-Year Plan (2006–10) gave priority to the complex capital goods sector, calling for the market share of domestic independent brand owners to exceed 50 percent of the automobile and machinery industries by 2010. Although adequate, progress has fallen short of plan targets; market shares of domestic automobile and machinery firms were 26 percent and 31 percent, respectively, in 2007 (World Bank 2008b).

As noted earlier and demonstrated by the recent experience of Germany, Japan, and the United States, complex capital goods, components, and electrical equipment are among the industrial products most suited for capital-abundant economies with a skilled and high-wage workforce.[13] This conclusion is apparent from the estimates of the RCAs of these countries (see tables 3.3–3.6), from Germany's top 10 export goods (see table 3.7), and from the rising share of these exports (see table 3.8). The fact that these industries have survived and prospered

---

[13]The most dynamic Japanese firms in the country's shrinking manufacturing sector are ones that specialize in components, in engineering, and in materials technologies. These companies contribute to the success of some of the latest Apple products and the newest generation of jet airliners (Schaede 2008).

Table 3.5   Selected German Exports with High RCA, 2006

Standard International Trade Classification	Short description	RCA	Technology class
7911	Rail locomotives, electric	5.0069	MT2
7264	Printing presses	4.3978	MT3
7913	Mechanically propelled railway, tramway, trolleys, and so on	3.8624	MT2
7423	Rotary pumps (other than those of heading 74281)	3.8014	MT3
7163	Rotary converters	3.6922	HT1

Source: UN Comtrade.
Note: Technology classification is based on Sanjaya Lall (2000): MT2 = process industry, MT3 = engineering, and HT1 = electronic and electrical.

Table 3.6   Selected Korean Exports with High RCA, 2006

Standard International Trade Classification	Short description	RCA	Technology class
8710	Optical instruments and apparatus	9.7947	HT2
7932	Ships, boats, and other vessels	8.8697	MT3
7938	Tugs, special purpose vessels, and floating structures	7.5444	MT3
7761	Television picture tubes, cathode ray	5.6905	HT1
7247	Textile machinery, not elsewhere specified, for cleaning, cutting, and so on, and parts not elsewhere specified	4.8618	MT3

Source: UN Comtrade.
Note: Technology classification is based on Sanjaya Lall (2000): MT3 = engineering; HT1 = electronic and electrical, and HT2 = other high-technology.

Table 3.7   Germany's Top 10 Exports, 2006

Commodities	Share of total exports (%)
Road vehicles	16.9
Electric machinery, apparatus, and appliances, not elsewhere specified, and parts, not elsewhere specified	7.9
General industrial machinery and equipment, not elsewhere specified, and parts, not elsewhere specified	7.1
Machinery specialized for particular industries	5.1
Medicinal and pharmaceutical products	4.2
Power-generating machinery and equipment	4.0
Miscellaneous manufactured articles, not elsewhere specified	3.7
Artificial resins and plastic materials, plus cellulose esters, and so on	3.3
Manufactures of metals, not elsewhere specified	3.3
Iron and steel	3.1

Source: UN Comtrade.

Table 3.8   Share of Engineering and Electronics Exports in Germany, Japan, and the United States, 1978 and 2006

Country	Share (%)	
	1978	2006
Germany	32.8	33.1
Japan	41.1	45.6
United States	28.9	35.7

Source: UN Comtrade.

in the advanced countries singles them out as the right candidates for China's premier industrial cities. However, there are other reasons for making these industries an integral part of a growth strategy.

A second category of manufacturing activities with growing appeal is profitable because these activities innovate incrementally and, every so often, introduce a revolutionary (disruptive) new product that redraws market boundaries and brings new firms to the forefront.[14] This category of manufacturing industries ranges from food processing and cosmetics to medical imaging and from nanotechnology to new materials. But all of these industries share several distinctive characteristics. They all are R&D intensive, often rely on research covering several fields, and frequently draw on the basic or applied research conducted in universities or specialized institutes (Boozer and others 2003; Jaruzelski and Dehoff 2007a; Jaruzelski, Dehoff, and Bordia 2005, 2006). Small and medium-size firms are the lifeblood of these industries because they are responsible for a significant share of innovation. Firms in industries associated with the life sciences and in advanced materials not infrequently are started by university faculty from nearby schools; draw on the research conducted in universities; and are heavy users of legal,[15] consulting, managerial, and financial services. Consequently, they integrate closely with the service providers in urban centers (see Bresnahan and others 2001). Both types of industries depend for their growth, profitability, and longer-term survival on knowledge deepening and on product differentiation through customization, innovation of all kinds (including

---

[14]Many innovative firms are reorganizing the way in which they conduct their R&D to promote radical innovation ("World's Most Innovative Companies" 2006). In the 2008 edition of *Business Week's* "The World's 50 Most Innovative Companies," no Chinese firms made the top 50, but two firms (Tata and Reliance) from India did so (http://bwnt.businessweek.com/interactive_reports/innovative_companies/). See also Christensen and Raynor (2003).

[15]Intellectual property protection is frequently a concern for high-tech firms in areas such as biotechnology and electronics.

business models), and packaging of products with services ("World's Most Innovative Companies" 2006).[16]

Industrial Productivity and Innovation

Retaining a manufacturing base that is knowledge intensive, combines strong technological capabilities with innovation to achieve competitiveness, and flexibly accommodates new industries as existing ones migrate critically depends on three types of services. First is the quality of the education imparted by urban schools, how effectively it instills science and math skills, and whether it nurtures a spirit of inquiry and an aptitude at solving problems (Yusuf 2009c). A solid base of primary, secondary, and technical or vocational schooling is the foundation of an industrially diverse global city. A sound university system with several world-class universities builds on this foundation and produces the advanced STEM (science, technology, engineering, and mathematics) skills and the talent for management, design, and marketing required by dynamic urban industries, whether manufacturing or services.[17]

The city's research establishment provides a third set of services. It usually centers on a few key universities and major firms but also embraces private and public research institutions,[18] which collaborate with leading local or multinational companies and contribute to the tenor of activities in the city. Openness and networking among local researchers and their interaction with peers around the world is a knowledge multiplier whose value is increasingly recognized.

Only Certain Industrial Sectors Are Innovative

From the U.S. experience, equipment, components, and materials-producing industries were among the 20 that registered the greatest gains in total factor productivity between 1960 and 2005; office equipment and electronic components

---

[16]The success of innovations in advanced materials has been closely associated with complementary innovations that can delay adoption or widespread use for many years. Realizing the full potential of glass fiber was paced by the evolution of laser technology, which brought the fiber-optic infrastructure into existence; Kevlar came into widespread use following advances in the design of body armor. Currently, proton exchange membrane fuel cells for automobiles are in a holding pattern waiting for other innovations that will reduce production costs and lead to superior catalysts and fuel cell stacks that together will result in an economically viable substitute for the internal combustion engine (Maine and Garnsey 2005).

[17]In the United States, math-related occupations are the best paid (Needleman 2009).

[18]Starting in 1999, China restructured and corporatized public research institutes while providing financial support, at least initially. Some of the reformed research institutes are now listed on the Shanghai and Shenzhen stock exchanges (Racine and others 2009).

were the first and the fourth on the list (Jorgenson and others 2007). Should such trends extend into the future, then some of the industries in Beijing and Shanghai will benefit doubly from a combination of technological catching-up, continuing growth of productivity in these subsectors in the advanced economies, and innovation arising from R&D in China. Productivity also rose in several service industries, such as wholesale and retail trade, real estate, telecommunications, and banks. However, much of this increase occurred after the mid-1990s and was the result mainly of major advances in information technology (IT), parallel reorganization of work practices, and logistics starting in the 1980s, coupled with innovations in business models (Brynjolfsson and Saunders 2009; Brynjolfsson and Hitt 2003; Oliner and Sichel 2000). A significant part of the gains has accrued from the introduction of new equipment (computers, other office equipment, and telecommunication equipment); that is, these gains are driven by improvements in hardware.[19] IT hardware has enabled providers of services to increase the efficiency of their supply chains and warehousing, to diversify their services, to consolidate their operations, and to outsource and massively reduce the labor intensity of their operations.

Arguably, this surge of productivity in services is unlikely to persist (it has been much less evident in other advanced countries[20] and has declined in the United States since 2005), absent significant breakthroughs in hardware, in the delivery of services, or in their quality.[21] Data from the U.S. Patent and Trademark Office show that leading companies in the most productive service activities took out few patents (see table 3.9). The firm with the most patents is Target, a retailer, with 441 patents since 1976. By comparison, during the same period, IBM (International Business Machines) was granted more than 49,000 patents, GE (General Electric) more than 27,000, and Intel—a relatively young firm compared to the first two—more than 16,000.

---

[19]Not just hardware, but also software, organizational changes, changes in work practices, and training contributed.

[20]This decline might be linked to the strength of labor unions and other laws protecting small service providers.

[21]Although process innovations associated with investment in IT hardware led to positive productivity growth for the financial sector, the financial crisis of 2008 to 2009 calls into question the merit of a number of product innovations in the financial sector (and the effectiveness of data-mining techniques), especially that of derivatives (Kay 2009). This is not to deny that derivatives—and securitization—have a positive side, because with them the market has been able to manage the volatility arising from the elimination of fixed exchange rates and regulated interest rates. However, by encouraging investors to believe that these financial instruments and other tools made it simple to manage risk, the readiness to leverage has hugely increased, and it is this excessive leverage that was at the root of the meltdown in 2008 and 2009.

Table 3.9 Patents Granted to Service-Oriented Firms

Firms	Cumulative number of patents since 1976
Accenture	284
United Parcel Service of America	210
American Express Travel	181
Citibank	112
Visa International Service Association	59
Citicorp Development Center	56
Goldman Sachs	50
GE Capital	45
Chase Manhattan Bank	31
Reuters	32
J.P. Morgan	29
GE Capital Commercial Finance	16
Bank One, Delaware, National Association	8
GE Corporate Financial Services	6
Restaurant Services	6
Fedex Corporation	3
Target	441
Wal-Mart	15

Source: U.S. Patent and Trademark Office (http://patft.uspto.gov/netahtml/PTO/search-bool.html).
Note: Patent search was conducted using the above assignee names. Data are current as of October 28, 2008.

Empirical findings have pointed to the high (private and social) returns that accrue from R&D and to the relationship between R&D and technological change, which feeds GDP growth (Wieser 2005). Only a subset of manufacturing and service activities benefit from R&D because, in a range of industries, the scope for conducting formal research is small or nonexistent. Most services fall into this category, as do a number of light industries. Figure 3.4 shows the R&D intensities (measured by R&D spending as a share of sales) among different subsectors based on the top 1,000 R&D spenders globally, and figure 3.5, which uses data from 10 leading OECD countries, presents the variation in research intensity across different subsectors. Clearly, the manufacturing industries, led by office and computing machinery, are in the forefront, followed by pharmaceuticals and by machinery and transport equipment. The contribution of the science-based industries such as electronics and pharmaceuticals and the specialized suppliers producing capital goods to productivity in the OECD countries is reinforced by Castaldi (2009: 721): "They remain fundamental contributors to technologies knowledge and aggregate productivity growth." Most processing and light industries contribute little to productivity. So also, surprisingly, do knowledge-intensive business services, although Castaldi

Figure 3.4　R&D Spending as a Share of Sales

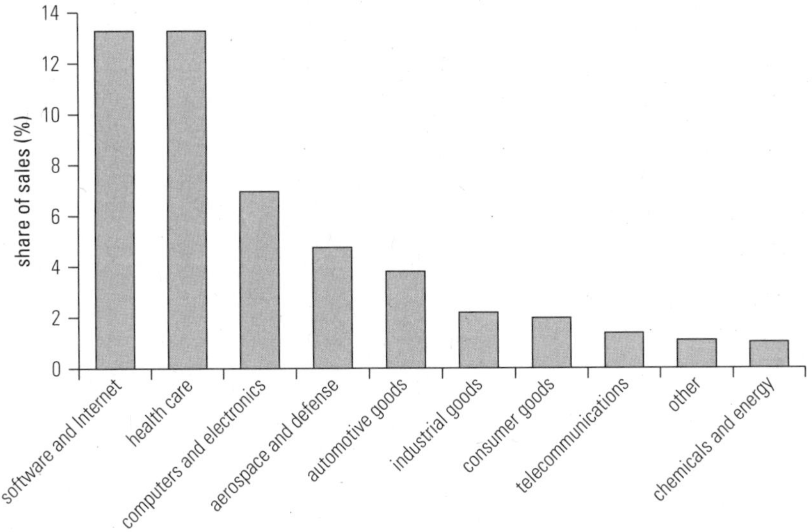

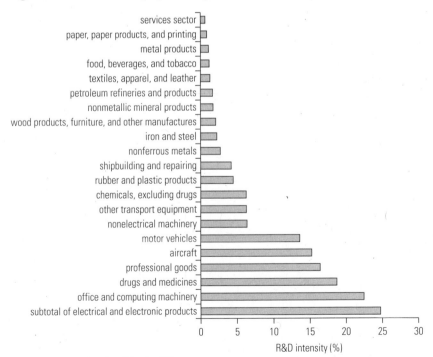

Source: Jaruzelski and Dehoff 2007b.

Figure 3.5　R&D Intensity by Industry in 10 OECD Countries

Source: Mathieu and van Pottelsberghe 2008.

Figure 3.6   Top R&D Spending Sectors among Top 1,000 R&D Spenders

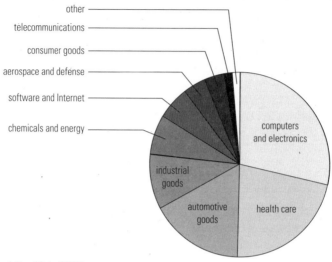

Source: Jaruzelski and Dehoff 2007b.

allows that there may be measurement problems and the contribution of such services might be indirect. In fact, the bulk of R&D spending is in just three areas: electronics, pharmaceuticals (including biotechnology), and machinery and equipment of all kinds, particularly automotive equipment (see figure 3.6).

The auto industry will remain among the most research intensive and one where the scope for innovation is wide for a number of reasons. First, the development of commercially viable "clean" automobiles and the supporting infrastructure will absorb a large volume of R&D in hybrid, electric, and fuel cell technologies, plus other alternatives, and in the physical facilities for delivering fuel or power.[22]

---

[22]The Chinese government plans to increase the production capacity of hybrid and electric cars to 500,000 units by 2011. In 2007, the total production of these hybrid cars was only 2,100. To stimulate the demand for hybrid and electric cars, the government is offering US$8,800 per vehicle purchased by taxi companies and local governments. It is also requiring the power companies to install charging stations for electric cars in Beijing, Shanghai, and Tianjin (Bradsher 2009). China was the largest lithium-ion battery producer in 2008, accounting for 43 percent of global production. China is expected to invest US$1 billion on lithium production. Companies such as BYD Auto and China BAK Battery are two of the largest battery producers. BYD Auto acquired a domestic automaker and is collaborating with Volkswagen to enter the electric car market by 2010. It began selling hybrid electric autos in 2008 (Tabeta 2009; Waldmeir 2009). Wanxiang, among others, is also entering the race to develop electric car technology.

Battery-electric cars were developed in the 19th century at about the same time as cars using an internal combustion engine. For close to a century, the big disadvantage of battery technology was the low energy density of lead acid batteries compared to gasoline (1: 300). Recently, lithium-ion and lithium polymer batteries have raised energy densities fivefold, narrowing the gap with gasoline, and zinc-air and aluminum-air batteries could raise densities further, although these batteries are not rechargeable. Over the near term, lithium technology is the best bet for rechargeable electric cars with a range of 250 to 300 kilometers on a single charge (Duke, Andrews, and Anderson 2009). SAIC (Shanghai Automotive Industry Corporation) and Volkswagen are already engaged in such research in collaboration with Shanghai's Tongji University.

Second, the increasing use of electronics in improving the performance of automobile engines, entertainment systems, dashboard displays, and safety and handling features opens fruitful opportunities for innovation, including in embedded software. Already, premium cars require 100 million lines of code to operate their electronic control units, and electronics accounts for almost 40 percent of the value of such vehicles. Third, the auto industry is also greatly interested in advanced materials that can reduce weight and facilitate the repair and recycling of the vehicle (Charette 2009; J. Zhao 2006).[23] As environmental regulations and their implementation are tightened in Beijing and Shanghai and across China, and with greater emphasis on energy efficiency, the pressure to innovate can only increase (S. Gallagher 2006; Gan 2003).

The share of the services sector in R&D is the smallest, which is not to deny that service industries do not innovate. In fact, they do, but formal R&D plays a small role, and policies that can influence R&D will have little effect on innovation in services. For services, business model and service-delivery innovations may be more important.

Patent data from the U.S. Patent and Trademark Office and from China underscore the relative importance of innovation in manufacturing. Invention patents are more numerous in manufacturing industries, notwithstanding a considerable jump in patents for services (inventions) over the past decade. Questions have been raised about the quality of patents issued for software and other services. Within manufacturing industries, only a dozen or so industrial subsectors account for 60 to

---

[23]Automobiles have evolved into highly complex systems, and the trend with hybrids, electric, and fuel cell-based automobiles is toward greater technical complexity entailing a vast amount of groundbreaking research. A premium car now has 70 to 100 microprocessor-based electronic control units, which can execute up to 100 million lines of code. This quantity is comparable to the number of electronic control units in the Airbus 380 (not including the aircraft's entertainment system). A car's electronics and software amount to between 15 and 40 percent of the vehicle's total cost, and as cars become smarter, this share could soon approach 50 percent (Charette 2009).

Figure 3.7   Share of U.S. Patents by Industry, 1986

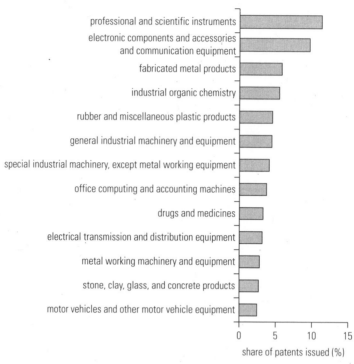

Source: Authors' calculation based on U.S. Patent and Trademark Office data.

70 percent of the invention patents. Comparing figure 3.7 and figure 3.8, one can clearly see that the distribution of patents seems to have become more skewed toward only a handful of the subsectors—electronic components, office machines, and professional and scientific instruments (see figure 3.8). This concentration is even more pronounced in Shanghai, as shown in chapter 5 (see table 5.48).

Interactions with Universities

Industrial competitiveness and industrial resilience in the face of demand shocks and shifting industrial fortunes can benefit from the capabilities of the education and research infrastructure in large cities, which contributes to the stock of usable scientific knowledge and skills. The depth and quality of the pool of skills are a determinant of productivity as well as the speed with which local industry can respond to competitive threats or new opportunities.[24]

---

[24]Glaeser (2005a) ascribes the revival of Boston in the 1980s to the abundant supply of human capital and ideas generated by the area's universities. However, other U.S. cities with world-class universities, such as Baltimore, Philadelphia, New Haven, and New York, have derived less advantage.

Figure 3.8   Share of U.S. Patents by Industry, 2006

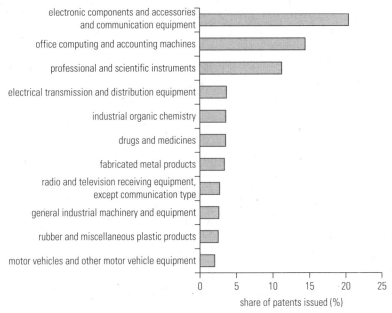

Source: Authors' calculation based on U.S. Patent and Trademark Office data.

Research universities are ideally placed to conduct the basic and interdisciplinary research that underpins innovation and that firms and specialized research institutions are unwilling (because of the low perceived commercial potential) or unequipped (because of its narrow focus or applied R&D orientation) to do. Moreover, close engagement between firms and local universities can be highly advantageous for three reasons. First, it energizes research in both firms and universities: generally, firms that link with universities do more research themselves (Adams and Clemmons 2008). Second, proximity to leading research universities is valuable to firms because the latest findings and state-of-the-art knowledge diffuse slowly and usually by word of mouth;[25] hence, physical closeness and formal or informal links with researchers matter. Third, interaction between firms and universities enables universities to raise funds and to create and staff suitably tailored programs for local firms. In addition, the business community can provide feedback to universities, directly and through internships, on how they can improve pedagogical practices, curriculum, practical training, and communication and teamwork skills to enhance students' readiness for careers after they graduate (Bramwell and Wolfe 2008; Lundvall 2007).

---

[25]Knowledge diffusion, especially at the early stage, is confined to a relatively short distance because the knowledge in question tends to be tacit and because face-to-face communication is often required for its diffusion (Keller 2002). Seminars and conferences organized by universities are venues for airing and discussing ongoing research (Bramwell and Wolfe 2008).

Tertiary education can, in turn, become a leading sector in its own right. It has high added value, substantial multiplier effects on the local economy, and potential for exporting its services and, in the process, for attracting talent from overseas, as Boston and San Francisco have been able to do by leveraging their world-class universities.[26]

---

[26]In terms of income and employment created, direct or "first round" contributions of major U.S. universities to local and state economies are substantial. In 2002, the eight universities in the Boston metropolitan area—Boston College, Boston University, Brandeis University, Harvard University, the Massachusetts Institute of Technology, Northeastern University, Tufts University, and the University of Massachusetts—employed 50,750 people, exceeding the number employed by Greater Boston's financial services industry. Four of these institutions and their five affiliated medical centers qualify as the top 25 employers in Massachusetts. In 2002, local employees earned approximately US$2.2 billion from all eight universities. In addition, new construction projects generated about 3,300 full-time jobs in 2000. Students and visitors spent US$850 million and US$250 million, respectively, in 2000. The estimated regional effect of the universities' US$3.9 billion spending (payroll, purchases, and construction), as well as expenditures by affiliated institutions and students and visitors, was US$7 billion in 2000. The concurrent employment generated was 37,000 full-time jobs (Appleseed 2003).

During fiscal year (FY) 2006/07, the University of California (UC), San Diego, made a net contribution of approximately US$463.1 million to the economy of southern California's San Diego area based on its expenditure of US$1.7 billion on salaries and wages, goods and services, and construction and on revenue of US$1.2 billion from within the county. The university is among the top three local employers, employing 16,760 people, second only to the State of California and the federal government. In FY 2006/07, UC San Diego spent more than US$625.3 million on purchases of goods and services and construction in San Diego County and US$1.1 billion on wages and salaries. Using the IMPLAN input-output model, CBRE Consulting (2008) estimated that the "total" economic consequences in FY 2006/07, incorporating direct, indirect, and induced effects of the university's spending on the mentioned activities, was, at the state level, approximately US$4.0 billion in total spending, 34,230 full-time equivalent jobs, and US$2.3 billion in income generated. Using the same model, CBRE Consulting estimated the "total" economic effects associated with spending incurred by students (including extension and international students), visitors, and retirees at US$600 million in total spending, 4,770 full-time equivalent jobs, and US$288 million income generated at the state level during FY 2006/07 (CBRE Consulting 2008).

Indirect or "second-round" effects of university research on the regional economy, in terms of start-up ventures and consequent income and jobs generated, have also been substantial in a few cases, as in the Boston area and in San Diego. Analog Devices, Biogen Idec, EMC, Lycos, and Staples are examples of major companies founded by alumni from the eight Boston area universities, four of which are listed in the top 25 employers in Boston. The universities started up 41 new ventures in 2000. Licensing of university technologies to private enterprises generated income of US$44.5 million. The economy in the Boston Area was also given a boost from the decision of national and international companies (such as Amgen, Cisco Systems, Merck, Novartis, Pfizer, and Sun Microsystems) to locate major research operations there (Appleseed 2003).

Technology-intensive manufacturing stimulates and can help partially finance university research, which has the potential for substantial spillovers. The proximity of industry and industry-university partnerships can lend focus to a university's applied research and facilitates quicker dissemination of the findings as well as their commercialization. If one important lesson can be drawn from the experience of Silicon Valley, it is that the presence of several companies operating at the frontiers of high-technology industries catalyzed the university-based research and training infrastructure and generated immensely fruitful symbiotic relationships between Silicon Valley firms and universities such as Stanford, UC Berkeley, and San José State. For example, GE's Electronics Research Center near Stanford gave consultancies to several faculty members, and Stanford's Honors Cooperative Program through the Stanford Center for Professional Development enabled researchers in companies to earn master's or doctoral degrees (Lenoir and others 2004). The presence of firms with a hunger for new technology set the stage for the emergence of a local innovation system. However, an integrated and productive system might never have emerged had universities not glimpsed an opportunity and taken the initiative to grasp it by setting up new departments, attracting talent from across the United States and overseas, and designing courses to meet the current and emerging needs of local firms[27]—in other words, by strengthening their capacity to meet the skilled labor and upstream research needs of an industry. However, the United States might be a special case. The quality of the R&D and the volume of innovative ideas generated are closely linked to the presence of foreign graduate students in science and engineering areas, foreign-born faculty, and foreign-born postdoctoral researchers. The openness of the United States to foreign talent has bolstered both the quality of the universities and the quality of their research (Stephan 2009). Replicating this model has proven difficult elsewhere in the United States and abroad.[28]

The Role of Small and Young Firms and of Patient Capital

Although those large corporations that have successfully routinized the art of (generally incremental) innovation constitute the vanguard of the innovation system in any

---

[27]Rosenberg (2003: 118) observes that "Stanford's responsiveness in the case of [integrated circuit technology] lay in the speed with which it diffused knowledge of an invention that had already been developed in industry and not in the academic world, a speed that was of great competitive significance for both Stanford and Silicon Valley." After integrated circuit technology was introduced, Stanford's Electrical Engineering Department launched a course on design and fabrication. Each time the technology improved, Stanford initiated new courses or modified its curriculum so that new generations of engineers were fully conversant with the latest technologies and could contribute to their further advancement (Rosenberg 2003: 114).

[28]On variant models, some of which have enjoyed success, see Yusuf and Nabeshima (2007).

Table 3.10 Major Innovations by Small U.S. Firms in the 20th Century

Air conditioning	Hydraulic brake	Pacemaker
Biomagnetic imaging	Kidney stone laser	Polaroid camera
Electronic spreadsheet	Microprocessor	Quick-frozen food
Heat sensor	Magnetic resonance scanner	Soft contact lenses
High-resolution CAT scanner	Optical scanner	Two-armed mobile robot

Source: Veugelers 2009.
Note: CAT = computed axial tomography.

country, in a number of dynamic scientific fields, such as the life sciences, advanced materials, and IT, young innovative companies are significant contributors and the source of most radical innovations. From the standpoint of innovation, the entry of many new firms and their presence in an urban economy are advantageous because they accelerate the technology refresh rate and raise growth rates (Rosenthal and Strange forthcoming). One reason the United States is the innovation front-runner is because it provides a hospitable environment for large numbers of young, innovative firms that contribute to both R&D and sales (see Veugelers 2009; table 3.10).

Two necessary conditions for the multiplication of promising new ventures are entrepreneurial talent[29] and ideas, and both depend on the existence of large firms and research universities. Large firms and universities are a source of experienced and talented people and of fruitful ideas springing from the entities' own research and knowledge of technologies and that of similar entities (Avnimelech, Kenney, and Teubal 2004).[30] Entrepreneurship with assistance from public providers can

---

[29]Antoinette Schoar (2009) draws an interesting distinction between "subsistence entrepreneurs" and "transformational entrepreneurs." Subsistence entrepreneurs set up small businesses with their own capital or the small amounts available from relatives, friends, and microfinance providers. These firms rarely grow. Transformational entrepreneurs have access to larger amounts of capital and are able to initiate ventures with the potential for growth. Such financing cannot be supplied by microfinance providers or venture capitalists; it must come from banks. Transformational entrepreneurship is also influenced by the regulatory environment, and innovation by smaller firms is promoted by competition with foreign firms (B. Hall, Lotti, and Mairesse 2008).

[30]Successful spinout institutions network closely with university faculty members, financial institutions, and providers of business services. Business angels also provide valuable support, especially with respect to the management of fledgling firms; most often, the quality of management rather than of technology determines success. Few scientists can substitute for managers with professional expertise. Promoting spinouts can on occasion be valuable for universities because their success and the technology that they commercialize are indicators of the nature and utility of the research being conducted by the university (European Commission 2002). See Kenney and Florida (2000) on the role of venture capital in Silicon Valley; Kenney, Han, and Tanaka (2004) on the development of venture capital in East Asia; and Zhang and others (2009) on China.

gradually enhance the supply of patient capital, the lack of which generally impedes the birth of firms. Much has been made of venture capital, but in the vast majority of cases, whether in the United States or in East Asia, banks—public or private— have provided the supplementary financing for start-up firms, whose primary source of funding is invariably the founders' own resources and those of family and friends. Venture capitalists, especially if they are highly experienced, well-established providers with deep pockets, can make a difference to the prospects of start-up firms with innovative ideas, but they do not change the pace of innovation itself (Hirukawa and Ueda 2008a, 2008b). Nevertheless, venture capitalists can make this difference only under certain conditions. First, they have to be highly selective and skilled in picking potential winners with the right venture capital–friendly technologies. Second, they need to be in a position to put up a significant amount of financing over a number of years with reference to performance and to assist firms actively in management, product development, and marketing. Third, venture capitalists' own profitability rests on investing in companies that can establish their worth in not much more than five years (Puri and Zarutskie 2008).[31] The refinement, testing, development, and marketing of most biopharmaceuticals and advanced materials can easily take 10 to 15 years, which is longer than venture capitalists are willing to wait. Hence, they either select firms promising an early payoff or provide mezzanine financing to companies with a proven product. Publicly owned providers of patient capital, which can be development banks or venture capitalists, can wait longer, but their success rate is also low.[32] International experience suggests that combining private with public financing gives better results and complementing financing with business services of the kind that technology-intensive small and medium-size enterprises find valuable also improves outcomes. Governments can also raise the odds against failure by building a monitoring and auditing process into public venture funding schemes as Israel and Taiwan, China, have done (Kenney, Han, and Tanaka 2003).

Perhaps the most successful model is the following:

- It includes several large firms that depend on growth through innovation and that are on the lookout for firms with good products.[33]
- It finances start-ups using public funds channeled through banks and other public agencies complemented by private venture capitalists.

---

[31]Interestingly, the likelihood of a new company succeeding with venture capital or other traditional sources of financing is about even, although at the end of five years, firms that received financing from venture capitalists are likely to be larger.

[32]In 2009, an evaluation of venture capital provided by the U.K. government of 782 firms indicated that the results were disappointing and the financing created only 1.8 jobs per company invested on average (Arnold 2009).

[33]Lewis Branscomb (2008: 916) notes that "Cisco is passionate about innovation [and] its most important innovation is its partnership with both customers and competitors making a true networked enterprise."

- It comprises emerging clusters of networked firms that provide a base of specialized suppliers and mutually reinforcing R&D activities that are a source of valuable technological spillovers.

Innovation Drivers

As measured by R&D and patenting, innovation seems to be influenced by five sets of policies and institutions:

- Policies affecting the composition of industry and of acquired technological capability and the contribution of FDI (and the diaspora) to this capability
- Policies affecting urban scale and urbanization economies as well as knowledge spillovers in urban centers[34]
- Education and research policies that determine the foundation-building strengths of primary and secondary schooling, the quality of tertiary education, and the volume and productivity of research[35]
- Sociopolitical institutions that assign status and recognition to learning and encourage intellectual achievement, safeguard intellectual property, and promote openness to ideas and to the circulation of knowledge workers
- Institutions that stimulate competition among producers of ideas, of goods, and of services that regulate performance and set standards

In other words, countries need first to build their knowledge base and to move closer to the frontiers of technology in selected fields. When countries reach this state, greater scope exists for sustained innovation. Acquiring this technological capability is no simple matter, however; the process of adoption and adaptation remains uncodified.[36] After countries have acquired substantial technological depth and are near the frontiers of knowledge, what might push the system they have created to deliver high and persisting levels of innovation or any significant innovation is difficult to determine. Spending on R&D can help; the innovation strategies of major firms can make a contribution, especially if they spin off innovative firms; new entrants can serve as bearers of technology; and the excellence of the research universities can feed the pool of skills, ideas, and entrepreneurship. Beyond this, there is little concrete to say. Whether research can fulfill the demands of national policy makers and chief executive officers who would like to make innovation routine remains an open question.[37]

---

[34]Florida (2002) has strongly championed the importance of such openness and the contribution diversity can make.

[35]Patenting by Korean residents has been influenced by both the spread of higher education and the increasing expenditure on R&D (Lee and Kim 2009).

[36]Nonetheless, the Japanese experience shows that investment in human capital is critical and that the government can assist firms in assimilating foreign technologies and developing indigenous technologies (P. Fan and Watanabe 2006).

[37]Not that there is a shortage of suggestions on how to improve innovation capabilities. See for example, World Bank Institute (2007).

4

Pitfalls of Early Deindustrialization

Starting in the 19th century, the industrial revolution unleashed a wave of urbanization that has spread from the West to the rest of the world and shows no sign of receding. This it did by enormously accelerating the generation of wealth and employment through a production system rooted in cities.[1] Industry flourished in cities because they made raising capital, hiring workers, finding buyers for products, obtaining needed services, gathering information, and finding housing and other amenities easier (see Hohenberg and Lees 1995). From at least the middle of the 19th century onward, modern manufacturing industry became one of the principal drivers, if not the principal driver, of growth in all the major cities (and some smaller towns) of Europe and the United States—and later of Japan as well. Industry maintained a dominant position through the middle of the 20th century; from then onward, the situation began changing in at least the leading cities of advanced countries. The share of industry began to shrink, and that of services began to expand. How quickly this change occurred and how radically it altered the urban landscape can be observed from the experience of four cities: Chicago,

---

[1]Hohenberg and Lees (1995: 176) observe that "the first phase of modern industrialization continued the emphasis on rural investment with the building of railroads and the progressive mechanization of manufactures. As the workers concentrated around mills and workshops, industrial capital simply became urban. In later phases, factories and their machinery were predominantly sited in urban places." Later, Hohenberg and Lees (1995: 194) note: "Modern industry [in the 19th century] meant principally iron, cotton textiles, and steam driven machinery."

Table 4.1   Share of National Income, 2005

City	Share of national income (%)
New York	8.3
Chicago	3.6
Tokyo (2000)	18.4
London	20.0

Sources: Statistical Research and Training Institute 2002; U.S. Census Bureau 2008.

London, New York,[2] and Tokyo.[3] These cities account for a substantial share of the national income of their respective countries (see table 4.1).[4]

---

[2] The many facets of life in old Shanghai that made it such a remarkable city are vividly conveyed by Sergeant (1998), and the more risqué side of life is described by Yatsko (2001). Both note the contribution of the White Russians to the vibrancy of the city in the 1920s and 1930s. Shanghai is often compared to New York and sometimes referred to as the "Chinese New York," among other nicknames such as the "Oriental Pearl" and the "Paris of the East" (H. Lu 2004). Partly, this name refers to large international concessions ceded to foreign powers after the Opium War (H. Lu 2004). Partly, it relates to the considerable standing Shanghai had achieved by the early 20th century as a center for industry and fashion (Yatsko 2001). The development of Shanghai during the first 15 years of reform is examined by Yusuf and Wu (1997).

[3] A cross-country analysis of the changing share of services in gross domestic product indicates that the growth of services occurs in two waves, with traditional services (mainly personal services) rising steadily until purchasing power parity–adjusted per capita incomes reach US$1,800 and then leveling off. A second wave commences as per capita incomes begin approaching US$4,000, and this wave encompasses business services, many affected by information technology, and pushes the share of services to higher levels at the expense of the primary and industrial sectors. Some studies find that the share of services is most strongly influenced by the openness of the economy to trade, by democratic institutions, and by proximity to a global financial center (Eichengreen and Gupta 2009). However, a study by Kollmeyer (2009) that explicitly tests for three leading factors responsible for the expansion of the services sector—rising income, faster productivity growth of manufacturing, and trade with other countries—finds that rising income is the most important factor contributing to the rise in the share of services in an economy.

[4] Using purchasing power parity rates, PricewaterhouseCoopers (2007) estimates that the 30 largest cities in the world were responsible for 16 percent of global GDP in 2005 and the top 100 cities for a quarter of the GDP. Four East Asian cities were among the top 30, ranked by GDP: Tokyo (1), Osaka-Kobe (7), Hong Kong, China (14), and Seoul (20) (PricewaterhouseCoopers 2007; see also the papers on global city regions in Scott 2001a).

Expansion of Services

Why have services squeezed out manufacturing from these cities? One explanation is the cost of land and labor in cities. Because manufacturing is land intensive, some analysts claim it moves out of the inner parts of major cities as rents rise and environmental regulations begin constraining those activities that are significant polluters (of air and water and the cause of noise). Manufacturing can transfer to the periphery of the city, where rental costs are lower, or it can seek greenfield sites in smaller and medium-size cities.

A second explanation is higher wage costs. It is argued that the cost of living in large cities drives up wages and forces manufacturing, which is labor intensive, to migrate to areas where labor is cheaper.[5] A third reason put forward is that services edge out manufacturing from the major cities because the demand for services grows most strongly in urban areas. Furthermore, urban densification favors services because of the effect it has on information flows and the transport cost advantages reaped by services (Glaeser 2005b).

Fourth and most important, city authorities, allied with urban residents (who are anxious to safeguard the quality of life) and developers, have in all these cases actively pursued the development of commercial real estate, housing, and services in the commercial business district and core areas through zoning laws,[6] real estate taxes, and preferential treatment. Urban planners believe that a concentration of services is more likely to contribute to longer-term prosperity (because services are less subject to fluctuations in demand, are arguably less footloose, and have better long-term prospects) and to urban revenues.[7] Municipal leaders, supported

---

[5]Glaeser (2009) points out that in 1970 workers demanded a hefty wage premium in large cities in the United States. However, as urban amenities have improved and crime has diminished, the premium also has vanished.

[6]Zoning specifies rules governing permissible activities, sizes of lots, numbers of buildings, and relationships between buildings.

[7]New York's zoning ordinance of 1916 favoring the Fifth Avenue retailers pushed out the garment industry with its workforce of poor immigrant women, and Thomas Adams's Regional Plan of 1929 brought skyscraper-based commercial activities to downtown areas and assigned industry to the periphery. In the 1980s, Michael Heseltine spearheaded initiatives that transformed London's governance and land use, especially in the Docklands (P. Hall 1998). The notion of a well-designed "compact city" that has high density, is served by an efficient public transport system, and is generously provided with public spaces was put forward by Richard Rogers in the early 1990s (Rogers 1997). The idea appealed to the Greater London Authority and the various boroughs. But because the public authorities lacked the vision, the planning capability, and the resources to upgrade transport and public spaces, achieving compactness while enhancing livability was left in the hands of developers, whose objective was to maximize the return from space by cramming in the maximum number of tower blocks.

by the business services community, have frequently championed the development of downtown service clusters. Noisy, polluting, low-value-adding manufacturing activities are seen more as a handicap than as an asset and are encouraged to relocate with a mix of negative and positive incentives. Developers and providers of real estate services actively support such policy initiatives.

The need for land-use regulation through zoning began to be felt in New York in the latter half of the 19th century with the appearance of tall buildings[8] that overshadowed smaller structures, blocked light, and impeded air circulation.[9] As early as 1860, a statute was introduced to ban commercial activities along the Eastern Parkway in Brooklyn. However, the construction of the 42-story Equitable Building in 1915 brought home the problems associated with such large structures with no setbacks (New York City Department of City Planning 2009). By 1916, New York had put in place the State Zoning Enabling Act.[10] This regulation and its subsequent extensions and modifications (in 1961, for example) came to determine the physical as well as the industrial characteristics of the city, and very quickly they were adopted by Chicago "as these two world cities were linked not only with one another but with European traditions and models" (Abu-Lughod 1999: 93). Zoning helped privilege housing to absorb the enormous influx of migrants to the city, it accommodated the creation of mass transit routes and the widening use of the automobile, and through setbacks, it ensured public plazas, green spaces, and amenities.[11]

---

[8]The height of buildings was affected by three developments: the invention of the elevator (the hydraulic and piston hydraulic varieties now superseded by electric elevators); the introduction of the traveling crane; and the construction of buildings using steel frames and curtain walls instead of stone, whose weight made constructing tall structures impossible. Use of steel frames originated in bridge building and was adopted by architects and engineers in Chicago in the 1880s. From there, it diffused to and was perfected in New York (P. Hall 1998). Chicago's architectural and engineering innovations were triggered by the Great Fire of 1871, which devastated 4 square miles of the city.

[9]Until the invention of fluorescent lighting (1940) and air conditioning (1930s), the occupants of buildings depended upon natural light and air circulation through windows. For this reason, offices were usually less than 30 feet deep. Thus, by blocking sunlight and the circulation of air, a tall building could create a serious problem for its neighbors (O'Flaherty 2005: 172).

[10]Zoning was first introduced in Frankfurt am Main, Germany, in 1891 (O'Flaherty 2005: 171).

[11]So that enough light and air reached buildings lit by dim incandescent bulbs and without space cooling, buildings had to be stepped back (or set back) as they increased in height with reference to a fixed angle from the center of the street. This requirement resulted in a wedding-cake configuration that endowed New York with its distinctive skyline (Abu-Lughod 1999: 94–95). Zoning bylaws in Melbourne, Australia, have preserved a Victorian skyline by requiring that tall buildings be constructed in courtyards behind existing buildings. Landry (2008: 150) observes that "as a result, Melbourne combines a distinctive cosmopolitan appearance with intimate walkable Victorian spaces."

Thus, zoning ensured that the building technologies, facilitating ever-taller buildings, did not choke the livability of the city. However, zoning also ushered most manufacturing activities out of the core areas of New York into smaller towns and cities on the far periphery. It started with regulations to protect the wealthy residential districts in Manhattan's Upper East Side from the pollution caused by the garment and textile industries, which had mushroomed in proximity (Freeman 2008). Thereafter, and gradually, rezoning that favored commercial offices and housing developments ratcheted up the incentives for factories to exit the city. By the early decades of the 20th century, with the spread of "banking, accounting, management, law, journalism, and advertising," a new form of "specialised human activity was firmly established—the white-collar office worker" (Reader 2006: 256). In recent years, environmental impact reviews and activities of the Landmarks Preservation Commission in New York, which has effectively blocked the construction of tall buildings in the better neighborhoods, have reinforced the effect of zoning on land use, lot sizes, and housing (Glaeser 2009). Glaeser, Gyourko, and Saks (2005) estimate the cost of regulation to be close to 100 percent of actual building cost.[12] They note further that inefficient regulation stems from the gradual transfer of property rights (or rents) from developers to homeowners, who have the incentives to restrict and exercise their political rights to prevent an additional supply of housing units so as to raise the prices of existing housing stocks. As a result, the number of permits approved for new housing units has declined in New York City and housing prices have increased dramatically since the 1980s, thus constraining the growth of the urban economy.

Each of the preceding reasons carries some weight; however, the exodus of manufacturing activities from the leading global cities and the rise of the financial sector are also the outcome of historical circumstances. Early in the 20th century, industry and logistics were the pillars of New York's economy. Garments, printing, sugar refining, footwear, electronics, and meatpacking industries generated US$1.5 billion worth of output in 1910 (Glaeser 2005b). New York was also a major transport hub serving its own producers and those in its hinterland.[13] A comprehensive regional plan for land use and transportation initiated the exodus of industry in the late 1920s. It was a slow process, but by the 1980s, New York was largely denuded of manufacturing, except for tiny pockets in the core city[14] and a few concentrations in the suburbs. New York's importance as a logistics hub also

---

[12]They came to this estimate even after accounting for possible negative externality associated with additional housing units, such as congestion.

[13]It was, in addition, a magnet for migrants from Europe.

[14]In 1950, New York had 2 million industrial jobs and was the leading industrial city in the United States; the number of industrial jobs declined to 500,000 by 2000. Most of the firms are small businesses in subsectors such as manufacturing, construction, wholesaling, utilities, and waste management. Manufacturing firms are in high-end garments, printing and publishing, furniture, and food processing. The last two industries are among the fastest growing.

diminished rapidly because of containerization, competition from other ports, and the role of trade with East Asia, which privileges ports on the West Coast.[15] Consequently, the city's economy became progressively more reliant on business and other services.[16] In particular, financial services,[17] already a significant force in New York's economy because of its earlier status as the country's biggest port, acquired ever-greater weight as a gradual dismantling of regulations from the early 1970s, a strategy favoring the services sector, and the start of globalization ushered in the golden age of finance (Eichengreen and Leblang 2008). By 1990, financial services, in conjunction with insurance, legal, accounting, and other professional services, accounted for 32 percent of total gross domestic product (GDP). Other services and creative industries, such as media, fashion, and Web-based services, also mattered, but New York's economy mainly revolved around the well-oiled, money-making machine extending from Wall Street to mid-Manhattan and reaching out to the far corners of the globe (Glaeser 2005b).[18] Yet, through much of the 1980s and 1990s, New York's economy grew slowly—at less than 1 percent per year—and even though the financial sector remained an island of prosperity, information technology (IT) facilitated outsourcing, and the high cost of employing staff in New York led to a steady outflow of back-office jobs to other medium-size cities in the United States. During the past decade, jobs have been offshored to India and Mexico, for example (O'Cléireacáin 1997; Rosen and Murray 1997).

London's Rise to Become a Global Financial Center

London and to a lesser extent Chicago have experienced similar seismic shifts. As recently as 1971, 27 percent of London's jobs were in manufacturing, a significant segment of which was located near the Docklands area. The decline of manufacturing since then was both sudden and sharp.[19] Containerization, which led to the closing of several of the docks and the concentration of port activities in downstream locations, denuded the Docklands economy. Overseas competition added to the pressure on local producers. In addition, by throwing its support behind the financial sector and incentivizing developers to convert industrial land into commercial real estate and housing, the government hurried manufacturing out of London. Through "a creative combination of public spending and private enterprises [the government ensured] that London would cease to be a center of goods

---

[15]However, air cargo traffic remains important.

[16]The growth of financial and business services in New York was accompanied by an expansion of the municipal government, which further enlarged the scale of the services sector (Crahan and Vourvoulias-Bush 1997).

[17]Abu-Lughod (1999) describes and compares the development of financial services in New York and Chicago.

[18]One consequence noted by Markusen and Gwiasda (1994) is that New York does not benefit from multiple layers of functions—political, industrial, financial, and industrial—which promote innovation and a variety of employment opportunities.

[19]Between 1970 and 2000, close to 800,000 jobs in manufacturing were lost (P. Hall 1998).

making and goods handling, and instead would devote itself wholeheartedly and enthusiastically to the new informational economy; the old spaces liberated from their traditional activities and lying derelict and unwanted would be recycled to meet the needs of the new economic world" (P. Hall 1998: 889).

However, financial and business services would not have so quickly gained ascendance in London—and in New York and Chicago—had a revolution in financial technology not occurred with the advent of securitization and swaps, strongly buttressed by computerization and advances in software. These developments, together with an easing of regulations, paved the way to financial globalization and an expansion of the financial industry in a few key centers—London being one of them.

Early on, from the 17th century, the financial center in the city of London was the beneficiary of the commercial and marine activities associated with London's port, including the insurance market, which was primarily engaged in insuring ships and cargoes. Three factors ensured that London remained at center stage of international financial centers, along with New York and later Tokyo, from 1890 to 2000 (Cassis and Bussière 2005). First, progressive financial specialization deepened expertise and helped build comparative advantage. By 1913, the city had almost 226 merchant banks, discount houses, and major joint-stock or large European banks, which effectively made London the payments center of the international economy. By the end of World War I, London retained the first rank in commerce, shipping, and marine insurance, and only New York was a larger source of financing.

Second was the city's ability to adapt to changing global challenges and opportunities. Despite the decline in the strength of the British economy and of sterling as an international currency after World War II, London benefited from the restrictions imposed by the U.S. government on the stock exchange and from legislation that kept commercial banks from engaging in investment banking. It exploited its location in the midst of time zones, the fact that English was the language of business, and the variegated expertise in brokerage and support services. Consequently, some U.S. banks opened offices in London. By the 1970s, the development of the Eurodollar market made London the center of attraction for banks that conducted international operations in money, foreign exchange, securities, and capital markets (exchange controls were lifted in 1979). From 82 foreign banks in 1961, the number doubled to 159 in 1970 and to 280 by 1978. Following the Louvre Accord, which led to the revaluing of the yen relative to the dollar, Japanese banks and finances also flooded into London. The resurgence of London as an international center for financial transactions was facilitated by personnel with technical knowledge retained from the heavily regulated years during the 1940s and 1950s. They relearned lost skills and willingly accepted foreigners,[20] especially from the United States and the former British Empire.

---

[20]This is one area in which Tokyo lags far behind London and New York (Yeandle and others 2009).

Third, the deregulation of the securities industry in 1988, along with the related financial market reforms known as the "Big Bang," further enhanced London's attractions and led to significant changes in business organizations. It resulted in dismantling of the traditional, specialized, and modestly sized British firms during the 1980s and 1990s, which were replaced by massive, globally active banks undertaking the full range of financial activities. A second set of complementary large firms comprising lawyers, accountants, and (private equity and hedge) fund managers also emerged. An enabling regulatory and legal environment (a single Financial Services Authority replaced a host of regulations in 2001), sound accounting standards, and relatively lenient immigration rules for knowledge workers further boosted London's financial sector.

By the beginning of the 21st century, London was consolidating its status as the foremost beneficiary of the globalization era (Cassis and Bussière 2005).[21] The city profited from the growth of international trade, which stimulated financial activities associated with trade, such as foreign exchange, ship and aircraft brokerage, and insurance. Through its leadership of the international banking industry and aided by the advances in technology, London became the principal center for offshore financial activities, in particular through the Eurobond market. The biggest impetus behind the economies of scale enjoyed by the city derived from the concentration of a large number of international services firms. Economies of scope arose from the availability of a critical mass of supporting specialist services, such as commercial lawyers, IT experts, and public relations consultants. The distribution of local employment clearly demonstrates the importance of the local workforce in terms of expertise in the financial sector. In 2000, about 40,000 people worked in the 481 foreign banks, while the domestic, head-office-type banks employed some 25,000. In addition, foreign exchange, investment banking, derivatives, fund management, insurance, and professional and specialist services employed another 200,000 people. Close to the total financial sector employment of 360,000 in New York in 2000, the aggregate number of the financial services workforce in London (335,000) far exceeded the 167,000 in Hong Kong, China (1997), and the almost 80,000 in Frankfurt, Germany.

As of 2007, the two financial hubs of New York and London remained far ahead of the rest of the world, and they mutually benefited from the network effects reinforced by the surge in cross-border mergers and acquisitions and in alternative investments ("Friends and Rivals" 2007).[22] In contrast to London, which tapped foreign interests to maintain its vitality and looked to profit from the legal, tax, and regulatory advantages it had compared to the rest of Europe, New York

---

[21]London is the only city in Europe that equals U.S. levels of productivity and competitiveness. Brussels is a distant second.

[22]Both cities have experienced population growth mainly through in-migration. In fact, almost 31 percent of London's population is foreign born.

looked inward and relied more on straightforward, heavily traded products such as equities.[23] New York prides itself in employing 15 percent of the local workforce in the financial sector. London, in contrast, leads the field in structured finance and new stock listings. It accounted for 24 percent of the world's exports of financial services (compared with 39 percent for the United States as a whole), and 66 percent of the European Union's foreign exchange and derivatives trading and 42 percent of the European Union's share trading were conducted in London.

The Transformation of Chicago

Chicago's importance as a transport node was first established by the building of the Erie Canal and the Illinois and Michigan Canal, which, respectively, connected Chicago to the coastal cities of New York via the Hudson and New Orleans via the Mississippi during an era when waterborne transport was the least expensive means of conveyance. The coming of railroads and later the refrigerated railcar made it the processing and transshipment point first for fattened hogs, then for cattle and dressed beef, and finally for grain, all of which flowed into the city's stockyards and abattoirs from the western prairie lands (Campante and Glaeser 2009). When the inventor of the mechanical reaper, Cyrus McCormick, moved to Chicago, it became the center of the farm-machinery industry and later also a focus of garment production and other manufactures (Glaeser 2009).[24] But all those industries are now a fading memory. Chicago's meatpacking, iron and steel, and railway wagon and farm-machinery industries have largely vanished along with their blue-collar workers; manufacturing employment fell from 45 percent in 1963 to 18 percent in 1998 (E. Johnson 2001). Their place has been filled by the mercantile exchange (CME Group)[25] and commodity exchanges and trading of derivatives, as well as by firms specialized in IT, the life sciences, telecommunications, and software. All these activities feed off the skilled workers and research findings generated by Chicago's universities and are attracted by the access to pools of capital. Chicago is the nation's fourth-largest employer of high-tech workers (E. Johnson 2001). Following the merger of the Chicago Mercantile Exchange and the Chicago Board of Trade in 2007 to form CME Group, Chicago became the leading center

---

[23]The New York Stock Exchange together with the National Association of Securities Dealers Automated Quotations (NASDAQ) accounted for almost half of the global trading in stocks in 2006.

[24]Printing was another industry that flourished in Chicago (as in New York, London, and Tokyo) from the late 19th century and gave rise to a thriving cluster of suppliers providing the printers with raw materials, parts, services, and skills (R. Lewis 2009).

[25]The Chicago Mercantile Exchange was started in 1898 to trade contracts in butter and eggs produced in Chicago's agricultural hinterland. In the early 1960s, the exchange expanded its scope to include pork bellies and live cattle futures.

of trade in derivatives. However, Chicago is keenly aware of the need to restore a broader economic base by rebuilding industrial corridors with the help of incubators, by enacting policy measures that will create industrial clusters, by introducing programs for upgrading workforce skills, and by reforming property taxes to free underused land for industrial purposes. These efforts are being buttressed by enhancements to Chicago's logistics capabilities and employment, which have improved the links between intermodal hubs, freight facilities, airfreight centers, and interstate highways (E. Johnson 2001).

Hollowed-Out Tokyo

Tokyo was services oriented but had substantial manufacturing subsectors until the early part of the 1980s. However, the appreciation of the yen following the signing of the Plaza and Louvre Accords in 1985 and 1987, respectively, and the economic bubble that grew through the latter part of the 1980s created cost pressures that drove manufacturing out of the city. Even though the bubble deflated in the 1990s, the industries that left did not return. The difference is that the leading Japanese manufacturing firms whose headquarters are located in Tokyo (and Osaka) still retain much of their research and development (R&D) operations close by, sustain their formal and informal links with researchers in the local universities, and do their prototyping and trial batch production at their research facilities. In other respects, Tokyo has begun to resemble New York and London in its reliance on services, except that the share of finance does not loom as large; finance is not the leading sector or the largest source of public revenues. Hence, manufacturing, mainly in the suburban prefectures, remains a considerable presence, even though its share of total metropolitan output has fallen to 10.7 percent.

As a financial center, Tokyo is not in the same league as New York and London, although it hosts the world's second-biggest market for equities. Tokyo's financial center mainly serves domestic borrowers.[26] Consequently, despite the scale of the Japanese financial market, Tokyo's financial sector does not dominate the urban economy to the extent that Wall Street, for example, dominates New York's economy. Only 4 percent of the workforce is directly employed by the finance and insurance industries (see table 4.2), and finance is not a major source of public revenue. The share of employment in business services is 15 to 16 percent.[27] That this lesser reliance on finance and insurance may be an advantage is a point elaborated on later in this chapter.

---

[26]The nature of the regulatory environment and differences in the accounting rules also discourage foreign participants.

[27]Business services is calculated as the sum of "other business services," "finance and insurance," "advertising," and "specialized services" in table 4.2.

Table 4.2 Subsectoral Breakdown for Tokyo by Establishments and Employees, 2006

Subsector	Establishments (%)	Employees (%)
Wholesale, retail	25.5	21.3
Manufacturing	9.1	10.3
Restaurants, hotels	14.6	8.9
Telecommunications	3.1	8.7
Other business services	2.3	7.2
Medical and social services	5.8	6.7
Construction	6.2	5.1
Transportation	3.0	4.7
Education	2.9	4.7
Finance and insurance	1.4	4.1
Specialized services	6.1	3.8
Government services	0.3	2.7
Clothes washing, beauty salons, bathhouses	5.2	1.7
Entertainment	1.2	1.3
Services related to lifestyles	1.1	0.8
Advertising	0.6	0.8
Academic and R&D	0.1	0.5
Electricity, gas, water	0.1	0.4
Other services	3.8	3.4

Sources: Tokyo Metropolitan Government.
Note: Sorted by the share of employees.

Early Industrialization and Industrial Turnover

New York, London, Chicago, and to a lesser extent Tokyo were among the early industrializers, and they attracted textiles, clothing, food processing, publishing,[28] metallurgical, and equipment manufacturing activities, all of which were the leading subsectors in the earlier stages of industrial development. These industries tended to be labor intensive and frequently employed numerous semiskilled and unskilled workers; the factory layouts for processing industries were sprawling, whereas production of apparel, tools, and machinery often took place in cramped and grimy workshops; and several of these activities caused severe air, water, and noise pollution. As land and labor costs increased and cities become more densely

---

[28]Edward L. Glaeser (2009) observes that New York rose as the publishing capital of the country because being the natural hub for trans-Atlantic trade gave the city a clear edge in pirating books published in England.

populated, these industries were pushed out (Glaeser 2005b). The rise and spread of service activities and a variety of regulatory measures (including antipollution measures) helped to ensure that new kinds of manufacturing activities did not return to these cities.

New York, London, and Chicago deindustrialized and bypassed the opportunity to benefit from a new generation of industries that use no more land than activities producing services, are less labor intensive than many services and employ a high proportion of skilled or technical workers, and generate little pollution thanks to advances in pollution abatement techniques. Moreover, the value added per worker in these new industries can match or exceed that of workers in service occupations. Unlike many, if not most, service activities, the new generation of manufacturing activities has three additional advantages. First, these new industries register high rates of increased productivity because of learning and continuing refinements in production techniques. Second, these industries are among the most dynamic in the technological sense, with backward links to research institutes and universities and forward links to some of the fastest-growing services, such as multimedia, design, digital entertainment, and health. And third, they have higher employment multipliers than service providers.[29]

New York, London, and Chicago were victims of premature deindustrialization after "old" manufacturing industries migrated either to provincial centers or, as in the case of textiles, overseas. The first two were quick to extend and consolidate a comparative advantage in financial services. Chicago built up the services sector following the success of the mercantile exchange. The rapid expansion of financial and related services created its own virtuous spiral of development, but it resulted in ever-greater specialization in business services, assisted by deregulation and the stripping away of exchange controls. The IT and digital revolutions have promoted financial innovation, and the creative industries have triggered some diversification, but mostly into other services, and have failed to attract a new generation of manufacturing industries.[30] Starting with Tokyo in the second half of the 1980s and extending to London and New York from the mid-1990s, real estate bubbles have erased all but a few economic activities and have profoundly gentrified the more exclusive neighborhoods. Because London, New York, and Tokyo are the iconic global cities, the assumption that the future of dynamic cities lies in services has now become axiomatic. This view deserves to be reconsidered.

---

[29]The auto sector in the United States has an employment multiplier of 7.

[30]Silicon Alley in New York failed to usher in new manufacturing activities mainly because soaring property values in Manhattan, fueled by the real estate bubble, not only prevented such diversification but also sharply constrained the expansion of Silicon Alley (Indergaard 2004).

Five Stylized Tendencies and Their Implications

The experiences of these four cities and of other cities in industrialized countries yield five stylized tendencies of relevance for Beijing and Shanghai as they map a future strategy.

Agglomeration Economies Bring Many Benefits

Size and industrial heterogeneity can deliver scale and urbanization economies, thereby permitting gains in productivity and innovation that contribute to the competitiveness of existing industries and to the emergence of new activities. In principle, heterogeneity enlarges the options for a city to diversify, and a sizable concentration of relatively affluent and discriminating consumers and businesses demanding innovation makes introducing new products and new lines of business easier.[31] The potential for cocreating valuable innovations with customers is also greater in cities (Prahalad and Krishnan 2008). The productivity gains arising from agglomeration and scale economies are a consequence of a greater circulation of interindustry information, "thicker" labor markets, and superior access to specialized services, as well as to better public infrastructure and public facilities (Melo, Graham, and Noland 2009). A review of research findings shows that the productivity advantages conferred by size and urbanization economies range from 3 percent to 14 percent of GDP (Pan and Zhang 2002; Rosenthal and Strange 2004).[32] Large cities that

---

[31]The strength of Tokyo as an innovation hotspot derives from the existence of a critical mass of sophisticated and adventurous consumers who are willing to try new products (K. Fujita and Hill 2005). Consumers in China, especially those in affluent urban areas, show some signs of becoming more discriminating. One reason multinational corporations set up R&D centers in China is to adopt and develop consumer durable goods for the Chinese market because they have had difficult times selling the older models in China in recent years. As a result, some corporations are now developing models in China and then introducing them to the global market (Y.-C. Chen 2008).

[32]Under favorable circumstances, with each doubling of the size of city, the urban GDP can increase by between 3 and 14 percent (Rosenthal and Strange 2004). Venables and Rice (2005) estimate that a doubling of the population of a city can raise productivity by 3.5 percent. Henderson concludes from his analysis of the size and productivity of cities in China that, because of past constraints on urbanization, most are suboptimal in size— that is, below 5 million (Au and Henderson 2006b)—and that productivity gains from achieving optimality would be about 4.1 percent if the city is 20 percent below optimal but as much as 35 percent if the city is half the optimal size (Henderson 2004; Rosenthal and Strange 2004). Although evidence on urbanization economies (arising from industrial diversity) is mixed (and greater for some industries than for others), that on the diversity of high-tech industries is much clearer. Overman and Venables (2005: 18) find that a one standard deviation increase in the diversity index raises productivity by 60 percent. See also Deichmann and others (2005); M. Fujita and Thisse (2002); S. V. Lall, Shalizi, and Deichmann (2004); Quigley (2008); and World Bank (2009c).

are absorbing young migrants, many of whom are educated and skilled, benefit from their energy, entrepreneurship, and human capital (D. Bloom and Williamson 1998; Parker 2007).[33] A growing population that deepens the urban labor pool can add 1 to 2 percent to economic growth if it also crowds more capital into local productive activities through new starts, which can, for example, spawn new industrial clusters (Glaeser and Kerr 2008).[34,35]

A Services Economy Is a Mixed Blessing

Leading cities emerged as centers of industry or as administrative and logistics hubs—often all three—in the late 19th and early 20th centuries.[36] Frequently, manufacturing was the engine of growth, with services playing a secondary role even when they generated a majority of the jobs. Mainly because of historical circumstances and location, a few of the very largest, strategically located cities diversified into financial and business services that initially served regional or colonial markets and, later, global markets. Financial globalization, expedited by new technologies, the progressive dismantling of capital and exchange controls, and the parallel partial deregulation of the financial sector, enabled the early starters—in particular London and New York—to rapidly expand the scale of their financial activities using a variety of instruments and to widen their international reach (Eichengreen and Leblang 2008; Obstfeld and Taylor 2003). Finance and associated business services provided a new growth engine for the global cities—and to some lesser ones as well—and hastened the departure of manufacturing. Finance can become the foremost leading sector when a city begins serving a large regional or a global market. In other words, the push exerted by the expansion of increasingly highly paid services employment, especially in finance, and the activities of urban developers catering to these services can reinforce the pull exerted by other lower-cost locations on manufacturing, thus resulting in a rapid shrinkage of manufacturing industry. The consequence is an increasingly monoindustrial economy, dominated by a few business services and retail and personal services, and declining industrial heterogeneity and layering, which was once the strength

---

[33]The influx of such talented immigrants from across Europe partly explains the "Irish miracle" and London's dominance in the U.K. economy.

[34]Clusters of firms modeled on the Italian industrial district's small firm cluster have emerged in the Pearl River Delta urban region as the thousands of Chinese workers and entrepreneurs who have gained experience in Prato, Italy, have returned to set up shop in China.

[35]Rosenthal and Strange (forthcoming) point to the benefits accruing from a concentration of college-educated workers, but they also find that the agglomeration benefits diminish the farther away one moves from the center of the agglomeration.

[36]A meta-analysis of the research on agglomeration economies also finds that proximity appears to produce larger gains in productivity for services than it does for manufacturing activities (Melo, Graham, and Noland 2009).

of the leading financial centers. The remaining and significantly attenuated urbanization economies arise from the diversity of service activities.

Most industrial cities are unable to make a transition to global cities led by finance and other business services.[37] Once manufacturing fades away, these cities cannot sustain earlier levels of prosperity (and exports) on the back of the services that remain or on new services attracted to these cities, most of which have a local (or at best a regional) clientele and rarely tap into the global market. The result can be a vicious downward spiral. As the economic and revenue bases narrow, industrial diversity is reduced. The supply of skilled workers becomes smaller as the most talented migrate, and the chances of a revival diminish. Even a large injection of capital from the central or subnational government is unable to jump-start these municipal cities after industry has been denuded, labor and entrepreneurs have departed, and the industrial fabric has developed large holes.

Productivity Growth Favors Manufacturing

Historical experience shows that productivity has grown fastest in manufacturing activities. Hence, the diminishing share of manufacturing in GDP eats into the contribution of productivity to growth. With national and urban economies in industrial countries drawing more of their growth impetus from productivity, the changing composition of economic activities—which has been labeled *Baumol's cost disease*—means a trend reduction in growth; there is little evidence to support the claim that most services can generate rates of productivity increase comparable to those of manufacturing industries (see Baumol 1967; Baumol and Bowen 1966). Table 4.3 shows the effect of changing GDP composition on total factor productivity (TFP) growth in the United States. Had the GDP composition remained fixed at the proportion reached in 1948, the annual TFP growth in the United States would have been 1.49 percent. The GDP composition as of 2001 results in an annual rate of TFP growth of 0.85 percent. Thus, changes in the composition of GDP between 1948 and 2001 are responsible for a reduction of 0.64 percentage point of TFP growth per year.

TFP growth is highest in services that are assimilating IT.[38] These include telecommunications, computer services, financial intermediation, and to a lesser

---

[37]Part of the reason is that these services tend to have much fewer links to other industrial sectors. For instance, the burgeoning business-process outsourcing sector in the Philippines has not stimulated the production in other industrial sectors (Magtibay-Ramos, Estrada, and Felipe 2008).

[38]Aral, Brynjolfsson, and Van Alstyne (2007) find that IT can raise the productivity of workers, but mainly through multitasking and not by speeding up work with the help of e-mail and database use. However, beyond a fairly low level, multitasking quickly degrades task completion and revenue generation. That IT is more effective in enhancing productivity when work practices and organizational structures have been suitably modified is supported by the findings of Motohashi (2008). Reformed Chinese state-owned enterprises benefited more from incorporating IT than did unreformed ones.

Table 4.3 Fixed-Shares Growth Rate for TFP for Different Periods in the United States

Period	Growth rate (%)				
	1948	1959	1973	1989	2001
1948–59	1.61	1.75	1.71	1.51	1.34
1959–73	1.44	1.39	1.26	1.03	0.78
1973–89	1.27	0.92	0.83	0.56	0.38
1989–2001	1.73	1.47	1.42	1.19	1.11
1948–2001	1.49	1.34	1.26	1.02	0.85

Source: Nordhaus 2008.

Table 4.4 Characteristics of Different Services

Service	Average annual TFP increase (%)		ICT producing or using[a]	Tradability
	1990s	1990–2005		
Group 1				
Public administration, defense	0.11	0.31	0	Nontradable
Retail trade	1.71	1.17	1	Nontradable
Transport and storage	1.85	1.01	0	Unknown
Wholesale trade	1.54	1.88	1	Unknown
Group 2				
Education	0.13	−0.5	0	Nontradable
Health, social work	−0.01	−0.53	0	Nontradable
Hotels and restaurants	−0.14	−1	0	Nontradable
Other community, social, and Nontradable personal services	−0.71	−0.86	0	
Group 3				
Post and communication	3.13	7.17	1	Tradable
Computer services			1	Tradable
Financial intermediation			1	Tradable
Legal, technical, advertising			1	Tradable
Other business activities			0/1	Tradable

Source: Eichengreen and Gupta 2009.
Note: ICT = information and communication technology.
a. ICT equal to 0 implies that the service neither produces nor uses ICT; a 1 indicates that the service uses or produces ICT.

extent, retail and wholesale trade.[39] In a range of other services, TFP growth has been slow or negative (see table 4.4; Eichengreen and Gupta 2009).

Therefore, the shift to services can be doubly disadvantageous. Aside from constraining urbanization economies and the scope for diversification, monosectoral urban economies—even very large ones—risk sacrificing growth over the long run.

---

[39]For retail and wholesale trade, this assimilation involves a one-time spurt followed by a slowing in productivity gains.

Innovativeness Is Greatest in Research-Intensive Activities

TFP and growth are intertwined with innovation. Large urban centers are, on balance, more innovative.[40] The level of innovation and its commercial outcomes are also a function of industrial composition. Some kinds of activities are more research intensive and innovative. It is not only R&D that leads to innovation; however, a robust relationship runs from R&D to patents and publications, which are widely viewed as proxies for innovation (Griliches 2000; B. Hall and Mairesse 2006; Jaffe 1986; Wieser 2005). Manufacturing industries—especially the high-tech ones—engage in more R&D and produce many more patents than service activities. If patents signal future commercial innovation, then the recent past suggests that manufacturing is more likely to spawn subfields and new starts, which can widen existing markets or give rise to new markets, and to introduce process innovations, which are widespread in manufacturing and have a higher probability of promoting productivity.[41]

Monosectoral Urban Economies Tend to Be Unequal

Large cities that transition rapidly from an economy based on manufacturing to one whose center of gravity lies in services face the challenge of finding alternative employment opportunities for workers and of sustaining an urban middle class. The experience of Hong Kong, China; London; New York; and Singapore suggests that services do not, on average, generate as many additional jobs or jobs that pay as well as the manufacturing activities they replace (Sassen 1991). Some services, such as finance, legal, and accounting, *do* create well-paid jobs, but only for highly educated workers and not for ex–factory hands. Retraining middle-aged factory workers or dockhands has been a failure wherever it has been tried, and many factory workers can end up being permanently unemployed, as has occurred across Europe. The result is rising inequality[42] and a shrinking middle class.[43] Too much of the city's income derives from a small number of activities, and it can become

---

[40]The size and the density of employment and industrial activities are also positively correlated with the innovativeness of a place (Bettencourt, Lobo, and Strumsky 2007; Carlino, Chatterjee, and Hunt 2007).

[41]Whether innovations in social networking and in data mining will prove to be productivity enhancing or, in the case of social networking, value subtracting remains to be determined.

[42]Galbraith and Hale (2009) find that the largest contributor to inequality in the United States was wage differentials between professionals (including technical services, finance, and insurance) and other occupations.

[43]Social tensions, rising rates of homicide, and slowing growth are some of the consequences of inequality (Glaeser, Resseger, and Tobio 2008; UN-HABITAT 2008). The income inequality may have contributed to the current financial crisis. In the United States, the top 1 percent of the population doubled its share of national income from 8 percent to

(continued on next page)

Table 4.5   Gini Coefficients in Selected Cities

Cities	Gini coefficient	Year
Beijing	0.22	2003
Hong Kong, China	0.53	2001
New York	0.54	2007
Singapore	0.49	2008
Shanghai	0.32	2004/05
Tokyo	0.31	2004

Sources: UN-HABITAT 2008; New York data from the U.S. Census Bureau's 2007 American Community Survey (http://www.census.gov/acs/www/).

concentrated in the hands of a few, generally mobile, workers.[44] Such a distribution of incomes affects real estate values, drives the lower- and middle-income workers from the core areas of the city, and unravels communities and neighborhoods. These factors lead to a homogenization of neighborhoods as well as to a diminishing diversity of people and of activities in the core city areas that saps the city's vitality and affects the urban quality of life (see table 4.5).[45]

(*continued from previous page*)

16 percent by the early 2000s. However, relatively few profitable investment opportunities existed for the additional wealth. The real median wages have been stagnant in the United States since the 1970s, resulting in flat income growth for middle-income families. Easy credit access, especially to middle-income families, was an expedient way of diffusing the class tension. The availability of easy credit and subsequent investment in housing also suited the wealthy (and the financial intermediaries) in search of investment opportunities. This debt-based growth strategy was feasible in the United States because of its ability to run current account deficits (Milanovic 2009), but it was a strategy that led to overleveraging, a bubble, and a painful crash.

[44]Glaeser, Resseger, and Tobio (2008) note the high income inequality in Manhattan (Gini of 0.6) and show that inequality in U.S. cities is related to the emerging skill mix in these cities and to the returns from skills. O'Cléireacáin (1997: 32–33) points out that "a significant share of personal earnings in the [financial] sector comes in the form of annual bonus payments. From the short-term perspective of the [municipal] budget, revenue forecasts and collections are thus hostage to a small number of firms' annual bonus payment decisions. . . . Increasingly the [city taxpayers] are foreign businesses," which are highly mobile, and this factor increases the uncertainty for New York's policy makers, because the city is becoming "dependent on a narrower and more mobile tax base than is healthy." The crisis of 2008 and 2009 has only reinforced concerns that were surfacing in the 1990s.

[45]In the past three decades, inequality in Hong Kong, China, has been steadily rising from 0.45 in 1981, to 0.48 in 1991, to 0.53 in 2001 (UN-HABITAT 2008), and closer to 0.6 currently. Inequality has also risen in Singapore, reaching 0.49 in 2008.

These stylized tendencies can inform development policies in Beijing and Shanghai. As noted earlier, however, times have changed, as have industrial life cycles. Chinese megacities are quite unlike New York in the earlier decades of the 20th century, and their opportunity sets and constraints also differ a great deal. How they could evolve will depend on a variety of factors, which the remainder of this volume discusses.

5

Economic Composition, Resources, and the Emerging Innovation Potentials in Beijing and Shanghai

In light of the discussion in the previous chapters, the first part of this chapter presents information on the evolution of the economic and industrial structure in Beijing and Shanghai since 1990.[1] The second part of the chapter examines the evolution of the capabilities that, in conjunction with policy actions and market signals, will affect future development and the pace of growth.

When discussing capabilities, this chapter makes an explicit distinction between *technological capability* and *innovation capacity*.[2] Technological capability refers to the assimilation, adaptation, and exploitation of knowledge for commercial purposes. Innovation capacity refers to the potential inherent within an urban environment variously furnished with universities, research entities, and firms to create new ideas, products, processes, and business models.

The Industrial Economy

Beijing and Shanghai account for a roughly similar share of China's population: 1.2 percent (16 million in 2008) and 1.4 percent (19 million in 2008), respectively (see table 5.1). Their economic weight is much larger: Beijing is responsible for close to 4 percent of the national economy and Shanghai for nearly 5 percent

---

[1]Shanghai (which means city on the sea) was designated as an "open city" (open for foreign direct investment) in 1984. During the 1980s, Shanghai did not experience the explosive growth that occurred in the four free trade zones and in the Pearl River Delta. It entered a period of rapid development following a decision in the early 1990s to transform Shanghai as the "dragonhead of development" for the Yangtze River Delta region (H. Lu 2004). The implication was that the city would be the economic locomotive for the region.

[2]This distinction also applies to policies. An innovation policy encompasses more than a technology policy might. A technology policy tends to focus narrowly on a certain area or issues, whereas an innovation policy needs to consider various supporting institutions.

Table 5.1   Share of National Population, 1995–2007

City	Share (%)		
	1995	**2000**	**2007**
Beijing	1.03	1.09	1.24
Hong Kong, China	0.26	0.26	0.25
Shanghai	1.17	1.32	1.41
Tokyo	9.39	9.51	10.01

Sources: For Beijing: Beijing Municipal Bureau of Statistics and Beijing General Team of Investigation under the National Bureau of Statistics various years. For Hong Kong, China: Hong Kong SAR Demographic Statistics Section, Census and Statistics Department, August 2008 (http://www.censtatd.gov.hk/hong_kong_statistics/statistics_by_subject/index.jsp). For Shanghai: Shanghai Municipal Statistics Bureau various years. For Tokyo: Tokyo Statistics Bureau, Ministry of Internal Affairs and Communications; Bureau of General Affairs, Tokyo Municipal Government; World Bank 2008c.

Table 5.2   Share of National GDP, 1995–2007

City	Share (%)		
	1995	**2000**	**2007**
Beijing	2.29	2.50	3.61
Hong Kong, China	19.80	14.12	6.32
Shanghai	4.05	4.59	4.81
Tokyo[a]	16.60	17.84	18.40

Sources: For Beijing: Beijing Municipal Bureau of Statistics and Beijing General Team of Investigation under the National Bureau of Statistics various years. For Hong Kong, China: National Income Section (1)1, Census and Statistics Department, August 2008 (http://www.censtatd.gov.hk/hong_kong_statistics/statistics_by_subject/index.jsp). For Shanghai: Shanghai Municipal Statistics Bureau various years. For Tokyo: Tokyo Municipal Government http://www.toukei.metro.tokyo.jp/keizaik/kk-data.htm; World Bank 2008c.
a. Data are for the years 1996, 2000, and 2005.

(see table 5.2). Together with Hong Kong, China, and Shenzhen, the two cities serve as the axes of China's largest urban industrial regions.

The Changing Shape of Industry

Manufacturing remains the engine of Shanghai's economy. The share of manufacturing in gross domestic product (GDP), although it is 8 percentage points lower than in 1995, was 44 percent in 2007 (see figure 5.1) and has remained more or less stable since 2000. In contrast, although manufacturing is an important driver of Beijing's economy, the city is rapidly shifting its orientation toward services. The share of manufacturing industry declined from 35 percent in 1995 to 22 percent in 2007. The detailed picture that emerges from the industrial census of Shanghai reveals three major and largely positive changes over the past decade: light, low-skill, labor-intensive industries, in particular those producing textiles, footwear, and garments, have lost shares, and in their place, transportation, engineering, electronics, and metallurgical industries have increased in prominence (see tables 5.3 and 5.4). Computers and electronic equipment generate about one-quarter of the industrial output in Shanghai. Close to two-thirds of the industrial output comes from just

Figure 5.1   GDP Composition, 1995–2007

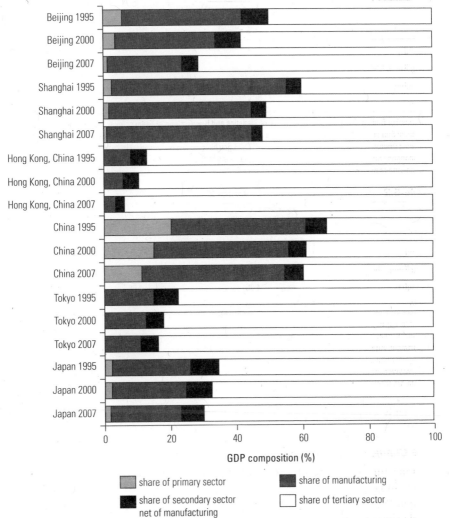

Sources: For Beijing: Beijing Municipal Bureau of Statistics and Beijing General Team of Investigation under the National Bureau of Statistics various years. For Shanghai: Shanghai Municipal Statistics Bureau various years. For Hong Kong, China: National Income Section (2)1, Census and Statistics Department, May 2008 (http://www. censtatd.gov.hk/hong_kong_statistics/statistics_by_subject/index.jsp). For China: National Bureau of Statistics of China various years. For Tokyo: Tokyo Municipal Government (http://www.toukei.metro.tokyo.jp/keizaik/ kk05pa1000.xls). For Japan: World Bank 2008c.

six subsectors, which account for 38 percent of the establishments and 46 percent of the employment in manufacturing as of 2007.

Manufacturing in Beijing comprises just a handful of subsectors (see tables 5.5 and 5.6). The communication equipment subsector alone is responsible for

Table 5.3   Subsectoral Composition of Manufacturing Activities in Shanghai, 1994

Manufacturing subsector	Share of establishments (%)	Share of employees (%)	Share of GVIO (%)
Smelting and pressing of ferrous metals	1.0	5.6	14.4
Transportation equipment manufacturing	4.8	7.7	9.6
Textiles	7.9	13.9	8.5
Electric machinery equipment and manufacturing	9.1	6.9	7.1
Raw chemical materials and chemical products manufacturing	5.1	5.1	6.3
General equipment manufacturing	7.8	8.0	5.9
Communication equipment, computers, and other electronic equipment manufacturing	3.4	4.1	5.5
Metal products manufacturing	9.0	5.7	4.8
Garments, shoes, and accessories manufacturing	7.0	5.3	4.1
Special-purpose equipment manufacturing	5.4	6.6	3.9
Chemical fiber manufacturing	0.4	2.0	3.1
Nonmetal mineral products	4.1	4.1	2.6
Smelting and pressing of nonferrous metals	1.1	1.3	2.4
Artworks and other manufacturing	3.7	2.0	2.2
Farm and sideline products processing	2.4	1.4	2.2
Oil processing, coking, and nuclear fuel processing	0.2	0.6	2.0
Medicine manufacturing	1.2	1.5	1.7
Instruments, meters, and culture and office equipment manufacturing	3.5	3.6	1.6
Plastic products manufacturing	4.7	2.0	1.5
Rubber products manufacturing	1.3	1.9	1.5
Leather, fur, and wool products manufacturing	2.4	1.8	1.4
Food manufacturing	3.1	1.9	1.4
Stationery, education, and sports goods manufacturing	2.6	2.1	1.3
Tobacco manufacturing	0.0	0.2	1.0
Papermaking and paper products manufacturing	2.2	1.4	1.0
Printing and record duplicating	3.8	1.5	0.9
Beverage manufacturing	0.7	0.6	0.9
Timber processing and timber, bamboo, rattan, coir, and straw products manufacturing	1.0	0.6	0.7
Furniture manufacturing	1.2	0.6	0.4

Source: Shanghai Municipal Statistics Bureau 1995.
Note: Ranked by gross value of industrial output (GVIO).

Table 5.4   Subsectoral Composition of Manufacturing Activities in Shanghai, 2007

Manufacturing subsector	Share of establishments (%)	Share of employees (%)	Share of GVIO (%)
Communication equipment, computers, and other electronic equipment	4.7	13.5	23.2
Transportation equipment	5.3	7.9	11.0
General equipment	11.7	9.5	8.8
Raw chemical materials and chemical products	7.1	4.1	7.6
Smelting and pressing of ferrous metals	1.1	1.6	7.5
Electric machinery equipment	8.3	9.0	7.3
Oil processing, coking, and nuclear fuel processing	0.3	0.8	4.5
Metal products	9.0	6.1	3.9
Special-purpose equipment	6.1	4.7	2.8
Plastic products	6.5	4.5	2.2
Garments, shoes, and accessories	6.9	7.9	2.0
Smelting and pressing of nonferrous metals	1.7	1.5	2.0
Nonmetal mineral products	4.1	2.9	2.0
Textiles	6.1	5.1	1.7
Instruments, meters, and culture and office equipment	2.2	2.3	1.5
Food	1.7	2.0	1.3
Tobacco	0.0	0.1	1.3
Medicine	1.5	2.0	1.3
Farm and sideline products processing	1.1	0.9	1.0
Furniture	1.7	2.0	0.9
Papermaking and paper products	2.2	1.3	0.9
Rubber products	1.6	1.6	0.8
Printing and record duplicating	2.5	1.7	0.8
Stationery, education, and sports goods	1.9	2.3	0.8
Beverages	0.4	0.4	0.6
Leather, fur, and wool products	1.5	2.0	0.6
Artworks and other	1.1	0.9	0.5
Chemical fiber	0.3	0.3	0.5
Timber processing and timber, bamboo, rattan, coir, and straw products	1.1	0.8	0.4
Waste resources and materials recycling and processing	0.3	0.1	0.2

Source: Shanghai Municipal Statistics Bureau 2008.
Note: Ranked by GVIO.

Table 5.5 Subsectoral Composition of Manufacturing Activities in Beijing, 1995

Manufacturing subsector	Share of establishments (%)	Share of employees (%)	Share of GVIO (%)
Transportation equipment	8.5	10.8	9.2
Smelting and pressing of ferrous metals	0.5	13.5	8.6
Nonmetallic mineral products	6.3	4.6	7.8
Textile wearing apparel, footwear, and caps	6.5	3.1	7.4
Textiles	3.2	3.7	6.7
General-purpose machinery	6.5	3.5	6.4
Communication equipment, computers, and other electronic equipment	4.8	12.9	5.5
Raw chemical materials and chemical products	6.4	6.7	5.2
Electrical machinery and equipment	5.6	2.9	5.0
Metal products	9.7	2.7	4.3
Special-purpose machinery	6.0	2.7	4.2
Printing and reproduction of recording media	4.4	1.8	3.1
Processing of petroleum, coking, and processing of nuclear fuel	0.6	8.6	2.6
Food	3.8	2.2	2.6
Measuring instruments and culture and office machinery	3.1	2.1	2.4
Plastics	4.1	1.8	2.3
Articles for culture, education, and sports activity	1.5	0.6	1.9
Artwork and other manufacturing	3.8	0.9	1.9
Processing of food from agricultural products	3.3	5.2	1.9
Medicines	1.3	1.7	1.8
Beverages	1.5	3.0	1.6
Rubber	0.7	0.9	1.3
Furniture	2.4	0.6	1.2
Leather, furs, down, and related products	1.3	0.5	1.1
Paper and paper products	1.9	0.9	1.1
Munitions and weapons	0.0	0.6	0.9
Smelting and pressing of nonferrous metals	0.8	0.6	0.8
Chemical fibers	0.3	0.2	0.5
Processing of timber, wood, bamboo, rattan, palm, and straw products	1.1	0.2	0.5
Tobacco	0.0	0.4	0.1

Source: Beijing Municipal Statistics Bureau and Beijing General Team of Investigation under the National Bureau of Statistics 1996.
Note: Ranked by GVIO.

Table 5.6   Subsectoral Composition of Manufacturing Activities in Beijing, 2007

Manufacturing subsector	Share of establishments (%)	Share of employees (%)	Share of GVIO (%)
Communication equipment, computers, and other electronic equipment	8.4	13.2	32.2
Transportation equipment	6.1	10.0	12.8
Smelting and pressing of ferrous metals	0.9	5.4	7.4
Processing of petroleum, coking, and processing of nuclear fuel	0.7	1.7	7.3
General-purpose machinery	7.5	6.0	4.2
Electrical machinery and equipment	6.5	4.7	4.0
Special-purpose machinery	8.2	6.6	4.0
Raw chemical materials and chemical products	6.8	4.0	3.8
Nonmetallic mineral products	6.9	6.1	3.1
Measuring instruments and culture and office machinery	5.7	3.1	2.6
Medicines	3.1	3.8	2.4
Metal products	6.4	3.9	2.3
Processing of food from agricultural products	3.4	2.8	2.2
Food	3.0	3.4	1.7
Beverages	1.0	2.3	1.5
Printing and reproduction of recording media	4.7	4.1	1.2
Artwork and other manufacturing	1.6	1.3	1.1
Textile wearing apparel, footwear, and caps	4.4	6.9	1.1
Textiles	2.5	2.7	0.9
Plastics	3.9	1.9	0.8
Smelting and pressing of nonferrous metals	1.5	0.7	0.8
Paper and paper products	1.9	1.0	0.8
Furniture	1.9	1.8	0.5
Tobacco	0.0	0.1	0.3
Rubber	0.7	0.8	0.3
Articles for culture, education, and sports activity	0.8	0.9	0.2
Processing of timber and manufacture of wood, bamboo, rattan, palm, and straw products	0.5	0.3	0.2
Leather, furs, down, and related products	0.6	0.3	0.1
Chemical fibers	0.3	0.1	0.0

Source: Beijing Municipal Statistics Bureau and Beijing General Team of Investigation under the National Bureau of Statistics 2008.
Note: Ranked by GVIO.

almost one-third of the gross value of industrial output (GVIO) (see table 5.6). Together with the transportation subsector, the two subsectors account for 45 percent of the industrial output. Smelting of ferrous metals and processing of petroleum and coking add another 15 percent. Three machinery subsectors (general, electrical, and special) together contribute 12 percent of the industrial output. Overall, the share of industrial output of these seven subsectors reaches 72 percent of Beijing's industrial output. Among these, the communication equipment and machinery subsectors are export intensive, especially the communication equipment subsector. More than half the production is exported, while the export intensity for various types of machinery is around 12 percent. In contrast, outputs from transportation equipment, smelting of ferrous metals, and processing of petroleum are sold mainly on the domestic market.

Manufacturing activities in Beijing are also shrinking because of the migration of labor-intensive industrial subsectors. Garment and textile industries accounted for 15 percent of industrial production in 1995 (table 5.5). By 2007, their share was just 2 percent (table 5.6). Industries producing communication equipment (including office machines), transportation equipment, machinery, and chemicals have partially filled the gap left by the textile industry. The growth of the communication equipment industry between 1995 and 2007 was remarkable. It increased from 6 percent in 1995 to close to one-third of industrial output in 2007 (see tables 5.5 and 5.6). In fact, two subsectors (communication and transportation equipment) accounted for nearly one-half of Beijing's industrial output in 2007, although their share of employment and of the total number of establishments was 14 percent and 23 percent, respectively. The growth of high-tech manufacturing has been insufficient to offset the overall decline in the share of Beijing's industrial establishment.

A comparison with Tokyo, which was also once an industrial heavyweight, suggests one possible future for the two Chinese megacities. Printing and publishing now dominate the substantially hollowed-out manufacturing activities of Tokyo (and New York), in terms of both establishments and number of employees (table 5.7).[3] Vestiges of Tokyo's past industrial strength can be seen in the continued presence of plants producing chemicals, electric machinery, telecommunication hardware, and metal products and those processing food. With the relocation of the bulk of manufacturing activity to other places, however, Tokyo has been transformed into a cultural and business center. If industry flees, this is what Beijing and Shanghai could become, albeit with less of a focus on printing and

---

[3]Publishing was and remains the major manufacturing industry in New York. Singapore also has a large publishing industry, although some of it has migrated to Bangkok.

Table 5.7   Share of Manufacturing Activities in Tokyo, 2001 and 2006

Manufacturing sector	2001 Establishments (%)	2001 Employees (%)	Manufacturing sector	2006 Establishments (%)	2006 Employees (%)
Printing, publishing	21.3	14.5	Printing, publishing	18.0	14.0
Machinery	11.9	10.0	Machinery	11.4	10.4
Chemicals	2.2	7.9	Chemicals	2.1	9.0
Metal products	12.9	7.2	Food processing	4.0	8.3
Electric machinery	4.9	7.2	Electric machinery	4.4	7.0
Food processing	3.8	6.6	Metal products	13.6	6.8
Telecommunications, IT hardware	1.6	6.1	Telecommunications, IT hardware	1.3	6.0
Transportation equipment	2.4	5.2	Transportation equipment	2.2	5.1
Electronic devices	3.1	4.9	Precision instruments	3.9	4.6
Others	6.7	4.9	Electronic devices	2.7	4.6
Precision instruments	4.0	4.4	Others	7.4	4.5
Plastics	4.7	3.6	Plastics	4.7	3.1
Garment	5.5	3.1	Garment	6.8	2.9
Pulp, paper	3.3	2.7	Pulp, paper	3.2	2.2
Glass, cement, ceramics	1.5	2.0	Glass, cement, ceramics	1.6	1.8
Leather products	2.7	1.7	Leather products	4.5	1.6
Nonferrous metal	1.0	1.7	Iron and steel	0.8	1.4
Iron and steel	0.9	1.6	Rubber products	1.5	1.3
Rubber products	1.4	1.2	Drinks, tobacco, feed	0.3	1.2
Drinks, tobacco, feed	0.3	1.1	Nonferrous metal	0.9	1.2
Furniture	2.3	1.1	Furniture	2.8	1.2
Textiles	0.8	0.6	Petrochemicals, excluding plastics	0.1	0.7
Petrochemicals, excluding plastics	0.1	0.6	Textiles	1.0	0.6
Wood products, excluding furniture	0.7	0.4	Wood products, excluding furniture	1.0	0.5

Source: Tokyo Metropolitan Government.

publishing. If the exit of manufacturing industry does continue and even accelerate, the cities will quite likely have to settle for rates of GDP growth in the 1 to 4 percent annual range.

The changing shape of industry in Beijing and Shanghai is mirrored in the shares of large firms compared with those of small and medium-size firms and

Figure 5.2   Share of Establishments, 1995

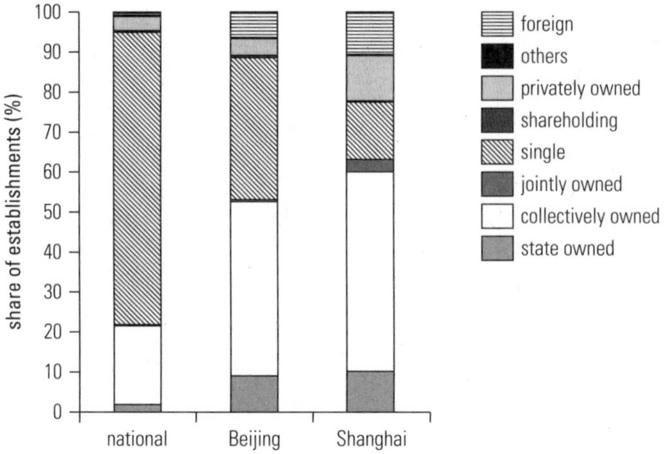

Source: Office of the Third National Industrial Census 1997.

in the increasing salience of private and multinational firms.[4] Comparing two industrial censuses (1995 and 2004) offers a foretaste of the emerging industrial landscape in Beijing and Shanghai. Most notable is the expansion of the private sectors, especially in Shanghai (see figures 5.2 and 5.3). In 1995, the share of foreign and private firms was little more than 20 percent of all establishments in Shanghai and 10 percent in Beijing. In 2004, the situation had reversed: the share of foreign and private firms had risen to more than 80 percent of all establishments in Shanghai. In Beijing, the growth of foreign and private firms was more muted, and their combined share is a little shy of 60 percent.

Although private firms have flourished in Beijing and Shanghai, their footprint is still relatively small compared with that of other types of firms. Foreign and private firms combined accounted for 30 percent of GVIO in 1995 in Shanghai (figure 5.4). Their share increased only to 55 percent in 2004, despite the large

---

[4]After the reform of state-owned enterprises, the footprints of such enterprises (and collectively owned enterprises) have diminished over the years in establishments, employment, and industrial output. For a detailed discussion on the reform of state-owned enterprises in China and elsewhere, see Yusuf, Nabeshima, and Perkins (2005).

Figure 5.3   Share of Establishments, 2004

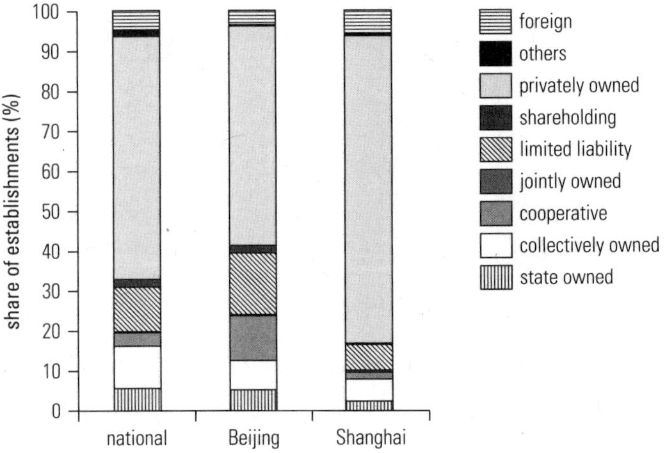

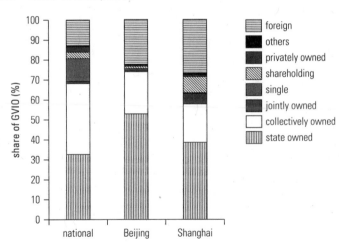

Source: National Bureau of Statistics of China 2006.

Figure 5.4   Share of GVIO, 1995

Source: Office of the Third National Industrial Census 1997.

increase in the number of private firms (figure 5.5). The situation in Beijing is similar although the magnitudes are lower. This finding suggests that although the number of private firms has increased in both cities, those firms tend to be among the smaller ones.

Figure 5.5   Share of GVIO, 2004

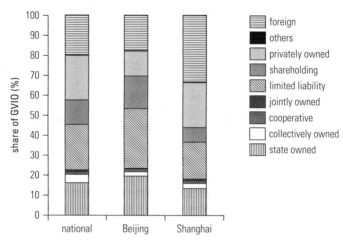

Source: National Bureau of Statistics of China 2006.

The data for firms with revenue of Y 5 million or more show that large firms accounted for 41 percent of the output in 2007 as against 50 percent in 1994. Private and foreign-invested firms produced 64 percent of GVIO in 2007, and they have increased Shanghai's integration with the global economy (see figure 5.6).[5] Key industries such as electronics and engineering export 70 percent and 22 percent of their output, respectively, and in the aggregate, more than 60 percent of Shanghai's GDP was traded in 2007. As is the case throughout China, a disproportionate share of Shanghai's exports (almost 77 percent) came from foreign-invested enterprises in 2007.[6] This imbalance mirrors the experience in other countries. The larger the share of foreign ownership is, the more likely a firm is to export. In addition, a few high-performing firms make the bulk of the exports (see table 5.8 for some European examples).[7] Although this situation broadly describes Shanghai's current businesses, the increasing share of smaller, private, and foreign-invested firms in the export sector and the concomitant decline in the share

---

[5] If firms from Hong Kong, China, and Taiwan, China, are included, the share increases to 76 percent.

[6] For China as a whole, the traded share of foreign-invested firms is 57 percent.

[7] Among European firms, the top 1 percent accounts for 40 percent of the total exports, and the top 5 percent accounts for 70 percent of the total (Mayer and Ottaviano 2008). Moreover, there is wide variation in productivity among firms. The lowest-performing ones are mainly focused on the domestic market, the better-performing ones tend to be exporters, and the top-performing ones are multinationals (Mayer and Ottaviano 2008).

Figure 5.6   GVIO in Shanghai, by Ownership Categories, 1994–2007

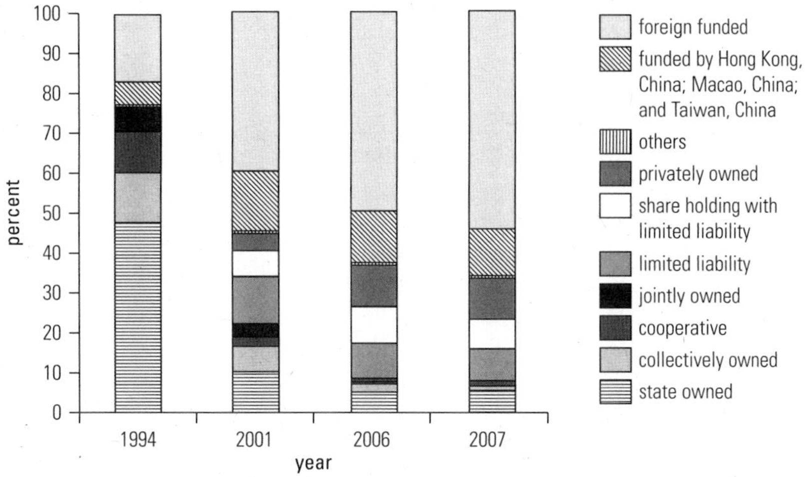

Source: Shanghai Municipal Statistics Bureau various years.

Table 5.8   Share of Exports for Top Exporters in Selected European Countries, 2003

Country	Share (%)		
	Top 1%	Top 5%	Top 10%
Belgium	48	73	84
France	68	88	94
Hungary	77	91	96
Italy	32	59	72
Norway	53	81	91

Source: Mayer and Ottaviano 2008.

of state-owned enterprises (SOEs) are welcome developments. SOEs tend to be less productive, profitable, and innovative on balance.[8] Nevertheless, some important exceptions have benefited from enterprise reform, corporatization, good management, and exposure to global competition. Firms such as Shanghai Automotive Industry Corporation, Baosteel, and Zhenhua Port Cranes (see Zeng and

---

[8]Industrial SOEs in China and elsewhere are less efficient than are private firms. The managerial, technical, and organizational capabilities of even those SOEs that have been corporatized continue to lag far behind those of multinational corporations operating in China, in large part because of the limited capacity of most SOEs to absorb and profit from new technologies, hard and soft, and to craft superior business models (Girma and Gong 2008; see also Dollar and Wei 2007; Y. Huang 2008; Yusuf, Nabeshima, and Perkins 2005).

Williamson 2007) are among the most dynamic firms in China today and could become the driving force behind incremental innovation in Shanghai, the role that large firms perform elsewhere.[9] When they are able to do so, a rising percentage of Shanghai's exports will be sourced from Chinese-owned firms, as should be the case.

Following the round of SOE reforms that began in the mid 1990s, the contribution of SOEs to Beijing's economy has diminished significantly. In 1995, 60 percent of industrial output in Beijing came from SOEs. In 2007, it was less than 10 percent, and shareholding companies and limited liability companies have expanded during this period (again reflecting the reform initiatives; see figure 5.7). Much like Shanghai, Beijing has attracted foreign direct investment (FDI) into a wide range of activities, including manufacturing, research and development (R&D), and business services. These activities now generate close to 40 percent of Beijing's GDP compared with more than half of Shanghai's industrial output. The government's efforts to promote new high-tech activities and services have also resulted in the entry of new firms in the science parks and elsewhere. These firms are mostly privately owned, and returnees from overseas have started a number of them.[10]

The Role of Large SOEs

Throughout the world, firms are responsible for the bulk of innovation. In particular, large firms have the resources to undertake sustained R&D and to routinize innovation in their business practices. China is no exception. In China, large and medium-size enterprises (LMEs) are almost invariably SOEs, former SOEs, or foreign firms. The state sector accounts for 44 percent of

---

[9]The durable innovation hotspots around the world—the ones that have given rise to resilient clusters of firms—share one common trait: the vital, procreative, and nurturing role of a few firms that struck root at an early stage, survived, innovated, built up competencies, grew in size, and (most important) were responsible for creating numerous spinoffs and for attracting many start-ups. This was the pattern for the clusters in Akron, Ohio; Bangalore, India; and Silicon Valley, California (Buenstorf and Klepper 2009; Smilor and others 2005). Drofiak and Garnsey (2009: 20) observe, "Competence accumulates through successive spin-outs of knowledge-based firms, as well as within specific firms. . . . Spin-outs from previous spin-out firms create new clusters of activity over time . . . [as for instance with the] Cambridge ink jet printing cluster and the ensuing display technology cluster, which originated from one university spin-out firm, CCL."

[10]One leading example is Li Hongyan, the founder of Baidu.com. To attract returnees, the Zhongguancun Science and Technology Park, located in Beijing, offers grants of Y 100,000 for qualified projects managed by returnees to promote start-up activities. As a result, by the end of 2005, 3,000 firms (of 17,000) were started up in Zhongguancun by overseas returnees (Zhou 2008).

Figure 5.7   GVIO in Beijing, by Ownership Categories, 1995–2007

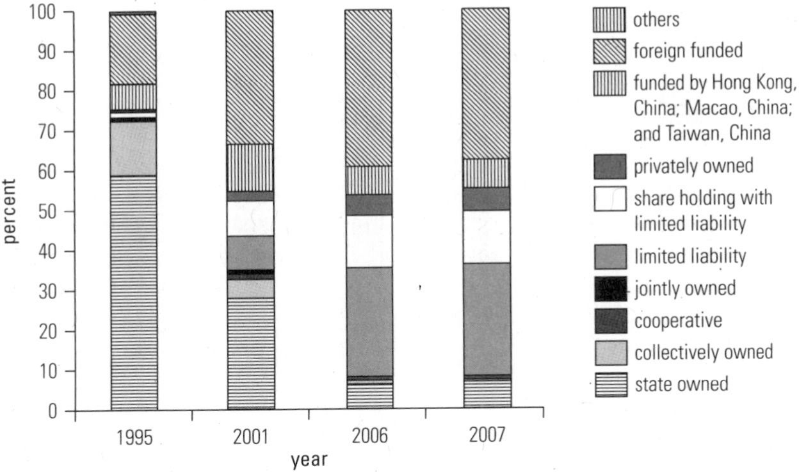

Source: Beijing Municipal Bureau of Statistics and Beijing General Team of Investigation under the National Bureau of Statistics various years.

Table 5.9   Share of LMEs in Various Sectors, 2006

Type of enterprise	Establishments (%)	GVIO (%)	Full-time equivalent scientists and engineers (%)	R&D spending (%)
State sector	43.6	55.2	73.0	66.2
Of which SOEs in state sector	9.7	12.2	14.2	10.1
Private sector	20.7	9.7	7.3	6.5
Foreign-invested enterprises	35.5	34.9	19.5	27.3
Others	0.2	0.2	0.1	0.1

Source: National Bureau of Statistics of China and Ministry of Science and Technology 2007.
Note: State sector is defined as domestic enterprises, excluding private firms. Foreign-invested enterprises include those from Hong Kong, China; Macao, China; and Taiwan, China.

LMEs in terms of establishments and for 55 percent of the industrial output of LMEs (see table 5.9). Various types of foreign firms encompass about one-third of the establishments and output. The growing private sector accounts for more than 20 percent of the establishments but only 10 percent of the output because privately owned firms are smaller than foreign firms or state sector enterprises.

Even in 2000, the share of R&D personnel (full-time equivalent) employed by China's LMEs exceeded that of other organizations, and this share rose to 46 percent in 2006 (see figure 5.8). Similarly, R&D expenditure by LMEs was higher

Figure 5.8·   Full-Time Equivalent of R&D Personnel

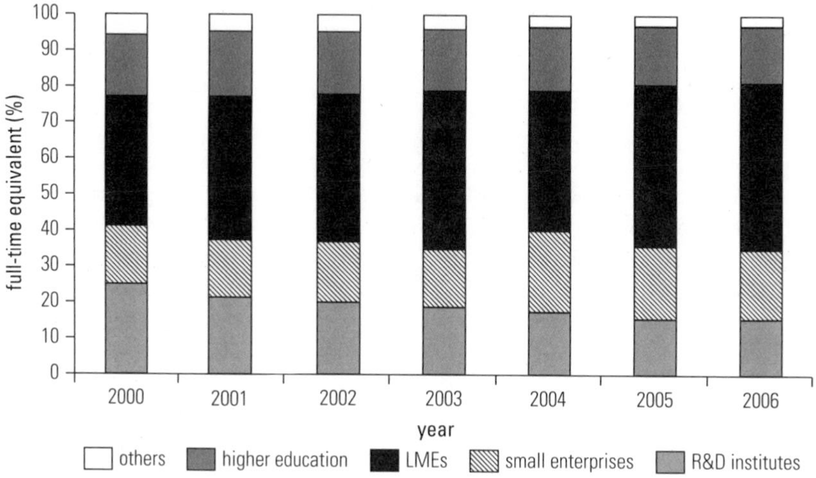

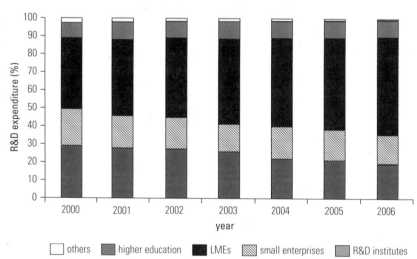

Source: National Bureau of Statistics of China and Ministry of Science and Technology 2007.

Figure 5.9   R&D Expenditure by Different Organizations, 2000–06

Source: National Bureau of Statistics of China and Ministry of Science and Technology 2007.

than that of other types of organizations and had risen to 54 percent of R&D expenditure in 2006 (see figure 5.9). Unfortunately, only a select few view innovation as an integral part of their strategy, and most SOEs in China's megacities have yet to weave research for the purposes of continual innovation into their business models.

Nevertheless, Shanghai and Beijing have a head start over other cities and a sharpening appetite for technology. The distribution of scientists and engineers engaged in R&D in these two cities is quite different relative to other locations in China (see table 5.10). The state sector accounts for two-thirds of R&D spending and employs three-quarters of scientists and engineers engaged in R&D (see table 5.9). In Beijing, the share of scientists and engineers is highest in R&D institutions because the city hosts the densest concentration of such institutions, followed by other entities (which include small firms). In Shanghai, LMEs maintain the largest research staffs, followed by higher education institutions and others. In Guangdong, LMEs are also dominant, followed by others (including small firms). The larger presence of LMEs with a research orientation in Shanghai—possibly influenced by the research intensity of the multinational corporations (MNCs) operating in the city and perhaps by the scarcity of innovative small firms in Shanghai relative to other places—can explain this difference. The distribution of R&D spending mirrors the shares of the scientists and engineers, although the dominance of LMEs is more apparent in Jiangsu and Guangdong than in Shanghai (see table 5.11).

Table 5.10   Scientists and Engineers Engaged in R&D, 2006

	Share of full-time equivalents (%)			
Location	R&D institutions	LMEs	Higher education	Others
National	14.5	44.3	19.3	21.9
Beijing	33.9	10.1	17.1	39.0
Shanghai	19.0	36.8	24.5	19.6
Jiangsu province	9.0	56.2	16.5	18.3
Guangdong province	3.0	66.6	9.8	20.6
Zhejiang province	3.4	49.8	13.6	33.3

Source: National Bureau of Statistics of China and Ministry of Science and Technology 2007.

Table 5.11   Distribution of R&D Spending in Selected Locations, 2006

	Distribution of R&D spending (%)			
Location	R&D institutions	LMEs	Higher education	Others
National	18.9	54.3	9.2	17.6
Beijing	43.8	13.6	8.6	34.0
Shanghai	20.9	51.7	10.2	17.2
Jiangsu province	11.4	69.0	8.1	11.6
Guangdong province	2.7	78.9	4.6	13.8
Zhejiang province	5.5	56.5	7.1	30.8

Source: National Bureau of Statistics of China and Ministry of Science and Technology 2007.

Table 5.12 Patent Applications and Grants, 2006

Type of firm	Invention patent applications (%)	Invention patents granted (%)
State sector	66.6	56.8
Of which SOEs	5.8	7.7
Private firms	7.3	15.8
Foreign-invested enterprises	26.0	27.2
Others	0.1	0.2

Source: National Bureau of Statistics of China and Ministry of Science and Technology 2007.
Note: State sector is defined as domestic enterprises, excluding private firms. Foreign-invested enterprises include those from Hong Kong, China; Macao, China; and Taiwan, China.

The state sector has the lion's share of patent applications and grants, followed by foreign firms (see table 5.12). Private firms have relatively few patent applications, but their share of grants is much larger, suggesting that patent applications of private firms may be of higher quality.

This configuration of R&D spending, employment, and outcomes poses a challenge for China in its drive to move toward an innovation-driven economy. Generally, SOEs are not known for efficiency in terms of both production and innovation (Deng and others 2007).[11] Given the lack of market incentives, SOEs are less likely to innovate than are other types of firms, especially private firms. In fact, even though the state sector's share of patents is large relative to the inputs, the private sector is more efficient in converting available resources into innovative outcomes. SOEs are the least profitable type of firm, but they are more likely to introduce new products than others, especially in markets where the degree of concentration is greater (Girma, Gong, and Görg 2009; S. Li and Xia 2008).[12] S. Li and Xia (2008) attribute this finding to SOEs' desire to fulfill the administrative requirement of introducing new products rather than to innovativeness.

One of the factors contributing to the lower innovation capability of SOEs is the lack of human capital. Because of the wage premium paid by MNCs, skilled workers tend to prefer working for them (Girma and Gong 2008).[13] Another is the appointment of chief executive officers of SOEs by the government (Girma and Gong 2008; Y. Li, Liu, and Ren 2007). Y. Li, Liu, and Ren (2007)

---

[11]See also Yusuf, Nabeshima, and Perkins (2005) for the history and analysis of SOE reform efforts.

[12]Girma, Gong, and Görg (2009) also find that older SOEs are more likely to engage in product innovation.

[13]In Girma and Gong's (2008) sample, the wage premium between MNCs and SOEs was 16 percent. The labor turnover at SOEs in Beijing since 1982 was 64 percent.

find that the government's appointment of chief executive officers of SOEs negatively affects innovation because the government cannot closely monitor the managers it appoints and has not designed incentives to circumvent this agency problem. In addition, the weakness of market pressures on SOEs affects the type of strategies adopted and, in turn, affects their innovation strategy. Those SOEs that have adopted strategies to make them market leaders tend to engage in product innovation (Y. Li, Liu, and Ren 2007). However, a majority of SOEs are pursuing cost saving as the main thrust of their corporate strategy, which entails reducing raw material and energy use and emphasizes process innovation.

Another strand of research examines the effect of FDI on the innovation performance of SOEs. In this literature, two different questions are explored. The first is whether spillovers are associated with FDI within and across industries. The second is whether foreign ownership stakes in SOEs affect their innovation capability.

Inward FDI has negative consequences for innovation outcomes of SOEs in a sector, which is similar to findings in other countries. However, certain types of SOEs do benefit from the presence of MNCs. These SOEs have a larger R&D spending and training budget; in other words, they have the absorptive capacity to take advantage of spillovers from FDI (Girma and Gong 2008; Girma, Gong, and Görg 2006, 2009). Bin (2008) finds that own R&D and foreign R&D are substitutes, whereas own R&D and domestic R&D are complements. This finding suggests that the absorptive capacities of Chinese firms are low, and although they can assimilate and benefit from R&D conducted by other Chinese firms (presumably at lower technological content), they are handicapped when it comes to assimilating technology from MNCs.[14] Technology spillovers from MNCs do not happen in the absence of proactive efforts on the part of potential domestic recipients to seek and exploit them. In this respect, SOEs have shown limited initiative by providing managers with incentives to be on the lookout for spillovers and to develop the in-house R&D capacity to target and assimilate new technologies (Girma and Gong 2008). What Shanghai and Beijing need are an increased number of smaller firms that are entrepreneurial, serial innovators and are out to exploit the spillover possibilities and ready to push the technology frontier. The large, established SOE does not fit this profile (Gittelman 2006; Hicks and Hegde 2005). However, those that do fit it find that foreign technology transfer contributes to improved labor productivity.[15]

---

[14]Chinese manufacturing firms are still focusing mainly on technology catch-up rather than on developing indigenous technology. The main avenues for interindustry R&D spillover are generally technology imitation and small improvements, reverse engineering, mobility of R&D workers, and skill exchange through an informal network (Bin 2008).

[15]Such spillovers seem to be limited geographically, however. SOEs do not benefit much from FDI in other regions (Girma, Gong, and Görg 2009).

SOEs with some foreign equity participation more frequently engage in product innovation (Girma, Gong, and Görg 2006), although the relationship seems to be nonlinear. Up to a certain point, foreign participation enhances the innovation activities of SOEs. However, as the foreign ownership share increases to 55 to 65 percent, such a positive effect on innovation declines. Most likely, these MNCs conduct their R&D elsewhere and use the subsidiaries in China mainly for manufacturing activities (Girma, Gong, and Görg 2009). Given that the average foreign ownership stake is about 25 percent, there is some scope for improvement in innovativeness of SOEs through an increase in foreign ownership share.

Foreign participation might well have catalytic effects, but the main impetus must come from a new breed of managers and through a search for better business models. That this change has begun to happen is apparent from the performance of several state sector firms, such as China International Marine Containers[16] and Chery Automobile, which have emerged as successful innovators through domestic consolidation; foreign acquisitions; the systematic search for and exploitation of foreign technology and design capabilities; and the leveraging of the domestic market. They are firmly establishing themselves as global competitors. The expanding domestic market has provided Chinese companies with a much-needed outlet for their products and an avenue for testing innovations. Both new and old state-owned and private enterprises are gaining valuable experience and leveraging local knowledge to build their domestic operations before attempting to enter the export market and, in some cases, to conduct a focused search for new technologies and intellectual property (Zhou 2008). As Khanna and Palepu (2006: 64) point out, "Many emerging market companies have become world class businesses by capitalizing on their knowledge of local product markets." They note, in particular, Haier's success in customizing its products to suit local needs first in China and now overseas and in building an effective distribution and service network.

Chinese SOEs wanting to build innovation capacity may have more to learn from large, bureaucratic, top-down management-style companies such as Canon, Toyota, Samsung, and Hyundai than from Western companies, which have very different managerial structures. Toyota has generated new knowledge and a steady stream of incremental innovations by carefully defining problems and systematically working to solve them, by diffusing the learning through the company, and by inculcating this problem solving through an innovation

---

[16]See Meyer and Liu (2004) and Zeng and Williamson (2007) for detailed accounts of the evolution of China International Marine Containers as the leading producer of maritime containers through selective acquisition of technology and of firms with intellectual assets, own innovation in the design of containers and the materials used, and diversification of the types of containers produced.

mentality across all levels of management (Spear 2008). Companies such as Samsung and Toyota have also demonstrated unusual agility and innovativeness in the teeth of global competition; whether Chinese SOEs can approach such levels of performance will be a key test. It will not be easy for reasons of size, which hinders radical innovation; bureaucratic structure, which can adversely affect the speed and quality of decision making; and public ownership, which discourages managers from being venturesome and induces them to prefer the security of the status quo.

The Financial Sector

China's banking-centered financial system has effectively channeled funds into infrastructure, urban real estate, and capital-intensive manufacturing activities. This system has typically favored SOEs[17] and entities affiliated with local governments that have adequate assets to offer as collateral for loans. As the economy diversifies, services multiply, and the role of smaller firms continues to increase, a deepening of financial markets and the provision of a wider menu of financial choices for private firms and new entrants would bolster economic performance.[18]

Beijing's financial industry accounts for almost 13 percent of municipal GDP (2007), compared with 10 percent for Shanghai's. The two cities complement each other. Beijing is the headquarters city for the banking and insurance industry and controls 90 percent of national bank loans and 65 percent of insurance premiums. It houses nearly 700 institutions, including 234 banks, 59 security institutions, and 117 insurance companies. Most important, Beijing is the epicenter of China's financial regulatory system, home to the head offices of the People's Bank of China, the China Banking Regulatory Commission, the China Securities Regulatory Commission, and the China Insurance Regulatory Commission. Beijing is vying with Shanghai to become the financial capital of China, and Beijing has more at stake because it depends on business services to a greater degree than does Shanghai for its growth and tax revenues. Whether Beijing is able to pull ahead remains to be seen; Shanghai's securities markets confer a longer-term advantage, which is reinforced by the size and dynamism of its hinterland and by the transactions associated with the thriving logistics

---

[17]On average, banks charged SOEs an interest rate a little over 2 percent for bank loans, whereas interest on such loans was close to 10 percent for private firms during 2001 and 2005 ("Red Flags" 2009).

[18]Many Chinese and Indian firms, especially small and medium-size enterprises, rely on alternative finances such as trade credits and informal financing for their daily operation and growth. It appears that the source of financing is not directly related to the performance of firms. As long as firms can obtain financing either from the capital market or from alternative sources, firms can perform well (Allen and others 2007).

Table 5.13   Deposit and Loan Balances of Financial Institutions in Shanghai, 2000 and 2007

Deposit and loan balances	Amount (Y billion)	
	2000	2007
Savings deposit balance of financial institutions	935.0	3,031.6
Chinese financial institutions	908.9	2,816.9
Chinese currency	777.2	2,704.5
Foreign currencies (converted into yuans)	131.7	112.4
Foreign-funded financial institutions	26.1	214.7
Foreign currencies (converted into yuans)	19.6	70.3
Chinese currency	6.5	144.4
Loan balances of financial institutions	725.4	2,171.0
Chinese financial institutions	642.8	1,801.9
Chinese currency	596.0	1,660.8
Foreign currencies (converted into yuans)	46.8	141.2
Foreign-funded financial institutions	82.6	369.1
Foreign currencies (converted into yuans)	63.6	170.3
Chinese currency	19.1	198.8

Source: Shanghai Municipal Statistics Bureau 2008.

industry. They are buttressed by a widening of the financial system. Shanghai's financial market has made solid progress in building the institutions, mobilizing the resources, and introducing the instruments to promote the expansion of industrial activity in the Yangtze River region. Between 2000 and 2007, savings deposits and loan balances have approximately tripled, and by 2007, in both Beijing and Shanghai, the deposit-to-GDP ratio had risen to 2 (see tables 5.13 and 5.14).

Other measures of financial depth for Beijing and Shanghai provide corroborating evidence, such as the number of operating banks and the savings and investment ratio. In 2007, 109 domestic banks and 84 foreign banks were operating in Shanghai (see table 5.15). Among the 84 foreign banks, 45 could accept deposits and loans in yuan and were able to compete against local banks Beijing has five times as many financial institutions, mainly banks, and twice as many insurance companies as Shanghai (see table 5.16). Financial institutions, both foreign and local, have taken the lead in introducing new financial instruments and practices that are contributing to better resource allocation, improving the access to finance of smaller firms and consumers, increasing mortgage financing, and helping enhance the growth potential of the entire urban region.

Investment accounts for a large share of the growth in China as well as in both megacities. It is supported by local savings, which have remained high. In 2007, the savings-to-GDP ratio in Shanghai was 249 percent, and the loan-to-GDP ratio was 178 percent. Although the savings-to-GDP ratio in Shanghai is much higher than the national average, it is only about one-half of that in Beijing (see table 5.17).

Table 5.14   Deposit and Loan Balances of Financial Institutions in Beijing, 2000 and 2007

	Amount	
Deposit and loan balances	2000	2007
Balance of savings deposits in standard and foreign currencies in financial institutions (Y billion)	1,152.6	3,770.0
Savings deposits (Y billion)	—	974.3
Fixed (Y billion)	—	602.9
Current (Y billion)	—	371.4
Chinese financial institutions		
Chinese currency (Y billion)	976.0	3,501.4
Savings deposits (Y billion)	—	911.3
Fixed (Y billion)	—	564.6
Current (Y billion)	—	346.7
Foreign exchange (US$ billion)	20.6	28.4
Foreign-funded financial banks		
Chinese currency (Y billion)	—	35.6
Foreign exchange (US$ billion)	—	3.5
Balance of loans from financial institutions to Beijing and other cities (Y billion)	640.8	1,986.1
Chinese financial institutions		
Chinese currency (Y billion)	601.3	1,736.0
Foreign exchange (US$ billion)	2.8	23.2
Foreign-funded financial banks		
Chinese currency (Y billion)	0.0	45.2
Foreign exchange (US$ billion)	0.9	4.9

Source: Beijing Municipal Bureau of Statistics and Beijing General Team of Investigation under the National Bureau of Statistics 2008.
Note: — = not available.

Table 5.15   Number of Financial Institutions in Shanghai, 2006 and 2007

Type of institution	2006	2007
Banking institutions	82	109
Insurance institutions	222	261
Security institutions	90	94
Foreign financial institutions operating in Shanghai	110	140
Foreign bank and finance companies operating in Shanghai	63	84
Number of foreign financial banks with permission to operate Chinese currency business in Shanghai	43	45
Total financial institutions	504	604

Source: Shanghai Municipal Statistics Bureau 2008.

A key factor that differentiates Shanghai from Beijing is that Shanghai hosts the largest stock exchange in mainland China (the other stock exchange is located in Shenzhen). Based on the market capitalization, the Shanghai Stock Exchange (SSE) is the fifth largest in the world. The SSE began operating in December 1990. The number of listed companies increased from 188 in

Table 5.16   Number of Financial Institutions in Beijing, 2006 and 2007

Type of institution	2006	2007
Financial institutions	3,032	3,174
Banking institutions	2,673	2,764
Insurance institutions	359	410

Sources: Beijing Municipal Bureau of Statistics and Beijing General Team of Investigation under the National Bureau of Statistics 2007, 2008.

Table 5.17   Share of Loans and Savings in Beijing and China, 2000 and 2007

	Share (%)	
City	2000	2007[a]
Beijing		
Savings	465.0	429.4
Loans	258.5	230.4
China		
Savings	124.8	156.0
Loans	100.2	104.9

Source: National Bureau of Statistics of China 2008.
a. Data for Beijing are from 2006.

Table 5.18   Basic Statistics on Shanghai Stock Exchange, 1995–2007

Item	1995	2000	2007
Number of listed companies	188	572	860
Number of stocks listed	220	614	904
Market value of stocks (Y billion)	252.6	2,693.1	26,983.9
Volume of stocks (Y billion)	55.8	212.8	1,236.7

Source: Shanghai Municipal Statistics Bureau 2008.

1995 to 572 in 2000 and 834 in 2005 (Shanghai Municipal Statistics Bureau 2007). The number of stocks listed rose from 220 in 1995 to 614 in 2000 and to 904 in 2007. Correspondingly, the market value of stocks grew from Y 253 billion in 1995 to Y 2,693 billion in 2000 and to Y 26,984 billion in 2007 (Shanghai Municipal Statistics Bureau 2008; see also table 5.18).[19] In 1995, the total volume of stocks issued was Y 55.8 billion, which went up to Y 213 billion in 2000 and to Y 1,237 billion in 2006 (Shanghai Municipal Statistics Bureau 2007). A unique characteristic of the SSE (and its counterpart in Shenzhen) is the classification of shares. "A" shares, denominated in renminbi,

---

[19]In February 2008, 861 companies were listed on the SSE, and the total market capitalization of the SSE was Y 23,340.9 billion (or US$3,241.8 billion).

were originally restricted to trading among domestic investors only. "B" shares, denominated in U.S. dollars, were open to foreign investors but were closed to domestic investors. Subsequent reforms have eased these restrictions, but limitations still exist on trading of these shares by domestic and foreign investors.

Between 2006 and 2008, Shanghai's stock market rose steeply as large current account surpluses increased the money supply, which then fed the demand for equities. This demand was augmented by the continuing paucity of alternative sources of investment (DeWoskin 2008). Although the Shanghai market followed the international bourses down after the collapse of Lehman Brothers, the market began reviving in April 2009, assisted by the government's fiscal stimulus policy and the expansionary credit policies of the banking sector. The market capitalization in mid-2009 was 73 percent of GDP, which is higher than that of the United States (68 percent), the United Kingdom (67 percent), and Japan (64 percent). The market's recent performance notwithstanding, it remains a highly managed and largely domestic entity with licensed foreigners accounting for little more than 1 percent of market capitalization. Furthermore, the stock market primarily serves the SOEs, many of which have diverted their productive assets into listed subsidiaries while retaining four-fifths of their shares, the bulk of which remain untraded, even though in theory, up to 50 percent of the shares should come onto the market as initial public offering lockups expire (Y. Huang, Saich, and Steinfeld 2005; "Shanghigh" 2009). Development of the financial futures market and other attempts at broadening may have to wait until the financial crisis has passed and the shape of the new international regulatory architecture and of domestic systemic regulation becomes clearer. However, China is preparing to launch its own version of NASDAQ (National Association of Securities Dealers Automated Quotations), the Growth Enterprise Market, which is scheduled to open in late 2009 at the Shenzhen Stock Exchange ("China to Establish" 2008). This board will provide an avenue for smaller high-tech companies to raise capital more easily from sources other than banks and family.[20]

According to the Global Financial Centers Index there are three East Asian cities in the top 30 global centers (Yeandle and others 2009): Singapore; Hong Kong, China; and Tokyo. In 2009, Shanghai was ranked 35th, and Beijing was in 51st place. The rankings are based on criteria factoring in the quality of a city's

---

[20]One purpose of establishing this second exchange is to assist the transformation of industry from labor intensive to more technology intensive ("China: GEM" 2009). To be listed on the Growth Enterprise Market, firms must have a minimum of Y 10 million of accumulated net profits in the two years prior to listing. The requirement for the main exchanges in Shanghai and Shenzhen is at least Y 30 million of accumulated net profits in the previous three years (Bi 2009).

workforce; the business environment; a market access index that takes account of the various instruments traded and the presence of financial companies; a measure of the infrastructure that amalgamates rental costs and other determinants, such as public transport; and an index of the general competitiveness of the economy, which reflects price levels and the quality of life. Both Singapore and Hong Kong, China, are solidly rated on all counts, with Hong Kong, China, lagging only in the area of insurance. Tokyo dropped out of the top 10 for the first time in 2009 because of fears of Japan's vulnerability to the global recession, the low level of consumer confidence, and the weak cultural acceptance of foreigners.

Even though Shanghai and Beijing are ranked low, when respondents were asked to rate East Asian centers with the greatest likelihood of becoming more significant, they ranked Shanghai first and Singapore second. Beijing trailed a distant fourth, with only a third of the respondents giving it their vote.

Shanghai and, to a lesser degree, Beijing derive—much like Hong Kong, China—considerable impetus from the dynamism and prosperity of their respective hinterlands. These factors are likely to push both Shanghai and Beijing higher on the Global Financial Centers Index. Singapore is attempting to offset the shallowness of its hinterland by attracting the hedge fund business and emphasizing private asset management. However, it faces competition from Mumbai in both areas, although more high-net-worth individuals might prefer to reside in Singapore.

From the preceding, it is apparent that both cities are actively promoting the financial sector and vying for the mantle of China's financial capital. Beijing has the edge in banking and insurance, and it enjoys the advantages that derive from the presence of state regulatory bodies. Shanghai hosts the country's leading stock market, is more commercially oriented, has a more industrially dynamic hinterland, is ranked higher on the Global Financial Centers Index, and has been nominated by the central government to become China's leading financial center by 2020.

Labor and Skills

The industrial firms and high-value-adding services are the economic building blocks for Beijing and Shanghai, but their performance over the longer term will depend on the quality and variety of human capital and on the potential of the local innovation systems. The labor markets of the two megacities are already fairly deep and diverse. Beijing and Shanghai each have a formal labor force of 3 million workers or more, which is supplemented by several million migrant workers who constitute the floating population. In Shanghai, more than 25 percent of the population in 2000 had graduated from high school, and 6 percent of the population had earned bachelor's degrees (see table 5.19). The likely cause of the small decline in the percentage of workers with high school degrees was the near doubling of Shanghai's population between 1990 and

Table 5.19 Educational Level of Population as a Percentage of Reference Population, 1990 and 2000

Minimum educational level	Beijing (%) 1990	Beijing (%) 2000	Shanghai (%) 1990	Shanghai (%) 2000	China (%) 1990	China (%) 2000
High school	17.8	16.9	30.1	27.1	11.4	12.0
College-level associate degree	4.6	7.9	5.6	7.1	1.2	2.5
Bachelor's degree	6.9	8.3	5.8	6.2	0.8	1.2
Advanced degree	—	1.3	—	0.6	—	0.1

Sources: For Beijing: Beijing Municipal Bureau of Statistics and Beijing General Team of Investigation under the National Bureau of Statistics various years. For Shanghai: Shanghai Municipal Statistics Bureau various years. For China: National Bureau of Statistics of China various years.
Note: — = not available. Reference population is six years of age and older.

Table 5.20 Educational Level of Population, 1990 and 2000

Minimum educational level	Beijing 1990	Beijing 2000	Shanghai 1990	Shanghai 2000	China 1990	China 2000
High school	1.6	2.2	2.1	3.3	89.9	138.3
College-level associate degree	0.4	1.0	0.4	0.9	9.6	29.0
Bachelor's degree	0.6	1.1	0.4	0.8	6.1	14.2
Advanced degree	—	0.2	—	0.1	—	0.9
Total population	8.8	13.0	6.9	12.3	789.2	1156.7

Sources: For Beijing: Beijing Municipal Bureau of Statistics and Beijing General Team of Investigation under the National Bureau of Statistics various years. For Shanghai: Shanghai Municipal Statistics Bureau various years. For China: National Bureau of Statistics of China various years.
Note: — = not available. Reference population is six years of age and older.

2000 (from 6.9 million to 12.3 million) partly because of the influx of less educated migrants (see table 5.20). The vast majority of the migrant workforce is engaged in construction, light manufacturing and assembly-type activities, household services, and other occupations—mostly unskilled or semiskilled jobs.

The average level of education in Beijing is much lower than in Shanghai. Only 17 percent of the population has completed secondary school. However, Beijing has more workers with tertiary degrees and above, and holders of advanced degree are far more numerous, reflecting the greater density of universities and research institutions in Beijing relative to Shanghai (see table 5.21). Nevertheless, Shanghai is closing the gap rapidly and has attracted significant numbers of highly skilled knowledge workers from other parts of China and overseas who fill the growing demand from Shanghai's technology-intensive activities. Close to 50,000 scientists and engineers are employed at large and medium-size manufacturing enterprises in Shanghai; 47,000 of these are in the machinery and materials-processing

Table 5.21   Number of Universities, 1995–2007

Location	1995	1996	2000	2001	2002	2006	2007
Beijing	—	65	58	61	—	80	83
Hong Kong, China[a]	—	—	—	—	30	35	35
Shanghai	45	41	37	45	50	60	60
Tokyo[b]	—	—	—	187	186	187	190
China	—	—	1,041	—	—	1,867	—
Japan	1,161	1,174	1,221	1,228	1,227	1,214	1,212

Sources: For Beijing: Beijing Municipal Bureau of Statistics and Beijing General Team of Investigation under the National Bureau of Statistics various years. For Hong Kong: Government of the Hong Kong SAR Education Bureau. For Shanghai: Shanghai Municipal Statistics Bureau various years. For Tokyo and Japan: Tokyo Metropolitan Government. For China: National Bureau of Statistics of China various years.
Note: — = not available.
a. Data are for the years 2002/03, 2006/07, and 2007/08.
b. Includes junior colleges and universities.

industries (see table 5.22). One-quarter of these scientific and engineering workers are employed in the electronics industry (including communication equipment and computer hardware). This capacity to attract knowledge workers is a tremendous asset for Shanghai (as it is for London and New York), and it needs to be enhanced by further augmenting the vitality and distinctiveness of the city and the convenience of living there.

Tertiary Education and the Innovation System

A technologically dynamic industrial economy relies mainly on the local production of knowledge workers and on the retention of graduates. In this respect, Beijing and Shanghai have been quick off the mark. The number of universities has risen from 65 to 83 in Beijing between 1996 and 2007 and from 45 to 60 in Shanghai between 1995 and 2006 (see table 5.21). Similarly, between 1996 and 2007, enrollment increased from 189,953 to 567,875 in Beijing and from 147,926 to 466,333 in Shanghai (see table 5.23). Approximately 40 percent of tertiary-level students major in science and engineering; hence, at least in terms of the numbers of graduates with science, technology, engineering, and math skills, Beijing and Shanghai are well supplied (table 5.24).[21] Furthermore, the attractions of the city

---

[21] As a percentage of the total, however, the number has dropped steadily from 52 percent in 1997 to 42 percent in 2001. Rising enrollment rates after 1999, which increased the supply of graduates and reduced the growth of salaries of science, technology, engineering, and math graduates, might be discouraging students from pursuing the hard sciences. Information gathered from interviews suggests that only the engineering and science graduates from the top schools are adequately prepared for entry into the job market and have good job prospects (Wadhwa and others 2007).

Table 5.22 Scientists and Engineers in Industrial Enterprises in Shanghai, 2005

Industrial sector	Number of employees
Manufacturing industry	49,795
Communication equipment, computers, and other electronic equipment manufacturing	12,393
Transportation equipment manufacturing	6,993
General equipment manufacturing	5,686
Electric machinery equipment and manufacturing	3,836
Smelting and pressing of ferrous metals	3,668
Special-purpose equipment manufacturing	3,002
Raw chemical materials and chemicals	2,962
Instruments, meters, and culture and office equipment manufacturing	2,197
Medicine manufacturing	2,146
Oil processing, coking, and nuclear processing	1,472
Nonmetal mineral products	680
Metal products manufacturing	655
Printing and record duplication	630
Textiles	513
Plastic products manufacturing	482
Rubber products manufacturing	458
Food manufacturing	429
Smelting and pressing of nonferrous metals	395
Stationery, education, and sports goods manufacturing	321
Tobacco manufacturing	195
Artworks and other manufacturing	157
Furniture manufacturing	143
Farm and sideline products processing	106
Chemical fiber manufacturing	79
Beverage manufacturing	63
Petroleum and natural gas exploitation	54
Papermaking and paper products manufacturing	38
Garments, shoes, and accessories manufacturing	37
Timber processing and timber, bamboo, rattan, coir, and straw products manufacturing	5

Source: Shanghai Science and Technology Commission 2007.
Note: Data are based on firms with revenues greater than Y 5 million.

Table 5.23 Number of Students, 1995–2007

Location	1995	1996	1997	2000	2001	2002	2006	2007
Beijing	—	189,953	—	—	340,284	—	—	567,875
Hong Kong, China[a]	—	—	—	—	—	169,600	184,500	188,300
Shanghai	—	147,926	153,804	226,798	279,966	331,649	442,620	466,333
Tokyo[b]	—	—	—	726,485	724,082	721,720	735,726	731,099
China	2,906,000	3,021,000	3,174,000	5,560,900	7,190,700	9,033,600	17,388,000	—
Japan	3,045,165	3,069,946	3,080,540	3,067,703	3,054,903	3,053,118	3,061,466	3,015,375

Sources: For Beijing: Beijing Municipal Bureau of Statistics and Beijing General Team of Investigation under the National Bureau of Statistics various years. For Hong Kong: Government of the Hong Kong SAR Education Bureau. For Shanghai: Shanghai Municipal Statistics Bureau various years. For Tokyo and Japan: Ministry of Education, Culture, Sports, Science, and Technology. For China: National Bureau of Statistics of China various years.

Note: — = not available.

a. Data are for the years 2002/03, 2006/07, and 2007/08.

b. Includes junior colleges and universities.

Table 5.24   Science, Technology, Engineering, and Mathematics Undergraduate Students, 1995–2007

Location	Share of total undergraduate students (%)						
	1995	1996	1997	2000	2001	2006	2007
Beijing	—	52.5	—	—	45.6	—	—
Hong Kong, China[a]	—	—	—	—	44.7	46.5	46.6
Shanghai	—	—	52.5	—	42.0	—	39.9
China	50.8	—	—	48.3	—	49.5	—
Japan[b]	28.4	—	—	28.3	—	28.4	28.5

Sources: For Beijing: Beijing Municipal Bureau of Statistics and Beijing General Team of Investigation under the National Bureau of Statistics various years. For Hong Kong: University Grants Committee (http://www.ugc.edu.hk/eng/doc/ugc/stat/apcfte_series.pdf). For Shanghai: Shanghai Municipal Statistics Bureau various years. For China: National Bureau of Statistics of China various years. For Japan: Ministry of Education, Culture, Sports, Science, and Technology.
Note: — = not available.
a. Data are for the years 2002/03, 2006/07, and 2007/08. The data are based on enrollment for undergraduate and graduate students at universities funded by the University Grants Committee.
b. Data include junior colleges and universities and cover science, engineering, and medicine students.

and opportunities for well-paid jobs relative to other parts of the country are such that the vast majority of graduates choose to remain in these cities.

Equally encouraging is the increase in the number of students enrolled in programs for advanced degrees. In 1995, about 15,000 students were enrolled in such programs in Shanghai (see table 5.25). This number rose to nearly 92,000 in 2007. The absolute number of students enrolled is still about half the number in Beijing,[22] which has a significant advantage over Shanghai in this respect. The number of students enrolled in PhD programs in Shanghai has also climbed tenfold in 12 years to 23,000 in 2007, still less than half the enrollment in Beijing but far above that of Hong Kong, China (see table 5.26).

The quality of graduates is a different matter, and scope exists here for substantial improvement to raise Beijing's and Shanghai's technological capacity and prepare the ground for innovation.[23] Employers find that graduates from even the finest universities have a number of limitations. Although the better graduates have a sound grasp of theory, they lag in their knowledge of the latest developments in

---

[22]In Beijing, 55 percent of graduate students received degrees in science and technology fields.
[23]The increase in class sizes since 1999 could be compromising quality. In this regard, Simon and Cao (2008) remark that a professor not uncommonly supervises as many as 10 doctoral students at one time. See N. Liu (2007) on the ranking and Xin and Normile (2008) for the challenges confronting Chinese universities as they attempt to improve the quality of instruction and research. China still faces some difficulties in effectively participating in and collaborating with international scientific organizations (Xu 2008).

Table 5.25   Students Enrolled in Postgraduate Programs, 1995–2007

Location	Number of students					
	1995	1996	2000	2001	2006	2007
Beijing	—	30,299	—	79,411	178,091	187,414
Hong Kong, China	—	—	—	10,197	8,411	8,517
Shanghai	14,713	—	30,614	—	—	91,763
China	145,443	—	301,239	—	1,104,653	—
Japan	153,423	—	205,311	—	261,049	262,113

Sources: For Beijing: Beijing Municipal Bureau of Statistics and Beijing General Team of Investigation under the National Bureau of Statistics various years. For Hong Kong: University Grants Committee (http://www.ugc.edu.hk/eng/ugc/publication/report/figure2007/figures/03.pdf). For Shanghai: Shanghai Municipal Statistics Bureau various years. For China: National Bureau of Statistics of China various years. For Japan: Ministry of Education, Culture, Sports, Science, and Technology.
Note: — = not available.

Table 5.26   Students Enrolled in PhD Programs, 1995–2007

Location	Number of students					
	1995	1996	2000	2001	2006	2007
Beijing	—	7,475	—	22,826	49,474	53,388
Hong Kong, China	—	—	—	4,033	5,465	5,627
Shanghai	2,333	2,670	8,236	10,503	21,882	23,105
China	—	—	—	—	55,955	—
Japan	43,774	—	62,481	—	75,365	74,811

Sources: For Beijing: Beijing Municipal Bureau of Statistics and Beijing General Team of Investigation under the National Bureau of Statistics various years. For Hong Kong: University Grants Committee (http://www.ugc.edu.hk/eng/ugc/publication/report/figure2007/figures/03.pdf). For Shanghai: Shanghai Municipal Statistics Bureau various years. For China: National Bureau of Statistics of China various years. For Japan: Ministry of Education, Culture, Sports, Science, and Technology.
Note: — = not available.

their fields; have weak communication and practical problem-solving skills; and given the emphasis on rote learning, tend to display limited initiative when on the job. According to Simon and Cao (2008: 192), many students who are "fresh out of universities have trouble handling tasks that require knowledge and skills beyond formal education." Most firms need to invest in three to six months of training to upgrade the technical and practical skills of their new hires and to instill the corporate culture. More than quantity, which has increased vastly, the tertiary education system in China's leading megacities now needs to focus on quality of skills, hard and soft, because innovativeness depends on both. Both cities are in much the same situation, and improvement will require years of effort not just by the universities but also by the municipality and the central government to embed a creative culture (Yusuf 2009c). Only about 10 percent of Chinese professors have doctoral-level qualifications—20 percent in elite institutions (Simon and Cao 2008). This short-coming is being remedied through new hires, but experience will remain in short supply for some time, and attracting some of the best and brightest to the teaching profession and research will require stronger inducements—financial and other. As Japan has found, attracting new talent is not easy, but a start can be made by giving the leading public universities more autonomy to manage staffing, salaries, and curricula.

To close the skill gap, the Shanghai government spent Y 27 billion on social security and job-related expenditure in 2007 (13 percent of fiscal expenditure, compared with 10 percent in 2006; see table 5.27) to provide more people with career-related training (see table 5.28). In 2007, more than 1 million persons (this includes double counting) received training through public training institutes, an increase of 25 percent over 2005. Similarly, Beijing offers training to more than 800,000 people. Raising the quality of education could lessen the need for such remedial training by public institutes and firms.

Two universities in Shanghai—Shanghai Jiao Tong University (SJTU) and Fudan University—are among the top (globally) ranked universities (see tables 5.29 and 5.30). These universities also rank in the top 10 within China (ex-cluding those in Hong Kong, China). Although these rankings typically do not change much from year to year, SJTU has moved up the global ranking from 404–502 in 2004 to 201–302 in 2008. Beijing is home to four high-ranking univer-sities: Peking University, Tsinghua University, University of Science and Technol-ogy of China, and China Agricultural University. The first two are the highest-rated schools in the country, and globally they are among the 201–302 most highly ranked schools worldwide. In the university pecking order, it would be fair to say that Beijing leads with Shanghai in second place.

Table 5.27   Spending on Training in Shanghai, 2006–07

Expense category	2006	2007
Social security and jobs (Y billion)	17.48	27.42
Social security and jobs as a percentage of local fiscal expenditure	9.6	12.5

Source: Shanghai Municipal Statistics Bureau 2008.

Table 5.28   Number of People Receiving Training, 2005–07

City	Thousand person times		
	2005	2006	2007
Beijing	637.2	522.0	882.0
Shanghai	971.2	1,103.8	1,105.3

Sources: Beijing Municipal Bureau of Statistics and Beijing General Team of Investigation under the National Bureau of Statistics 2007, 2008; Shanghai Municipal Statistics Bureau 2008.

Table 5.29 Rankings of Universities in Beijing; Hong Kong, China; Shanghai; and Tokyo, 2008

World ranking	Regional ranking	National ranking	Institution	City
19	1	1	Tokyo University	Tokyo
101–151	9–16	5–7	Tokyo Institute of Technology	Tokyo
201–302	23–41	1–3	Chinese University of Hong Kong	Hong Kong, China
201–302	23–41	1–3	Hong Kong University of Science and Technology	Hong Kong, China
201–302	23–41	10–12	Keio University	Tokyo
201–302	23–41	1–6	Peking University	Beijing
201–302	23–41	1–6	Shanghai Jiao Tong University	Shanghai
201–302	23–41	1–6	Tsinghua University	Beijing
201–302	23–41	1–3	University of Hong Kong	Hong Kong, China
201–302	23–41	1–6	University of Science and Technology of China	Beijing
303–401	42–68	4–5	City University of Hong Kong	Hong Kong, China
303–401	42–68	7	Fudan University	Shanghai
303–401	42–68	4–5	Hong Kong Polytechnic University	Hong Kong, China
303–401	42–68	13–18	Tokyo Medical and Dental University	Tokyo
303–401	42–68	13–18	Waseda University	Tokyo
402–503	69–100	8–18	China Agricultural University	Beijing, China
402–503	69–100	19–31	Nihon University	Tokyo
402–503	69–100	19–31	Tokyo Metropolitan University	Tokyo
402–503	69–100	19–31	Tokyo University of Agriculture and Technology	Tokyo

Source: Center for World-Class Universities, Shanghai Jiao Tong University (http://www.arwu.org/rank2008/en2008.htm).
Note: Institutions within the same ranking range are listed alphabetically.

The volume of science and technology skills and the quality of the workforce are indicators of technological capacity of relevance to advanced manufacturing industries. The level of R&D and its productivity is a gauge of innovation capacity. Shanghai invested 2.6 percent of its GDP in R&D in 2007, up from 1.3 percent in 1995 and more than a percentage point higher than the average for China (see table 5.31).[24] By comparison, Beijing invests 6 percent, an enormous

---

[24]Europe is losing ground in research and innovation because spending on R&D has stagnated at around 2 percent for 10 years and because of the low academic attainment of most European universities. These factors have affected the quality of graduates and postgraduate students and induced many of the brightest to emigrate to the United States (Patten 2006).

Table 5.30 Times Higher Education Global Ranking of Universities, 2007

2007 ranking	2006 ranking	Name	City
19	17	University of Tokyo	Tokyo
26	18	University of Hong Kong	Hong Kong, China
39	53 (tie)	Hong Kong University of Science and Technology	Hong Kong, China
42	38	Chinese University of Hong Kong	Hong Kong, China
50 (tie)	36	Peking University	Beijing
56	40	Tsinghua University	Beijing
61	90 (tie)	Tokyo Institute of Technology	Tokyo
113	85 (tie)	Fudan University	Shanghai
141	155 (tie)	University of Science and Technology of China	Beijing
144 (tie)	163 (tie)	Shanghai Jiao Tong University	Shanghai
147 (tie)	149 (tie)	City University of Hong Kong	Hong Kong, China
180 (tie)	180 (tie)	Waseda University	Tokyo

Source: Times Higher Education (http://www.timeshighereducation.co.uk/hybrid.asp?typeCode=243&pubCode=1&navcode=137).

Table 5.31 R&D Spending as a Share of Regional GDP, 1995–2007

Economy	Share (%)		
	1995	2000	2007
Beijing[a]	—	8.9	6.0
Hong Kong, China[b]	0.4	0.6	0.8
Shanghai	1.3	1.7	2.6
China[a]	0.6	1.0	1.4
Japan[b]	3.0	3.2	3.0

Sources: For Beijing: Beijing Municipal Bureau of Statistics and Beijing General Team of Investigation under the National Bureau of Statistics various years. For Hong Kong: Science and Technology Statistics Section, Census and Statistics Department, May 2008. For Shanghai: Shanghai Municipal Statistics Bureau various years. For China: National Bureau of Statistics of China various years. For Japan: World Bank 2008c.
Note: — = not available.
a. End year is 2006.
b. Data are for the years 1998, 2002, and 2006.

amount that reflects an aggressive strategy to build research capacity and to ground its future growth in innovation. As is the case in the rest of China and in industrial countries, firms do two-thirds of the R&D. The distribution of R&D in Shanghai and in Beijing is shown in figures 5.10 and 5.11, respectively. The bulk of research is in experimental development areas, although R&D in Beijing focuses more on basic and applied research. The R&D trend in Shanghai

Figure 5.10 Distribution of R&D Expenditure in Shanghai, by Type of Activity, 2001–06

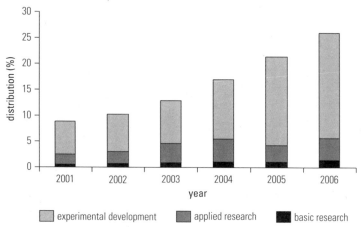

Source: Shanghai Science and Technology Commission 2007.

Figure 5.11 Distribution of R&D Expenditure in Beijing, by Type of Activity, 2002–07

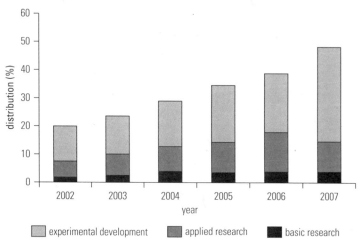

Source: Beijing Municipal Bureau of Statistics and Beijing General Team of Investigation under the National Bureau of Statistics various years.

is in the direction seen in the advanced industrial economies, away from government institutes and toward firms and universities (see figure 5.12), whereas close to half of R&D is conducted by universities and research institutions in Beijing (see table 5.32). However, the productivity of R&D in many of the SOEs is questionable. Most of these companies do not yet have in place the business

Figure 5.12 R&D Expenditure in Shanghai, by Type of Institution, 2001–06

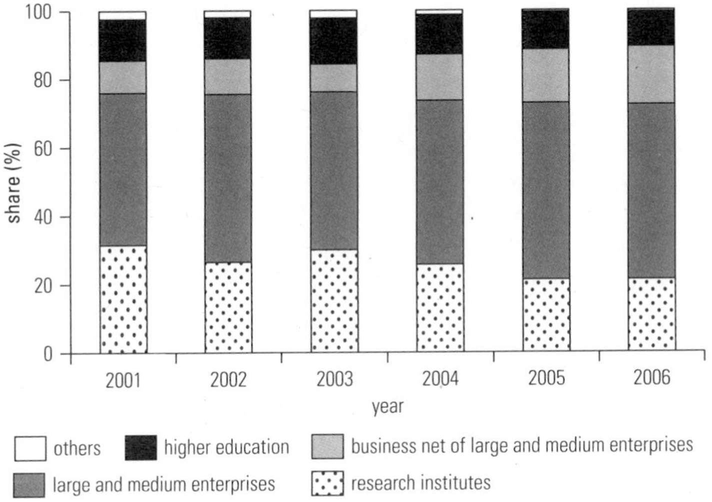

Source: Shanghai Science and Technology Commission 2007.

Table 5.32 Expenditure on R&D and Its Composition in Beijing, 2005 and 2006

Spending institution	Amount (Y billion)		Share (%)	
	2005	2006	2005	2006
Scientific research institutions	27.00	32.41	35.96	37.05
Institutions of higher education	7.86	9.02	10.47	10.32
Enterprises	38.52	43.21	51.30	49.40
Medium-size and large industrial enterprises	8.37	11.48	11.15	13.12
Others	1.70	2.83	2.27	3.24
Total	75.10	87.48	100.00	100.00

Sources: Beijing Municipal Bureau of Statistics and Beijing General Team of Investigation under the National Bureau of Statistics 2006, 2007.

models, incentives, and experienced managerial and supervisory staff to organize research activities effectively, to derive adequate benefits from R&D by integrating it closely with production and marketing, and to routinize incremental innovation throughout the firm. Some SOEs exhibit signs of change and are learning how to harness their R&D more effectively. The value of R&D by MNCs and its spillovers also raise questions. Whether MNCs are doing enough core R&D in Shanghai is difficult to say, and given worries over intellectual property, they are probably doing relatively little. Because hardly any researchers leave major MNCs to start their own firms, few of these much-needed spinoffs would seem to occur, although employee turnover in the MNCs does transfer knowledge to local producers.

The share of universities in research was about 10 percent in 2006, about the same as in 2001 in both Beijing and Shanghai. Research institutions are far more numerous in Beijing and account for 37 percent of the research, compared with about 20 percent in Shanghai. In 2006, Beijing had 351 research institutions and Shanghai, 170. Because most of the basic and upstream applied research vital for innovation in high-tech industries is likely to be conducted in universities and research institutions, they will have a major role in pushing outward the frontiers of potentially commercializable knowledge and in imparting the skills relevant for dynamic, fast-growing industries (see figure 5.12).[25] Thus, growth in the share of universities and research institutions and in the share of basic research in total research is a desirable development.

R&D by MNCs

MNCs are gradually transferring their R&D activities outside their home countries.[26] For example, foreign affiliates, mainly in advanced countries, conducted 13 percent of U.S. MNCs' R&D and 43 percent of Swedish MNCs' R&D. Worldwide, this percentage is on the rise, with 16 percent of R&D conducted by foreign affiliates of MNCs, compared with 10 percent in 1993. East Asian economies—China especially—are benefiting disproportionately from the internationalization of research. MNCs are attracted to East Asian economies because of the elastic supply and low wages of science and technology workers, the heavy investment by these countries in their innovation systems and particularly in tertiary education, and the quality of the information and communication technology infrastructure that facilitates easy communication between R&D centers spread across a number of countries. China ranked third after the United States and the United Kingdom as

---

[25]"From the point of view of the unthinking market mechanism, investment in basic research is largely a wasteful expenditure because the outlay offers no dependable promise of addition to the profits of the firm" (Baumol 2004: 24). Basic research will depend largely on state funding because of its nature as a public good. That such research can initiate cycles of innovation is supported by the experience of government funding in the United States for integrated circuits, biotechnology, the Internet, and of digital search technology. To cite just one currently famous example, the firm Google was the outcome of a National Science Foundation grant to Stanford University to research digital libraries.

[26]In 1980, close to half (45 percent) of MNCs conducted R&D only in their home countries. By 2000, this share had decreased to 27 percent. In 2000, the median number of countries where MNCs operated R&D activities was 4, while a handful of MNCs conducted R&D in more than 10 countries (Quintás and others 2008).

Figure 5.13   Locations of R&D Investments by MNCs, 2004

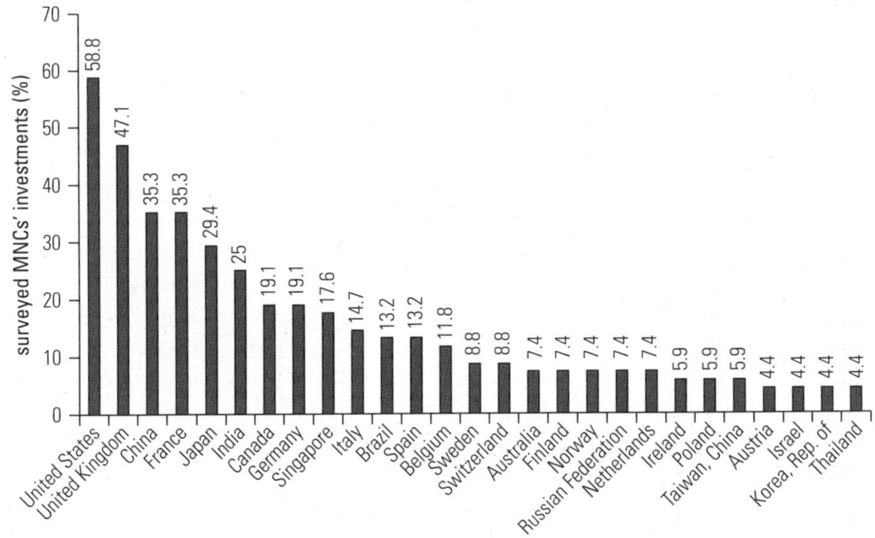

Source: UNCTAD 2005: figure IV.8.

a destination for R&D investments, with India ranked sixth (UNCTAD 2005). By the end of 2007, MNCs had set up 1,160 research centers in China ("China: Foreign R&D" 2008). Some of these R&D facilities are there purely to meet the conditions imposed by the government and do testing and product customization for local purposes. Others are starting to do real R&D work, which is surfacing in the patenting statistics.[27]

Relative to other countries, foreign firms are attracted by the opportunities presented by the scale of China's innovation system and its pace of expansion as well as by the potential size of the domestic market. China was the top choice for MNCs from 2005 to 2009, followed by the United States and India (see figures 5.13 and 5.14). Developing innovation capability takes a long time, not only because training skilled workers takes time, but also because building experience in managing R&D takes time. By attracting foreign R&D operations, China is attempting to accelerate a deepening of innovation capability. In addition to technology transfer mediated by MNCs, China is attempting to make full use of the intellectual capital inherent in its diaspora.[28] These Chinese, who were educated and gained experience abroad and

---

[27]See Sun, Du, and Huang (2006) for a detailed look into MNCs' R&D operations in Shanghai.
[28]According to Chinese government estimates, more than 2,500 PhDs, 20,000 master's degree holders, and 3,000 other Chinese have returned to China (J. Li and Yue 2005).

Figure 5.14   Prospective R&D Locations Considered Most Attractive, 2005–09

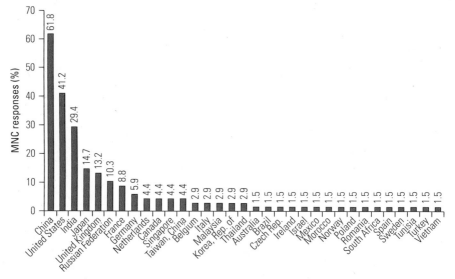

Source: UNCTAD 2005: figure IV.11.

subsequently returned to China, are an important asset because they help facilitate managing a diverse group of researchers that includes foreigners, domestic Chinese without any experience outside of China, and overseas Chinese.[29] By mobilizing experienced returnees who can understand and manage a multicultural and disparate group of people, China can increase the effectiveness of the R&D activities in China (Y.-C. Chen 2008; Sun and Wen 2007a).

---

[29]On the difference between Chinese and Japanese engineers, one returnee Chinese who oversees the R&D center of a Japanese MNC commented: "Chinese engineers are more like businessmen while Japanese engineers are much more like craftsmen. Chinese engineers would choose to stop working on a project once the technology or product is acceptable to the market, while Japanese engineers will continue improving the technology. For Japanese engineers, technology development is not simply for market demand: in many cases, such efforts become a personal hobby" (Sun and Wen 2007a: 440). Similarly, "most American engineers take a job because they are interested in such jobs themselves first, while many Chinese engineers take job not necessarily because of the intrinsic nature of the project or the job itself, but because of the pay and other aspects of the job. Many people from the USA and other countries would like to stick with their technological field, while most Chinese love to become managers [or] government officials" (Sun and Wen 2007a: 440).

Foreign R&D operations in China are concentrated mainly in Beijing and Shanghai.[30] A closer examination of their activities and aims suggests that R&D operations in Beijing favor pure research whereas those in Shanghai tend to focus on development (and service) activities associated with manufacturing.[31] In addition, the coverage of industries is different in these two megacities. Firms affiliated with the information technology (IT) industry are responsible for a disproportionate number of R&D centers in Beijing. In contrast, firms drawn from a wide range of industrial subsectors, such as automotive, electronics, chemicals, and materials, have established R&D activities in Shanghai and capitalize on its industrial diversity (Sun, Du, and Huang 2006).

Beijing is attractive to research-oriented MNCs because of the concentration of major research institutions and universities. Beijing is home to China's top universities, such as Peking University and Tsinghua University, and to other technology-oriented universities, such as Beijing Polytechnic University, Beijing University of Aeronautics and Astronautics, and Beijing University of Post and Telecommunication. In addition, 41 research units of the Chinese Academy of Sciences (CAS) are located in Beijing (Y.-C. Chen 2008). This concentration of tertiary institutions complements and reinforces the abundant supply of graduates in science and engineering fields. The number and diversity of universities and research institutions provide a wider spectrum of engineering expertise in Beijing relative to other cities in China (Y.-C. Chen 2008). In addition, IT-related foreign R&D operations benefit from being in Beijing because it is the largest IT cluster in China. Beijing is also the seat of the central government, where telecommunication-related regulations are formulated (Sun and Wen 2007b).

For instance, Microsoft set up its fundamental research facility, Microsoft Research China, in Beijing in 1998 with US$60 million. The center is developing Chinese-language and user-interface technologies and next-generation multimedia. Other technology-related firms, such as Fujitsu, IBM, Intel, Lucent, Motorola, and Nokia, are also located in Beijing (J. Li and Yue 2005). Because these R&D centers in Beijing engage in fundamental research as well as in downstream research, they are collaborating with local universities through various channels, such as joint research labs (Lucent and Tsinghua University), joint research projects (Intel and Tsinghua

---

[30]Although the exact distribution is hard to calculate, many studies point to the share of foreign R&D centers in Beijing and Shanghai as being around 70 percent (Sun and Wen 2007b). Others are located in Guangzhou–Shenzhen, Chengdu, Tianjin, and Dalian.

[31]This is not to say that Shanghai has no research-oriented foreign R&D centers. Some exist, such as Unilever's, which was established in 2002. However, the point is that, relative to Beijing, Shanghai has fewer research-oriented R&D centers (Sun, Du, and Huang 2006).

University), internship programs,[32] training programs (Motorola and Peking University), and exchange of personnel (Y.-C. Chen 2008).

Because R&D centers support the manufacturing activities of MNCs, most R&D centers in Shanghai are co-located with manufacturing plants. The R&D operations supply support services, help in adaptation to the local conditions and needs, and develop products specific to the Chinese market. For instance, Hewlett-Packard's China Software Solutions Center shares the site with the manufacturing plant to facilitate communication with the production unit. The Infineon Shanghai Center, which customizes the platform designs used in mobile phones in China, is located in Shanghai to be close to the actual manufacturing activity (Sun, Du, and Huang 2006). Some R&D centers have become major global product development centers for MNCs. Initially, Sharp's R&D center was geared toward product development for the Chinese domestic air-conditioner market. However, it is now developing products that are manufactured in Thailand and eventually will be manufactured in Japan (Sun, Du, and Huang 2006).[33]

MNCs now regard China as a major innovation node in their global R&D strategy.[34] Interviews with MNCs' R&D managers reveal that infrastructure[35] and institutional constraints are not a major concern, although improvements are welcomed (Sun and Wen 2007a).[36] Human resource management, however, is a key challenge for companies operating R&D centers in China. Their concerns center on rising wages, high mobility and turnover, lack of experience among recent graduates, limited creativity, and cultural differences (Simon 2007). Although the technical understanding of subjects among Chinese scientists and engineers is

---

[32]Internship programs are beneficial to firms and students. Firms gain skilled workers inexpensively (often free) to meet short-term needs. Students gain valuable experience. Microsoft, for example, has more interns than permanent staff members. Because of the worsening traffic in Beijing, locating closer to campus is advantageous to accommodate interns, who must shuffle between school and work (Y.-C. Chen 2008).

[33]Other firms, such as Motorola, use their R&D centers in China to develop products for the global market, sometimes testing the waters in the Chinese market first (Y.-C. Chen 2008).

[34]In 2008, China ranked higher than the United States as the preferred location for the R&D facilities of MNCs: 61 percent of those polled preferred China, and only 41 percent polled for the United States. Between 1998 and 2003, U.S. companies' investment in their R&D operations overseas was twice (52 percent) the rate of their investments in the United States (26 percent). See Auerswald and Branscomb (2008).

[35]One constraint is the lack of suppliers for lab materials. Sourcing of inputs that would arrive in only a few days in advanced countries can take weeks in China (Sun and Wen 2007a).

[36]Regulations concerning the importation of equipment to be serviced pose some issues. Thus, product service centers tend to be located in Hong Kong, China, or in Singapore, where bringing in these products duty free is easier (Sun and Wen 2007a).

adequate, many MNCs express their dissatisfaction with a lack of creativity among these scientists and engineers (Sun and Wen 2007a). In the past, workers tended to work for a single firm for a long time, but SOE reform dealt a blow to the tenure culture. Job-hopping has become a social norm, and it has resulted in high labor turnover, even in the R&D activities of MNCs. Turnover is a major concern for MNCs because typically these engineers need one to two years of training before they are ready and acculturated enough to engage productively in R&D (Sun and Wen 2007a).

University-Industry Links

Both universities and firms are important components of a national innovation system. With globalization and intensifying competitive pressure, many countries are now seeing the collaboration between universities and the industrial sector as a means of spurring innovation.[37] The experience from the United States shows that productivity in terms of innovation increases when universities and firms collaborate (Darby, Zucker, and Wang 2003).[38,39] National and local governments have introduced a number of schemes to encourage key universities to increase research and to engage with firms to stimulate innovative activities in their locale. Beijing and, to a lesser degree, Shanghai have adopted an activist stance in stimulating research.

China has two broad vehicles for university-industry links. The first consists of the traditional mechanisms, such as licensing, consulting, and collaborative R&D

---

[37]The best research universities strive to create an environment that encourages interdepartmental and interdisciplinary collaborative work. They work hard to attract and nurture the very best talents, and they attempt to deepen the research in fields with the greatest perceived potential. Stanford, for example, got it right when the university decided to build its research capacity in solid state electronics by hiring new faculty members, expanding graduate programs, and setting up specialized laboratories (Lenoir and others 2004).

[38]The U.S. government-sponsored SEMATECH (Semiconductor Manufacturing Technology) consortium supported collaborative R&D among electronics producers to attack specific problems and constraints. It helped establish priorities and allocate funding, and through industry cost sharing, it directed funds to research of importance to businesses themselves and increased the likelihood of both adoption and diffusion of such research through the spillovers induced by the temporary assignments of personnel to the consortium (Alic, Mowery, and Rubin 2003).

[39]This conclusion is based on the behavior of firms participating in the Advanced Technology Program (ATP) in the United States. Participating in the ATP increases the number of patents firms apply for. This behavior is further enhanced through partnerships with universities. The ATP was introduced in the United States after the successful implementation of R&D consortia in Japan (Fukuda and Watanabe 2008). For analysis of R&D consortia in Japan, see Sakakibara (1997, 2001) and Sakakibara and Cho (2002).

activities. The establishment of six state technology-transfer centers in key universities formally encouraged such mechanisms. SJTU is one such center. The other vehicle is the establishment of university start-ups and spinoffs in many industrial subfields, few of which are high tech (K. Chen and Kenney 2007).[40] Often these university enterprises were established to supplement a university's budget and to absorb surplus university personnel, although this practice is declining (Wu 2007).[41]

Fudan University and SJTU are the two premier universities in Shanghai. Their technology licensing revenue in 2003 was Y 73.3 million for Fudan and Y 224.5 million for SJTU (Wu 2007). The state technology-transfer center at SJTU has branch offices in the Yangtze River Delta and Pearl River Delta regions to extend its reach. Fudan University established a Commercialization and University Enterprise Management Office to promote spinoff activities. By 2003, the office managed more than 100 spinoff firms. Some have gone public, such as Fudan Fuhua Pharmaceuticals and Shanghai Fudan Microelectronics Company Limited, an integrated circuitry firm. SJTU also has a number of spinoff firms, Angli Ltd. being the most well known. Both universities find the absorptive capacity of local domestic firms, especially that of small and medium-size enterprises, to be weak, with first-generation owners evincing little interest in building their intellectual assets and pursuing in-house applied research to encourage incremental innovations or more (Zhang and others 2009). These universities engage with MNCs mainly through joint R&D efforts, often focusing on localizing foreign technologies for the Chinese market (Wu 2007).

In 2007, the contract value of technologies transferred by universities in Shanghai was Y 171 million (see table 5.33). About one-quarter of this contract income is from the sale of patents. SOEs are the most frequent users of the technology developed in universities, followed by private enterprises. Foreign firms are not actively involved in university-industry links, except in certain areas of upstream or basic research, because they can draw on the parent firm's expertise, the expertise of buyers and suppliers, and in-house research centers with the relevant specialized skills.

---

[40]During 1997 to 2004, Chinese universities spun off 42,945 firms, although most of them are not high-tech operations and many were created to provide employment for redundant university staff members. Nevertheless, this achievement is striking and points to the role that universities can play (M. Hu and Mathews 2008).

[41]Most university-linked enterprises have been unsuccessful because of inappropriate business models and the inexperience of university administrations in managing these enterprises, a problem exacerbated by excessive interference in their operations. A state council directive in 2001 began the process of modifying the corporate governance of university-affiliated businesses so as to arrive at viable outcomes for both universities and enterprises (Xue 2006b). Fudan University, for instance, restructured all existing university enterprises so that these enterprises are separate from the university (Wu 2007).

Table 5.33   Technological Transfer from Universities in Shanghai: Science, Engineering, Agriculture, and Medicine, 2006

	Number of contracts	Contract value (Y thousand)	Real income at present year (Y thousand)
Total	329	170,630	123,342
Patent sale	62	40,763	27,933
Sale of other intellectual property rights	131	37,380	34,280
By type of technological transfer			
State-owned enterprises	126	90,223	60,475
Foreign-funded enterprises	31	17,692	18,215
Private enterprises	131	52,530	35,784
Others	41	10,185	8,868

Source: Shanghai Science and Technology Commission 2007.

Among the universities in China, Peking University and Tsinghua University derive the largest revenue from their affiliated firms (see table 5.34).[42] Affiliated firms of Peking University generated Y 16.3 billion of income in 2003 and those of Tsinghua University had total revenues of Y 14.5 billion. These figures dwarf the revenues accruing to other universities. Close to 45 percent of university-affiliated firms are classified as high tech, and they are responsible for more than 80 percent of revenues (K. Chen and Kenney 2007). Some of the most famous firms linked to the two universities or to the Chinese Academy of Sciences are Lenovo from CAS,[43] Founder from Peking University, and Tongfang from Tsinghua University. Following the example of universities in member states of the Organisation for Economic Co-operation and Development (including those in China), CAS established a Technology Licensing Office to commercialize some of its research results. In addition, CAS established a Science and Technology Development Center in partnership with the Beijing municipal government, again to commercialize CAS technology. To support start-up firms by its scientists and engineers, CAS created the China Science and Technology Promotion and Economic Investment Company. By 2004, more than 400 firms had been spun off or had received investment from CAS (K. Chen and Kenney 2007). Tsinghua University established its own science park[44] and incubators (Tsinghua Business Incubator) to stimulate the spinoffs and created the Tsinghua Holding Company in 1995 to manage spinoff firms and to invest in new ones. Among the universities in China, Tsinghua University has received the largest number of patents from the U.S. Patent and Trademark Office (M. Hu and Mathews 2008).

---

[42]Peking University was founded in 1898, and Tsinghua University was established in 1911 as a technical university (K. Chen and Kenney 2007).

[43]See Q. Lu and Lazonick (2001) for the details on how Lenovo was spun off from CAS.

[44]The park has more than 300 firms, including national laboratories, headquarters of university-affiliated firms, and R&D centers of MNCs (K. Chen and Kenney 2007).

Table 5.34 University Revenues from Affiliated Firms, 1999 and 2003

	1999				2003		
Rank	University	Income (Y billion)	Location	Rank	University	Income (Y billion)	Location
1	Peking University	8.7	Beijing	1	Peking University	16.3	Beijing
2	Tsinghua University	3.2	Beijing	2	Tsinghua University	14.5	Beijing
3	Harbin Institute of Technology	1.0	Harbin	3	Zhejiang University	3.4	Hangzhou
4	Zhejiang University	0.9	Hangzhou	4	Xi'an Jiaotong University	2.6	Xi'an
5	Northeastern University	0.9	Shenyang	5	Northeastern University	2.4	Shenyang
6	Shanghai Jiao Tong University	0.8	Shanghai	6	Tongji University	2.2	Shanghai
7	University of Petroleum (East China)	0.8	Dongying	7	Shanghai Jiao Tong University	1.9	Shanghai
8	Tongji University	0.7	Shanghai	8	Harbin Institute of Technology	1.5	Harbin
9	Tianjin University	0.6	Tianjin	9	University of Petroleum (East China)	1.4	Dongying
10	Nankai University	0.6	Tianjin	10	Fudan University	1.4	Shanghai

Source: K. Chen and Kenney 2007.

In 1993, the Chinese authorities issued the Law on the Progress of Science and Technology of P.R.C. to encourage R&D collaboration between universities and MNCs.[45] Following passage of this law, Tsinghua University and other universities in Beijing began collaborating with MNCs. In 2005, Tsinghua University was involved in 323 projects with a total contract value of US$29 million (actual disbursement was US$15 million) (B. Wang and Ma 2007).

Public research institutions in Shanghai are also engaging more actively in technology acquisition and transfer. In 2006, the total amount expended on acquiring technologies was Y 25 million (see table 5.35). This amount is almost equally divided between natural sciences and engineering. These institutions received Y 570 million from technology transfers. More than three-quarters of the revenues come from technology transfer in engineering, followed by natural sciences and medical science (see table 5.35). Clearly, the comparative advantage in engineering is substantial.

---

[45]The law was in part intended to reduce dependence on government funding for research. The share of research funding from the government decreased from 75 percent in 1985 to about 55 percent in recent years (Johnes and Yu 2008).

Table 5.35 Technological Acquisition and Transfer by Natural Sciences Research and Technology Development Institutions in Shanghai, 2006

Subject	Amount (Y thousand)	
	Expenditures for technology acquisition	Revenue from technology transfer
Total	25,127	569,129
Natural sciences	13,074	104,129
Agriculture science	0	0
Medical science	0	25,670
Engineering	12,053	439,330
Social sciences and humanities	0	0

Source: Shanghai Science and Technology Commission 2007.

Table 5.36 Technical Contracting in Shanghai, 2006

Type of contract	Number of contracts	Contract value (Y million)
Technological development	6,165	14,279.2
Technological transfer	2,172	16,517.7
Technological consulting	3,592	760.2
Technological service	16,262	2,885.6
Total	28,191	34,442.7

Source: Shanghai Science and Technology Commission 2007.

More than 28,000 technical contracts were issued in Shanghai, valued at Y 34 billion (see table 5.36). This figure represents a significant increase over the almost 24,000 technical contracts signed in 2001. The largest single type of contract in terms of value was in the area of technology transfer, followed by technological development, although the majority of contracts were for technology services. In contrast, the provision of technological services dominated technical contracting in Beijing in terms of both the number of contracts and their total value (see table 5.37). Technological development was a distant second. This finding reflects the orientation of research in Beijing and the industrial composition of the city as well as the higher concentration of research institutions and universities and the concentration of the communication equipment industry in Beijing.

Closer inspection of the purpose of such technical contracts reveals that industrial promotion has the largest share in Shanghai and the second highest in Beijing after social development (see tables 5.38 and 5.39). Within the industrial promotion category in Shanghai, electronics and IT dominate other areas. Advanced

Table 5.37 Technical Contracting in Beijing, 2007

Type of contract	Number of contracts	Contract value (Y million)
Technological development	11,889	20,255
Technological transfer	1,574	4,539
Technological consulting	5,804	2,883
Technological service	31,705	60,579
Total	50,972	88,256

Source: Beijing Municipal Bureau of Statistics and Beijing General Team of Investigation under the National Bureau of Statistics 2008.

Table 5.38 Technical Contracting in Shanghai, by Objectives, 2006

Social and economic objective	Number of contracts	Contract value (Y million)
Agriculture, animal husbandry, and fishery	66	42.7
Promotion of industry	5,472	11,270.7
Promotion of energy production, allocation, and use	968	974.6
Promotion of infrastructure	1,258	3,211.9
Environmental protection and treatment of pollution	2,840	294.0
Public health (excluding pollution)	1,056	2,351.3
Social development and services	8,031	5,786.0
Exploration and use of the Earth and atmosphere	14	30.5
Knowledge development	369	279.3
Civil space	515	4,290.1
National defense	158	80.5
Other	7,444	5,831.4
Total	28,191	34,443.0

Source: Shanghai Science and Technology Commission 2007.

manufacturing technology was ranked second, and medicine and medical equipment came third (see table 5.40). Not surprisingly, technical contracting in Beijing leans toward national-level objectives of energy efficiency and diversification, infrastructure development, and environmental management.

Shanghai is still at the intermediate stage of industrialization, and firms are attempting to upgrade technology. When these firms seek technological support, they look to public research institutions and universities to identify and adopt new technologies to meet their requirements. Therefore, the resulting intellectual properties tend to be trade secrets (since these technologies would be rather firm specific) and computer software (most likely embedded software for either

Table 5.39 Technical Contracting in Beijing, by Objectives, 2007

Social and economic objective	Number of contracts	Contract value (Y million)
Development of farming, forestry, and fishery	913	947
Promoting industrial development	7,936	16,825
Production and reasonable use of energy	4,238	13,893
Development of infrastructure	4,498	8,203
Environmental control and protection	2,140	7,066
Health (excluding pollution)	2,034	956
Social development and services	12,035	17,254
Exploration and use of Earth and aerosphere	201	450
Development of knowledge	1,179	1,736
Civil space	1,150	1,162
National defense	2,011	1,830
Other	12,637	17,933
Total	50,972	88,255

Source: Beijing Municipal Bureau of Statistics and Beijing General Team of Investigation under the National Bureau of Statistics 2008.

Table 5.40 Areas of Technical Contracting in Shanghai, 2006

Area of technology	Number of contracts	Contract value (Y million)
Electronic information technology	6,921	15,739.1
Aviation and aircraft technology	181	78.7
Advanced manufacture technology	2,657	5,416.3
Biology, medicine, and medical equipment	2,886	3,469.4
New material and its application	789	3,269.5
New energy and high-efficiency energy saving	1,384	1,687.1
Environmental protection and comprehensive resource use technology	3,331	439.2
Nuclear application technology	62	19.0
Agricultural technology	158	66.7
Modern traffic	1,430	2,321.0
Urban construction and social development	8,392	1,937.0
Total	28,191	34,443.0

Source: Shanghai Science and Technology Commission 2007.

Table 5.41   Technical Contracting in Shanghai by Type of Intellectual Property, 2006

Intellectual property	Number of contracts	Contract value (Y million)
Technical secret	22,189	17,320.7
Patent	586	4,003.8
Computer software	3,812	8,448.2
New animal or plant product	2	0.4
Designing integrated circuit layout	94	3,057.3
New biology or medicine product	329	1,055.1
Intellectual property not involved	1,179	557.3
Total	28,191	34,442.8

Source: Shanghai Science and Technology Commission 2007.

Table 5.42   Origination of Technical Contracting in Beijing, 2007

Contract source	Number of contracts	Contract value (Y million)
Beijing	24,938	26,421
Other Chinese provinces	24,819	40,743
Foreign	1,215	21,092

Source: Beijing Municipal Bureau of Statistics and Beijing General Team of Investigation under the National Bureau of Statistics 2008.

machinery or the final products); only a few result in patents because not many firms are engaged in developing new technologies (see table 5.41). This finding is also consistent with the fact that most of the entities seeking technology are SOEs and local private firms that have limited in-house R&D.

About half the technical contracts (as well as half by contract value) entered into by entities in Beijing originate from other provinces in China (see table 5.42). Notably, the contracts with foreigners account for one-quarter of the total contract values even though they are only a small fraction of contracts. This finding suggests that foreign contracts are larger in scale and amount than those originating in China. Clearly, Beijing is emerging as a center for research for China as a whole and on a world scale.

The composition of science and technology activities in Shanghai reflects its status as China's premier industrial region and a focus of FDI. The majority of the technical contracts entered into originated in Shanghai, followed by the neighboring provinces of Jiangsu and Zhejiang (see table 5.43). Now, however, more contracts (and in terms of the value, the second largest) come from abroad, as business accrues to the increasing number of R&D centers run by foreign firms. Because R&D activities are typically associated with activities of

Table 5.43   Origination of Technical Contracting in Shanghai, 2006

Contract source	Number of contracts	Contract value (Y million)
Beijing	847	2,344.2
Tianjin	129	108.3
Shanghai	20,742	18,781.5
Jiangsu	1,403	620.0
Zhejiang	1,134	390.2
Guangdong	498	540.6
Hong Kong, China; Macao, China; and Taiwan, China	149	648.7
Abroad	1,410	8,894.2
Other provinces	1,879	2,115.1
Total	28,191	34,442.8

Source: Shanghai Science and Technology Commission 2007.

the parent firms instead of affiliates, these contracts may be classified as "foreign" in origin. Shanghai appears to be on the threshold of joining Beijing as a regional innovation hub for industrial research, a promising development that—if it does materialize—should benefit local industries through technology spillovers.

Innovation Outcomes

Expenditure on R&D is a highly imperfect indicator of innovation capability because a lot of what is classified as R&D by firms is little more than minor product development and testing. Calling such activity R&D brings tax credits or other financial benefits, but it does not lead to innovation. The indirect measures of innovation capacity are invention patents, papers published in refereed scientific journals, and new products. The newness of these last is often suspect, and newness cannot be equated with innovation; nevertheless, it is a pointer. Patents and papers infrequently lead to commercial innovation; however, these two contribute to the pool of scientific knowledge and usable ideas out of which come innovative products, processes, or services that can be profitable over the longer term.

Strong encouragement by central and municipal governments, starting in 1999, produced a sharp increase in these three indicators of innovation capacity in China, after 2001. Table 5.44 indicates how Beijing and Shanghai have performed relative to China as a whole.[46] Although the shares of applications from Shanghai are close to

---

[46]Patenting in China has increased dramatically, especially since 2000. It stems from the reform of the patent law, clearer assignment of property rights, and FDI inflow to both production and research activities (A. Hu and Jefferson 2006).

Table 5.44 Share of Domestic Invention Patents from Beijing, Shanghai, and Hong Kong, China, 1990–2006

Year	Applications (%)			Patents granted (%)		
	Beijing	Shanghai	Hong Kong, China	Beijing	Shanghai	Hong Kong, China
1990	14.2	5.1	—	18.8	8.6	—
1995	12.5	3.6	—	21.4	4.7	—
2000	13.4	18.6	0.6	17.4	4.9	0.5
2006	11.6	9.9	0.5	15.4	10.5	0.6

Source: National Bureau of Statistics of China and Ministry of Science and Technology various years; Shanghai Science and Technology Commission 2007.
Note: — = not available. Only invention patents are included in the figure.

Table 5.45 Change in Spatial Rank of Invention Patents' Distribution in China over Time, 1985–2005

Rank	1985	1990	1995	2000	2005
Top 5	Beijing	Beijing	Beijing	Beijing	Beijing
	Liaoning	Shanghai	Liaoning	Liaoning	Shanghai
	Jiangxi	Liaoning	Shandong	Shandong	Guangdong
	Shanxi	Jiangsu	Sichuan	Jiangsu	Jiangsu
		Hubei	Shanghai	Shanghai	Zhejiang
Bottom 5		Neimeng	Neimeng	Guizhou	Neimeng
		Qinghai	Gansu	Neimeng	Xinjiang
		Xinjiang	Ningxia	Ningxia	Ningxia
		Ningxia	Qinghai	Qinghai	Qinghai
		Tibet	Tibet	Tibet	Tibet

Source: F. Liu and Sun 2009.
Note: Very few patents were granted in 1985: 23 for Beijing, 2 for the next three provinces, and 1 for each of the next nine provinces. Hence, only the top four provinces are listed.

those from Beijing, patent applications emanating from Beijing seem to be approved more frequently, suggesting that the quality of patents from Beijing is higher.[47] A spatial mapping of invention patents shows that Beijing has led since 1985, with Liaoning, the main focus of China's heavy industry, in second or third place through 2000. Shanghai briefly occupied second place in 1990, but then dropped to the fifth rung, only to regain the second spot in 2005 in response to the focus of the municipal authorities on the knowledge economy. Surprisingly, Liaoning was not in the top 10 provinces as of 2005 (see table 5.45) (F. Liu and Sun 2009).

Although the share of patent applications (including invention, utility, and design) from universities and colleges has increased in recent years, in Shanghai

---

[47]Beijing leads other provinces in terms of number of invention patents granted. However, Guangdong and Zhejiang receive more patents overall (mainly utility and design patents) than other regions in China (D. Lu and Hu 2008).

Table 5.46   Share of Patent Applications in Shanghai by Different Types of Organizations, 1996–2006

Year	Universities and colleges (%)	Research institutions (%)	Industrial and mining enterprises (%)	Government agencies and organizations (%)
1996	2.1	4.7	32.7	11.2
2000	4.5	5.3	51.9	0.9
2003	2.8	3.1	81.9	0.5
2006	9.6	5.2	69.3	1.7

Source: Shanghai Science and Technology Commission 2007.
Note: Individuals applied for the remaining patents.

Table 5.47   Share of Patent Applications in Beijing by Different Types of Organizations, 1996–2006

Year	Universities and colleges (%)	Research institutions (%)	Industrial and mining enterprises (%)	Government agencies and organizations (%)
1996	2.7	9.3	16.9	1.1
1999	3.7	9.4	24.0	0.5
2003	10.0	11.5	30.9	0.9
2006	10.6	10.2	38.5	0.5

Source: Beijing Municipal Bureau of Statistics and Beijing General Team of Investigation under the National Bureau of Statistics various years.
Note: Individuals applied for the remaining patents.

more than two-thirds of patent applications come from firms (see table 5.46).[48] Not unexpectedly, the share of patents applied for by universities, research institutions, and individuals in Beijing is larger, and the share of firms is relatively small because the industrial sector also happens to be smaller (see table 5.47). Universities submit 25 percent of the invention patents in Shanghai, but the majority of such patents are still granted to firms (table 5.48).[49]

In Shanghai, firms in communication equipment, computers, and other electronic equipment industries are in the forefront of applicants for invention patents and also gain the largest number of approvals.[50] In 2006, firms in this

---

[48]In the United States, universities and colleges account for at most 4 percent of patents granted in any given year.

[49]Even so, the contribution of universities to innovative outcomes in China is much larger than in other economies in East Asia (Tuan and Ng 2007).

[50]From his analysis of data on patents from China's State Intellectual Property Office, A. Hu (2008: 261) finds that most patents go to the machinery industry, followed by other chemicals, radio and television, and basic chemicals.

Table 5.48   Share of Invention Patents in Shanghai by Different Types of Organizations, 2006

Invention patents	Natural sciences R&D (%)	Universities (%)	Private R&D (%)
Applications	11.2	25.0	41.2
Grants	15.5	4.9	34.8

Source: Shanghai Science and Technology Commission 2007.

subsector applied for 1,289 patents (more than half of all applications for invention patents) and were granted 430 patents (about one-third of all invention patent grants; see table 5.49). Firms in smelting and pressing of ferrous metals, general machinery, chemicals (including petrochemicals), medicine, and machinery (transportation equipment) follow the electronic industry in terms of patents. Firms in other manufacturing subsectors rarely apply for patents.

The number of papers published by entities in Beijing and Shanghai has increased dramatically since 1998. The growth of publications by entities is faster in Beijing than in Shanghai, owing to the greater concentration of universities and research institutions in Beijing (see figures 5.15 and 5.16). However, the productivity of universities in this respect is low and declining relative to the injection of resources. Improving the quality of university teaching and research could raise productivity. Using research publications and awards as a measure of output, Ng and Li (2009) find that social science research suffered from deteriorating productivity because of technical inefficiencies and scale inefficiencies. In other words, universities were producing far below their potential output and were subject to decreasing returns to scale. This finding is not surprising given the pace at which tertiary-level institutions have grown and how many resources have been pumped into research, but it does highlight the widening gap between actual and potential output and also the implicit costs to municipal economies.

Introduction of new products to the market is also viewed as an indicator of innovativeness, and by this yardstick, Shanghai has registered a healthy improvement commensurate with the acceleration in R&D spending. In 2007, revenues from such new products accounted for more than 21 percent of GVIO in Shanghai, compared with 13 percent in 2001 (see table 5.50). In a number of subsectors, the share of revenues from new products exceeded the average for Shanghai. Notably, equipment producers of various kinds lead the field. Three subsectors stand out: general equipment; transportation equipment; and communication equipment, computers, and other electronic equipment. These three subsectors account for more than 70 percent of the output of new products, suggesting that their outputs are much larger than those coming from other subsectors, even innovative ones. Judging from table 5.50, one can say these three subsectors also have the highest share of new products in exports,

Table 5.49   Distribution of Patent Applications and Grants in Shanghai among Manufacturing Subsectors, 2006

Manufacturing subsector	Number of applications	Number of grants
Processing of food from agricultural products	0	2
Manufacture of foods	4	7
Manufacture of beverages	1	1
Manufacture of tobacco	2	12
Manufacture of textiles	17	10
Processing of timber and manufacture of wood, bamboo, rattan, palm, and straw products	4	1
Manufacture of paper and paper products	2	3
Printing and reproduction of recording media	9	4
Manufacture of articles for culture, education, and sports activities	10	1
Processing of petroleum, coking, and processing of nuclear fuel	42	118
Manufacture of raw chemical materials and chemical products	128	130
Manufacture of medicines	70	117
Manufacture of rubber	6	10
Manufacture of plastics	6	1
Manufacture of nonmetallic mineral products	17	24
Smelting and pressing of ferrous metals	323	266
Smelting and pressing of nonferrous metals	3	4
Manufacture of metal products	15	16
Manufacture of general-purpose machinery	151	144
Manufacture of special-purpose machinery	81	35
Manufacture of transportation equipment	74	51
Manufacture of electrical machinery and equipment	22	62
Manufacture of communication equipment, computers, and other electronic equipment	1,289	430
Manufacture of measuring instruments and machinery for cultural activity and office work	9	5
Production and supply of electric power and heat power	11	19
Production and supply of water	5	1
Total	2,301	1,474

Source: Shanghai Science and Technology Commission 2007.

although export intensity and the revenues from new products are not correlated. Some subsectors have high export intensity (for example, metal products, chemical fibers, and rubber products), but they do not introduce many new products.

Figure 5.15 Number of Papers Published in International Journals, 1998–2005

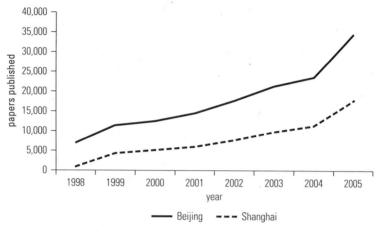

Source: National Bureau of Statistics of China and Ministry of Science and Technology various years.

Figure 5.16 Number of Scientific Papers Published in International Journals According to Science Citation Index, 1998–2005

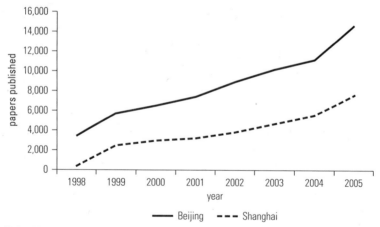

Source: National Bureau of Statistics of China and Ministry of Science and Technology various years.

Since 1994, manufacturers of general equipment; transportation equipment; and communication equipment, computers, and other electronic equipment have introduced the largest number of new products in Shanghai (see figure 5.17).

By ramping up R&D spending higher than Shanghai, Beijing has pulled far ahead of its sister megacity in terms of both published papers and share of new

Table 5.50   New Product Development of Industrial Enterprises in Shanghai, 2007

Manufacturing sector	Share of new products in GVIO by subsector (%)	Share of new product output in Shanghai (%)	Share of new product exports in Shanghai (%)	Export intensity[a] (%)
Overall manufacturing	21.5	—	—	17.1
Farm and sideline product processing	0.4	0.0	0.0	6.4
Food	3.2	0.2	0.1	5.1
Beverages	0.8	0.0	0.0	0.0
Tobacco	11.9	0.7	0.1	3.2
Textiles	4.6	0.4	0.1	5.4
Garments, shoes, and accessories	0.4	0.0	0.0	20.2
Furniture	27.8	1.2	1.3	18.4
Papermaking and paper products	0.9	0.0	0.0	0.0
Printing and record duplication	12.6	0.5	0.0	1.1
Stationery, education, and sports goods	2.4	0.1	0.1	10.4
Oil processing, coking, and nuclear processing	9.7	2.1	0.0	0.0
Raw chemical materials and chemicals	11.5	4.0	1.6	6.9
Medicine	26.4	1.6	0.3	3.5
Chemical fibers	0.5	0.0	0.0	36.7
Rubber products	17.5	0.6	1.2	33.6
Plastic products	2.0	0.2	0.3	22.9
Nonmetal mineral products	4.9	0.4	0.4	14.5
Smelting and pressing of ferrous metals	22.2	7.7	2.0	4.4
Smelting and pressing of nonferrous metals	3.9	0.4	0.1	2.5
Metal products	4.1	0.7	2.7	62.0
General-purpose equipment	27.9	11.4	18.4	27.4
Special-purpose equipment	14.7	1.9	1.7	15.4
Transportation equipment	57.5	29.4	21.5	12.5
Electric machinery equipment	15.7	5.4	9.3	29.8
Communication equipment, computers, and other electronic equipment	27.3	29.4	33.6	19.5
Instruments, meters, and culture and office equipment	21.5	1.5	5.0	57.0
Artworks and other	0.9	0.0	0.0	31.7

Source: Shanghai Municipal Statistics Bureau 2008.
Note: — = not available. Data are based on firms with revenues greater than Y 5 million.
a. Export intensity is calculated as the share of new product exports over the revenue from the new products.

products, especially by the communication equipment industry (see table 5.51). In 2007, more than half the industrial output was composed of new products. Because this industrial subsector is the largest in Beijing, it accounts for half of all new product output in Beijing. This industrial subsector is also the most export

Figure 5.17   Changes in Share of New Product Output in Shanghai, 1994–2006

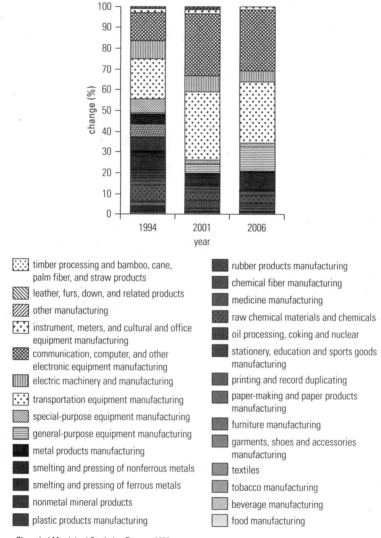

timber processing and bamboo, cane, palm fiber, and straw products

leather, furs, down, and related products

other manufacturing

instrument, meters, and cultural and office equipment manufacturing

communication, computer, and other electronic equipment manufacturing

electric machinery and manufacturing

transportation equipment manufacturing

special-purpose equipment manufacturing

general-purpose equipment manufacturing

metal products manufacturing

smelting and pressing of nonferrous metals

smelting and pressing of ferrous metals

nonmetal mineral products

plastic products manufacturing

rubber products manufacturing

chemical fiber manufacturing

medicine manufacturing

raw chemical materials and chemicals

oil processing, coking and nuclear

stationery, education and sports goods manufacturing

printing and record duplicating

paper-making and paper products manufacturing

furniture manufacturing

garments, shoes and accessories manufacturing

textiles

tobacco manufacturing

beverage manufacturing

food manufacturing

Source: Shanghai Municipal Statistics Bureau 2008.

intensive. Even the remnants of the textile industry in Beijing derive one-quarter of their output from new products.[51]

---

[51]U.S. experience suggests that high-end garments and textiles thrive best in megacities with a wealthy and sophisticated consuming public. In the United States, this industry is concentrated in New York and Los Angeles.

Table 5.51 New Product Development of Industrial Enterprises in Beijing, 2007

Manufacturing sector	Share of new products in GVIO by subsector (%)	Share of new product output in Beijing (%)	Export intensity[a] (%)
Processing of food from agriculture products	8.2	0.5	6.7
Manufacture of foods	6.8	0.3	7.1
Manufacture of beverages	3.2	0.1	1.5
Manufacture of tobacco	0.7	0.0	4.1
Manufacture of textiles	27.3	0.7	31.9
Manufacture of textile wearing apparel, footwear, and caps	5.2	0.2	38.5
Manufacture of leather, furs, down, and related products	0.9	0.0	37.2
Processing of timber and manufacture of wood, bamboo, rattan, palm, and straw products	1.4	0.0	21.8
Manufacture of furniture	1.5	0.0	26.4
Manufacture of paper and paper products	1.9	0.0	5.5
Printing and reproduction of recording media	4.4	0.2	1.4
Manufacture of articles for culture, education, and sports activity	4.1	0.0	44.4
Processing of petroleum, coking, and processing of nuclear fuel	37.5	8.0	0.3
Manufacture of raw chemical materials and chemical products	21.0	2.4	5.4
Manufacture of medicines	28.6	2.0	3.4
Manufacture of chemical fibers	20.5	0.0	11.9
Manufacture of rubber	13.4	0.1	30.6
Manufacture of plastics	7.1	0.2	8.8
Manufacture of nonmetallic mineral products	14.4	1.3	4.5
Smelting and pressing of ferrous metals	25.8	5.6	8.1
Smelting and pressing of nonferrous metals	39.8	0.9	18.5
Manufacture of metal products	16.0	1.1	11.7
Manufacture of general-purpose machinery	25.7	3.2	18.1
Manufacture of special-purpose machinery	30.9	3.6	14.1
Manufacture of transportation equipment	20.4	7.6	4.0
Manufacture of electrical machinery and equipment	26.4	3.1	13.1
Manufacture of communication equipment, computers, and other electronic equipment	56.7	53.3	52.4
Manufacture of measuring instruments and machinery for cultural activity and office work	46.5	3.5	16.4
Manufacture of artwork and other manufacturing	61.9	2.0	26.9
Recycling and disposal of waste	5.0	0.0	0.0

Source: Beijing Municipal Bureau of Statistics and Beijing General Team of Investigation under the National Bureau of Statistics 2008.
Note: Data are based on firms with revenues greater than Y 5 million.
a. Export intensity is calculated as the share of new product exports over the revenue from the new products.

Table 5.52   Value of Exports of High-Tech Products in Shanghai, 2001–06

	Amount (US$ billion)					
	2001	**2002**	**2003**	**2004**	**2005**	**2006**
Value of exports of high-tech products	5.4	7.5	16.4	28.9	36.3	44.3
Total value of exports	27.6	32.1	48.5	73.5	90.7	113.6
Value of exports of high-tech products/total value of exports	19.6	23.4	33.8	39.3	40.0	39.0
By technology field						
Computers and telecommunications	3.2	4.2	11.3	19.1	24.4	30.2
Electronics	1.7	2.8	4.1	7.1	7.8	10.6
Life sciences	0.2	0.3	0.4	0.5	0.7	0.9
By trade mode						
Processing with imported materials	3.3	4.7	12.0	20.4	27.2	34.8
General trade	0.5	0.7	1.4	2.6	3.2	4.4
By ownership						
State-owned and collectively owned	0.5	0.7	0.8	0.8	1.1	1.6
Cooperative	2.4	2.0	2.6	3.9	3.9	3.7
Foreign funded	2.4	4.7	12.7	23.8	30.4	37.9
By destination						
European Union	1.3	1.5	4.1	7.9	10.6	12.3
Hong Kong, China	0.8	1.2	2.0	3.5	4.6	6.0
Japan	0.6	0.9	1.6	2.6	2.8	3.2
United States	1.3	1.5	4.6	7.9	10.2	12.6

Source: Shanghai Science and Technology Commission 2007.

Another indicator of technological, if not innovation, capacity is the changing share of high-tech components and capital goods in exports from these cities. Close to 40 percent of total exports from Shanghai are high-tech products—up from 20 percent in 2001 (see table 5.52). The bulk of the high-tech exports are computer and telecommunication-related goods. This trend is promising, although thus far, foreign-invested firms using imported inputs produce most of these exports.

The level and distribution of FDI offer an additional indirect perspective on how foreign investors perceive a city's comparative advantage.[52] This perspective is useful because such investors are able to compare the medium-term potential of Beijing and Shanghai with that of other cities in China and abroad and to make decisions that weigh a variety of options. By selecting specific industries, MNCs are factoring in incentives as well as technological capacity, the quality and productivity of the workforce, the adequacy of the physical infrastructure, and the livability of the city.

From the information contained in figure 5.18, one can see how rapidly FDI in Shanghai has risen since 1990. In 1990, the total FDI inflow was US$0.2 billion, and hardly any wholly owned foreign firms existed. By 2007, the actual

---

[52]On the links between FDI and development in China's two major urban regions enjoying substantial agglomeration economies (the Yangtze and Pearl River Deltas), see Tuan and Ng (2007).

Figure 5.18   FDI Inflow to Shanghai, 1990–2007

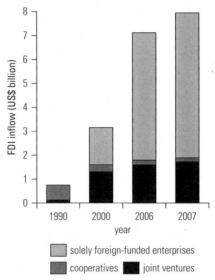

Source: Shanghai Municipal Statistics Bureau 2008.

FDI flow had increased to US$7.9 billion, three-quarters into wholly owned foreign subsidiaries. These trends are encouraging because they suggest that foreign businesses are beginning to view Shanghai as a center for advanced manufacturing activities that is making progress in perfecting a local innovation system.

FDI into Beijing also increased rapidly, although a drop occurred after 2000, caused by the bursting of the IT bubble in the United States. The inflow (and the use of the actual contract amount) of FDI resumed the upward trend in 2004 to reach US$5 billion in 2007 (see figure 5.19). Beijing's smaller industrial sector and shift toward services explain both the lower level of FDI and its distribution.

Venture Capital

Much of the patient capital raised by firms in the two megacities comes from the banking sector, which reflects a pattern seen throughout East Asia. As the dominant financial institutions, banks do engage in venture financing, partly as a way of building their lending business.[53] However, bank lending is only a partial substitute for the kind of risk capital innovative firms need; hence,

---

[53]See Hellman, Lindsey, and Puri (2004) on venture lending by U.S. banks.

Figure 5.19   FDI Used in Beijing, 1987–2007

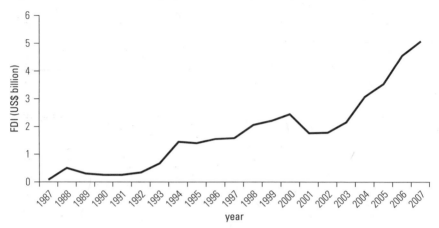

Source: Beijing Municipal Bureau of Statistics and Beijing General Team of Investigation under the National Bureau of Statistics 2008.

attention in China and elsewhere has focused on the venture capital industry. Venture financing, at its best, can provide the intellectual capital to help industry mobilize its technical, managerial, and marketing expertise and seek fresh opportunities.[54] In Taiwan, China, and in Silicon Valley, venture capital has contributed importantly to the reorienting of a local production system and assisted in the formation of a cluster. More often, when venture capitalists are inexperienced, venture capital is likely to follow rather than lead innovation. In 2007, the 236 venture capital firms (including foreign venture capital) in Shanghai had an investment in excess of Y 30 billion (see table 5.53). The venture capital industry in Shanghai accounts for 40 percent of all venture capital activities in China (Shanghai Venture Capital Association 2008).

As one would expect, the type of subsectors that venture capitalists invest in are high-tech areas such as software and multimedia, biotechnology, microelectronics, and new materials, as well as financial services (see table 5.54). In recent years, the spread among different subsectors is lessening. The venture capital industry's areas of

---

[54]H. Chen and others (2009) list the several empirically validated gains from the presence of venture capital firms in urban centers. Venture capital fosters entrepreneurial communities, patents, and new business. In addition, venture capital–backed firms demonstrate faster operational growth, better performance after the initial public offering, more innovation, and more scale potential. Therefore, at least in the United States, the number of venture capital firms in an area and the active involvement of venture capitalists in the firms they support not only increase venture capital investment but also can contribute to the performance of the companies receiving risk capital.

Table 5.53   Number of Venture Capital Firms and Capital Committed in Shanghai, 2004–07

	2004	2005	2006	2007
Number of firms	106	204	215	236
Capital under management (Y billion)	16.8	25.0	28.0	30.46

Source: Shanghai Venture Capital Association 2008.

Table 5.54   Areas of Investment by Venture Capitalists in Shanghai, 2004–07

	Distribution (%)			
Sector	2004	2005	2006	2007
Software and networks	25.0	20.9	16.2	14.3
Biotechnology and medical care	21.3	20.9	16.2	13.7
Financial services	5.0	7.0	5.4	8.6
Microelectronics	7.5	8.1	9.9	7.4
New material	7.5	8.1	12.6	7.4
Telecommunications	5.0	9.3	8.1	6.9
Energy technology	1.3	2.3	9.9	6.3
Traditional manufacturing	2.5	0.0	3.6	6.3
Computer hardware	2.5	1.2	3.6	2.9
Environment	0.0	0.0	0.0	2.9
Agriculture	0.0	0.0	1.8	2.3
Others	22.5	22.1	12.6	21.1

Source: Shanghai Venture Capital Association 2008.

focus overall are stable, but those by foreign venture capitalists shift from one year to the next. In 2004, investments in software and biotech accounted for almost half of foreign venture capital investment; however, by 2006, the attention had shifted to telecommunications and traditional manufacturing. Broadly, the areas of concentration are similar between domestic and foreign firms in 2007, although foreign firms are more active in telecommunications and less so in biotech (table 5.55).

Venture capital investment in Shanghai is concentrated in the growth and expansion stage of the firm and not in the very early stages. Compared to the distribution in 2006, that in 2007 (the latest year for which information is available) has not changed radically, although more emphasis is on the seed stage (see table 5.56). Foreign venture capitalists also tend to prefer growth and expansion stages. This pattern of venture capital investment is also seen in the United States and elsewhere. Typically, seed capital comes from angel investors rather than from venture capital (Auerswald and Branscomb 2003).

Table 5.55   Areas of Investment by Foreign Venture Capitalists in Shanghai, 2004–07

Sector	Investment share (%)			
	2004	2005	2006	2007
Software and networks	31.3	18.8	0.0	10.7
Microelectronics	12.5	18.8	15.4	10.7
Financial services	12.5	6.3	0.0	10.7
Telecommunications	12.5	18.8	23.1	8.9
Computer hardware	6.3	6.3	0.0	7.1
Biotechnology and medical care	18.8	6.3	7.7	7.1
New material	0.0	6.3	0.0	7.1
Traditional manufacturing	0.0	0.0	15.4	7.1
Energy technology	0.0	0.0	15.4	5.4
Agriculture	0.0	0.0	7.7	3.6
Environment	0.0	0.0	0.0	3.6
Others	6.3	18.8	15.4	17.9

Source: Shanghai Venture Capital Association 2008.
Note: Foreign venture capitalists include those from Hong Kong, China; Macao, China; and Taiwan, China. This table is based on 16 foreign firms among the 85 venture capital firms sampled that returned the survey.

Table 5.56   Distributions of Venture Capital Investments in Shanghai, 2006 and 2007

Type of investment	Distribution (%)	
	2006	2007
Seed	21.6	23.1
Growth	36.4	34.6
Expansion	29.6	30.8
Mature	12.3	11.5

Source: Shanghai Venture Capital Association 2008.

In a survey by the Shanghai Venture Capital Association, the sampled venture capital firms singled out market prospects as the most important consideration before making an investment, followed by the quality of the management team, the financial condition of the firm, and the technological capability of the firm (see table 5.57).[55] Foreign firms assign similar weights to these factors, except for technological capabilities. Instead, foreign venture capital firms put more emphasis on the integrity of corporate governance.

---

[55]Firms in the famous Silicon Fen cluster in Cambridge, United Kingdom, have relied mainly on local banks for their borrowings, and the volume of lending was constrained by the scarcity of bank managers acquainted with the technologies being developed in the cluster. Venture capital firms, although active in Cambridge, have financed no more than 10 percent of the firms (Drofiak and Garnsey 2009).

Table 5.57 Factors Considered Important by Venture Capitalists Prior to Investment, 2006 and 2007

Factor	2006	2007
Market prospects	32.6	32.4
Management team	24.5	23.1
Financial condition	16.3	14.7
Technology	11.4	12.2
Corporate governance	6.5	6.3
Stock price	4.3	6.3
Investment location	2.2	3.4
Other	2.2	1.7

Source: Shanghai Venture Capital Association 2008.
Note: Based on responses by 83 firms sampled in 2007.

Table 5.58 Modes of Exit by Start-Up Firms in Shanghai, 2004–07

Exit mode	2004	2005	2006	2007
Acquisition by domestic nonlisted firms or natural persons	32.0	43.9	25.0	29.3
Listing abroad	20.0	20.5	18.8	26.0
Acquisition by estate management	17.3	9.1	29.5	15.4
Acquisition by foreign nonlisted firms	17.3	18.9	7.1	13.8
Listing domestically	9.3	5.3	10.7	13.8
Acquisition by listed foreign firms	4.0	2.3	8.9	1.6

Source: Shanghai Venture Capital Association 2008.

The vehicle most often used for exit is acquisition by domestic nonlisted firms or natural persons (see table 5.58). Listing on the stock exchange abroad ranks as the second most-favored method. This method combined with domestic listings accounts for close to 40 percent of the exits. The balance is through acquisition by various types of firms. Notably, the acquisition by listed foreign firms is quite small, representing only 1.6 percent of the total.

The number of people working for venture capital firms in Shanghai more than doubled from 2003 to 2007 (table 5.59). The number of professional managers also increased during this period. However, the increase in the supply of professional managers seemingly was not able to keep up with the expansion of the venture capital industry, and the share of professional managers decreased until 2005.[56] Since then, the supply of managers has begun outpacing the

---

[56]The lack of mature and experienced venture capital is also identified as one of the key problems facing firms in Zhongguancun Science Park in Beijing (Cao 2004).

Table 5.59 Number of Employees at Venture Capital Firms in Shanghai, 2003–07

	2003	2004	2005	2006	2007
All sampled firms					
Number of employees	405	711	765	868	962
Number of professional managers	166	270	242	319	365
Share of professional managers (%)	41.0	38.0	31.6	36.8	37.9
Number of sampled firms	51	70	81	65	83
Foreign firms					
Number of employees	—	—	113	99	140
Number of professional managers	—	—	38	54	67
Share of professional managers (%)	—	—	33.6	54.5	47.9
Number of sampled foreign firms	—	—	15	7	16

Source: Shanghai Venture Capital Association 2008.
Note: — = not available.

expansion of the industry. Foreign venture capital firms are more often staffed with professional managers relative to the overall sample. The trend should enhance the effectiveness of the venture capital industry and facilitate the growth of more technology-intensive firms. Nevertheless, more capable venture capitalists can make a contribution only if innovative ideas are forthcoming. Venture capital cannot push innovation. It is pulled by innovation, generally of the kind where the payback period is in the region of five years.[57] A shortage of promising new start-ups with cutting-edge technologies might be a bigger constraint than a shortage of venture capital (Wu 2007).[58]

Megacities: Moving to a More Innovative Economy

Beijing and Shanghai are China's megacities with the largest economic footprints. The experience of other advanced and industrializing countries suggests that the development of these two megacities will significantly affect the future innovativeness and productivity growth of the national economy. Because the evolution of these two cities has proceeded down different paths, as is reflected in their economic structures and industrial mix, and the experiences that they have accumulated differ, their future development paths will not be the same. Instead, these two cities will develop somewhat differently, taking advantage of their individual

---

[57]Hirukawa and Ueda (2008a, 2008b) find that although the growth of venture capital is positively associated with the patent propensity of an industry, venture capital investments do not necessarily lead to an increase in factor productivity. In fact, the growth in total factor productivity is what attracts venture capital.

[58]Own resources, family, and friends are the principal sources of seed capital in advanced economies with mature capital markets. The complaints voiced by entrepreneurs in New York are little different from those of individuals starting up firms in Shanghai.

experiences and accumulated endowment and focusing on different areas, but complementing each other.

Shanghai's development was based on commerce and manufacturing industry, and its comparative advantage and capabilities are strongest in these areas. Recent changes in the composition and capabilities of Shanghai's economy have been mainly in the right direction. The share of manufacturing industries producing complex capital and high-tech goods is increasing. The growth of these industries is supporting the city's innovation agenda, because they are the industrial subsectors with the greatest propensity to innovate and the most scope for enhancing productivity. A substantial deepening of financial and business services—which have leveraged an earlier tradition and reputation and are supported by a policy of openness—has occurred, and these services support the rapid expansion of manufacturing activities. Creative industries are beginning to mature. Shanghai's tertiary education and research sectors are expanding rapidly and beginning to forge links with industry. Incentives to conduct R&D and to patent are bearing fruit. Venture capital is more abundant, and the investors themselves are gaining in experience. Finally, the quality of urban infrastructure itself has vastly improved over what it was 15 years ago. Shanghai's industry has accumulated manufacturing and technological capabilities comparable to those of an advanced middle-income economy. To derive more of its future growth from innovation, however, Shanghai will need to

Table 5.60   Value Added of Selected Creative Industries in Beijing, 2005–07

Creative industry	Added value (Y billion)			Proportion to GDP (%)		
	2005	2006	2007	2005	2006	2007
Cultural and artistic	3.2	3.6	3.9	0.5	0.5	0.4
Journalism and publication	11.5	13.4	14.1	1.7	1.7	1.5
Broadcast, television, and film	7.8	7.3	10.2	1.1	0.9	1.1
Advertisements and exhibitions	5.1	4.8	5.8	0.7	0.6	0.6
Transaction of artwork	0.9	0.8	1.0	0.1	0.1	0.1
Design service	7.5	8.2	10.5	1.1	1.1	1.1
Electronic information transmission services	35.4	37.7	45.5	5.1	4.8	4.8
Computer service and software	23.0	31.1	40.1	3.3	3.9	4.3
Other information-related service	13.5	14.7	17.7	2.0	1.9	1.9
Scientific research, technical service, and geological prospecting	34.2	42.5	53.9	5.0	5.4	5.8
Total	142.1	164.1	202.7	20.6	20.9	21.6

Sources: Beijing Municipal Bureau of Statistics and Beijing General Team of Investigation under the National Bureau of Statistics 2007, 2008.

sustain and further refine its current industrial strengths and to develop innovative capacity across a range of activities through a mix of initiatives affecting firms, knowledge producers, and the quality of life in the city itself.

Beijing, in contrast, will need to derive more of its growth from the high-tech industry and high-value-adding services industry, including the creative industry. By 2007, such creative industry already accounted for more than one-fifth of Beijing's output (see table 5.60). Urban and industrial policies and rising incomes have increased the share of services, which even at the outset was larger than that of Shanghai. As the seat of the central government, Beijing has been particularly hospitable to highly regulated activities, including telecommunications and finance. The development of IT-related firms (both in hardware and software) and the emergence of large financial and nonfinancial sectors reflect this advantage. The government's determination to build China's knowledge capabilities and expand research has been translated most directly into action in Beijing through investment in the universities, investment in science parks, and support for R&D. Arguably Beijing has the strongest fundamental research capability in China, with two premier research universities and a constellation of public research institutes. Using its strength in research to stimulate innovation in selected manufacturing and services activities that can flourish in the metro area will be the challenge for the city and the means of sustaining high growth.

The measures both cities might take to improve their growth prospects foreshadowed in earlier sections are explored next in chapter 6.

6

Making Industries Innovative

Although some research suggests that the optimal economic size of a Chinese city is reached when its population is in the region of 5 million (Au and Henderson 2006a), other findings indicate that well-managed cities can continue growing in size without encountering decreasing returns. In fact, Overman and Venables (2005) observe that, for a city, being too small is more of a disadvantage than being too large. The implication is that both Beijing and Shanghai have ample scope for exploiting the productivity-enhancing benefits of scale and agglomeration economies.[1] Shanghai may be further advantaged because it is a remarkably industrial city. The share of manufacturing in gross domestic product (GDP) is twice that of Beijing, four times greater than that of Tokyo, and six times that of New York. Even 40 years ago, manufacturing industries generated no more than one-quarter of Tokyo's GDP and one-fifth of New York's GDP. Shanghai's manufacturing sector, moreover, is highly diversified—much more so than that of Beijing. Of the top six manufacturing sub-sectors, four comprise equipment of various kinds: general, communications, electronics, and transportation. If to these are added special-purpose equipment and instruments and office equipment, the six subsectors account for 55 percent of industrial GDP. Metallurgical and chemical industries together contribute 25 percent of the output, and industries producing textiles, food, furniture, paper, and plastic and wood products make up the rest. The strong export orientation of the leading industries is a good indicator of their competitiveness. With this product mix and industrial diversity, Shanghai can reap the benefits of urbanization economies as well as the advantages accruing from a strong focus on industries producing complex

---

[1]This is especially so because the population density is also high, and agglomeration economies—specifically the induced accumulation of human capital—are particularly beneficial at earlier stages of development (Brülhart and Sbergami 2009). In addition, Shanghai has the advantage of its location at close to the midpoint of China's coastline (H. Lu 2004).

capital goods, high-technology components, and key industrial materials. These industries have multiple links with other sectors and have a history of high-productivity growth and of research and development (R&D) intensity. A comparison of the scale and composition of Shanghai's industrial activities with those of Tokyo suggests that Shanghai is better placed to maintain a strong industrial lead well into the future by complementing its technological capabilities with the capacity to innovate, even as wages and land costs rise and certain kinds of labor-intensive industries migrate to other parts of China and to other countries. Moreover, the global financial crisis of 2008 to 2009 and the industrial restructuring it has triggered in China and throughout the world economy increase the opportunities for radical innovations by dynamic firms (Bers and others 2009)[2] and for an acceleration in labor productivity.

Between 1995 and 2003, industrial reform, which catalyzed the restructuring of industrial enterprises and a reallocation of resources, contributed more than 40 percent of the annual 20 percent increase in labor productivity. Scope remains for further reallocation and "creative destruction"[3] in Beijing and Shanghai and for a closing of the "efficiency gap" between Chinese firms and their overseas competitors (in services and manufacturing industries). The factors could deliver a continuing productivity bonus over the course of a decade (J. Zheng, Bigsten, and Hu 2009).[4] Between 1995 and 2003, labor productivity in Chinese industry rose by 20 percent annually, on average; the restructuring of firms and the redistribution of resources within and between industries contributed the major share of this change. Predictably, foreign-invested firms registered the highest gains in productivity. Nevertheless, the restructuring of state-owned enterprises (SOEs) and the shedding of redundant workers by these firms made a large contribution. SOEs were among the least productive firms at the beginning of the period, and they trailed the others in 2003. However, they showed more rapid gains during 1998 to 2003 than some of the other types of firms (including domestic private firms), which underscores the potential for achieving further gains from continuing SOE restructuring (Deng and others 2007).

In contrast, Beijing's strength lies in the research-intensive industries and other industries that are regulated by the central government. Clearly, Beijing

---

[2]Two examples of firms that have made remarkable strides in cost innovation are the battery maker BYD, which has drastically reduced the prices of lithium-ion cells, and Zhongxing Medical, which has scaled down the costs of direct digital radiography (Williamson and Zeng 2009). BYD is now eyeing the electric car market because of its strength in battery technology. The firm employs 5,000 battery engineers and 5,000 automotive engineers (Bradsher 2009).

[3]This creative destruction will lead to the disappearance of weaker companies and of the considerable excess capacity in several industries (see Foster and Kaplan 2001).

[4]See, for instance, the comparison by Crafts and Toniolo (2008) of the persisting productivity differences between the United States and European countries. See also W. Lewis (2004).

Table 6.1 R&D Expenditure, 2006

		R&D expenditure (Y billion)		
	Total	R&D institutions	Large and medium-size enterprises	Institutions of higher education
National	300.3	56.7	163.0	27.7
Beijing	43.3	19.0	5.9	3.7
Shanghai	25.9	5.4	13.4	2.7

Source: National Bureau of Statistics of China and Ministry of Science and Technology 2007.

Table 6.2 R&D Personnel, 2006

		Science and engineering full-time equivalents		
	Total	R&D institutions	Large and medium-size enterprises	Institutions of higher education
National	1,224	177	542	237
Beijing	147	50	15	25
Shanghai	68	13	25	17

Source: National Bureau of Statistics of China and Ministry of Science and Technology 2007.

occupies center stage in Chinese research capabilities. Of 1,867 higher education institutions in China, 80 are located in Beijing. There are more R&D institutions in the higher education sector in Beijing than in any other Chinese city, including Shanghai (National Bureau of Statistics and Ministry of Science and Technology 2007). Beijing dominates the other cities in R&D spending and in the volume of research conducted at universities and research institutions (52 percent of the total, compared with 31 percent in Shanghai and 28 percent nationwide; see table 6.1). Almost 50 percent of researchers in Beijing work in research institutions and universities, compared with 44 percent in Shanghai and 33 percent in China as a whole (see table 6.2). Along with universities and research institutions, Beijing has a number of science parks.[5] Among them, the most famous is the Zhongguancun Science and Technology Zone, often referred as China's Silicon Valley (Zhou 2008). It compares favorably with other well-known science parks and high-tech clusters around the world with respect to national prominence, public investment, innovativeness, and "new Argonaut links" (see table 6.3). Zhongguancun is located in the

---

[5]China's first university-associated science park was created in 1989. Since then, every science-based university has sought to establish an adjacent commercially administered park in conjunction with local authorities. Xue (2006b) remarks that a science park is viewed as a symbol of a top-class university.

Table 6.3 International Comparison of Science Parks and Cities

Factors	Zhongguancun, China	Zhangjiang Park, China	Daedeok, Republic of Korea	Hsinchu Science Park, Taiwan, China	Tsukuba, Japan	Silicon Valley, United States	Science Cities, United Kingdom	Kista, Sweden	Oulu, Finland
Greenfield location		√√	√√	√√	√√	√			
Regional development goals		√√	√√	√√	√√		√√		√√
Dominant national role	√√		√√	√√	√√			√√	
Dedicated public investment	√√	√√	√√	√√	√√			√√	
National program				√√			√		
Major research institutions	√√	√√	√√	√√	√√	√√	√√	√√	√√
National R&D leader	√√				√√	√√		√√	
Partnership models				√√		√	√√	√√	√√
Flexible network models	√			√		√√	√	√	√
Orientation to innovation	√√	√	√	√√	√	√√	√√	√√	√√
"New Argonaut" links	√√			√√		√√			
Strong venture capital presence						√√			
Public science education							√√		

Source: OECD 2008.

Note: √√ = strongly present; √ = partially present. More √√s or √s denote that more factors are present, not that having more factors leads directly to better outcomes.

Haidan district of Beijing, near Peking University, Tsinghua University, and the Chinese Academy of Sciences (CAS). The main street through Zhongguancun, Baiyi Boulevard, is called "Electronic Street" because of the large number of stores selling computer hardware and software. It has evolved into a large concentration of firms specializing in information technology (IT) and electronic equipment—mainly domestic firms such as Lenovo, Founder, Datang, Baidu, UFIDA, aigo, Sina.com, and Sohu.com. Earlier firms were spinoffs (or related firms) from CAS, Peking University, and Tsinghua University. For instance, Lenovo was spun off from CAS,[6] Founder from Peking University, and Tongfang from Tsinghua University. The early success of these firms stimulated the emergence of other firms, especially those started by overseas Chinese.[7] By the end of 2005, 3,000 firms (out of 17,000) in Zhongguancun had been started up by more than 7,600 returnees.[8] One of these returnees is Li Hongyan, the founder of Baidu.com, which is China's equivalent of Google and its main competitor (Zhou 2008).

Beijing's status as the seat of China's central government contributed to the development of the IT industry.[9] When the personal computer (PC) industry was born in the 1980s and 1990s, virtually no demand from private consumers existed for PCs and software. Instead, the bulk of the demand for hardware and software initially came from government ministries, which sought to create a homegrown computer industry and prompted universities, CAS, and SOEs to invest in computerization. These government institutions required localization of both hardware and software so that Chinese characters could be used effectively on PCs and backed this requirement with procurement from Chinese vendors (Y.-C. Chen 2008).[10] The need for Chinese characters first triggered innovation by firms such

---

[6]CAS shifted its research focus from defense-related technologies to more commercializable technologies in the 1980s (K. Chen and Kenney 2007).

[7]Of students who received degrees in computer science from Peking University and Tsinghua University, 30 percent have gone abroad. Of those who went to the United States, an estimated 14 percent have returned. A study by the National Science Foundation in the 1990s found that 88 percent of Chinese students in advanced degree programs intended to stay abroad (Gregory, Nollen, and Tenev 2009).

[8]Zhongguancun offers grants of Y 100,000 for qualified projects managed by returnees to promote start-up activities (Zhou 2008).

[9]Similarly, the telecommunication industry is a highly regulated industry not only in China but also in other countries. Therefore, the telecommunication industry tends to cluster around the capital city because of the constant interactions needed with sector regulators (Zhou 2008).

[10]Centralized political control and a fairly interventionist government enhance the attractiveness of the capital city for firms. The concentration of economic activities in Tokyo is a reflection of the "developmental state" stance taken by the Japanese government (K. Fujita 2003).

as Founder and Legend (now known as Lenovo). Soon local demand was large enough to stimulate the entry of new firms to Beijing.[11]

This experience mirrors to a degree that of Silicon Valley. Although private initiative was surely a part of the story, U.S. government support for R&D and demand for high-tech products mainly for defense purposes were the crucial complement (Sturgeon 2000). Abundant government funding and encouragement were critical to the coalescence of the Silicon Valley industrial cluster. Government support, spread over decades, provided the essential underpinnings for the mixed public and private tertiary education and research ecosystem that has sustained Silicon Valley's legendary technological dynamism and ability to transition from one generation of a technology to the next and from one technological domain to another. This ecosystem is now a vast and vibrant service industry in itself, employing large numbers of people. It is tightly linked not only to firms in Silicon Valley and California but also to services, venture capital providers, and industries throughout the United States and in India, Israel, and Taiwan, China, to name some of the most prominent countries (Bresnahan and others 2001).

One sign of the resilience of Zhongguancun is that even though much of the production of the actual hardware has shifted to cheaper locations (mainly in the south),[12] firms in the park are demonstrating the capacity to move into new areas, such as Web services.[13] The explosive growth of Internet users in China, along with a large number of start-up firms catering to them, made this move possible. Internet firms Sina.com and Sohu.com are among the notable start-ups. Even though the share of Internet users in Beijing is not high relative to its population size, Beijing had close to 20 percent of the domain registration in China at the end of 2006 (Zhou 2008). Increasing integration of IT in business activities and government continues to stimulate the software industry, especially the enterprise software segment.[14] Again, being close to the government is beneficial to firms located in Beijing (Zhou 2008).

One of the factors differentiating Beijing from Shanghai is entrepreneurship. Following the success of the small new entrants in Beijing, some of them affiliated with

---

[11]The initial innovation was the creation of an add-on card so that computers can display Chinese characters. This innovation has led to the development of Chinese word processors (Q. Lu and Lazonick 2001).

[12]By 1994, close to two-thirds of PC hardware production had moved out of Zhongguancun to Guangdong, where a cluster of PC peripherals was forming (Y.-C. Chen 2008).

[13]This kind of gradual transition to the next "big thing" mimics the resilience and flexible innovativeness of the Silicon Valley (Kenney 2008).

[14]The output of the software industries (including IT-enabled services) in China and India is comparable. Whereas the Indian software market exports mainly to the United States, the bulk of the sales of Chinese software are in the domestic market (Gregory, Nollen, and Tenev 2009). The outsourcing business gained by Chinese firms is from Japan, with which China shares cultural affinities and the writing system. These business process outsourcing firms cluster in northeast China, particularly in Dalian, because of the advantages of proximity to the client (Tajima and Furuya 2008).

established universities and research institutions. Beijing, especially Zhongguancun, is seen as the place to start firms, the sort of sentiment that is notably absent in Shanghai (Y.-C. Chen 2008; Su and Hung 2009). Beijing's lead in new starts may also stem from its having a deeper pool of engineers and scientists owing to the larger number of universities and research institutions. These institutions, in turn, have attracted many R&D centers owned by multinational corporations (MNCs) (Y.-C. Chen 2008).[15]

Urban Strategy and Policy Directions

China's central and municipal authorities are actively promoting the development of technological and innovation capabilities that will help urban centers upgrade existing industries and extend their comparative advantage to new industries with higher profitability and better growth prospects.[16] Beijing and Shanghai are at the epicenter of these efforts.

Proposals for Shanghai

Starting in the mid-1990s, Shanghai launched a program to develop six pillar industries: information, finance, trade, automobiles, complete sets of equipment, and real estate. More recently, the city has turned its attention to building business services, with an emphasis on finance, in an effort to eventually make Shanghai a world city akin to New York and London.[17] In pursuit of these strategic initiatives, Shanghai is taking initiatives to encourage technological adoption, deepening, and innovation. By strengthening the individual components of a "municipal innovation system" and its links, Shanghai seeks to accelerate industrial change in directions that will be advantageous for growth and employment. Similarly, Beijing is emphasizing the development of financial services, of creative and logistics industries, and of software and information and communication technology industries.

Space and data limitations prevent evaluation of the effectiveness of existing fiscal and financial incentives given to pillar industries to enhance Shanghai's innovation capacity. However, a list of the major incentives in table 6.4 suggests that they are comprehensive and comparable to incentives provided for high-tech industrial development in the Organisation for Economic Co-operation and Development (OECD) countries. In view of the uncertainties regarding the effectiveness of these instruments, adding to the list of incentives or making current incentives more generous may not be warranted. Moreover, the feedback from

---

[15]Part of the reason for this depth in engineers and scientists is the restrictions imposed by the United States on the issuance of student visas after the events of September 11, 2001. As a result, the Zhongguancun area now has an oversupply of engineers (Y.-C. Chen 2008).

[16]Technology policy requires the coordinated action of national, provincial, and local governments. The near-term objectives need not be systemwide innovation but innovation in specific industries and fields and in specific geographic locations.

[17]New York and London are the most competitive cities in the world. Shanghai ranks 41st and Beijing 66th ("Urban Competitiveness" 2008).

Table 6.4 Fiscal Incentives for Innovation Offered in China

Fiscal incentives for R&D and related activities	Import tariff exemptions are provided to • Facilitate technological renovation and product upgrading in existing SOEs. In addition, targeted industries such as those in the electronics sector were exempted from tariffs and import-related value added tax (VAT) on equipment during the 9th and 10th five-year periods. • Promote technical transfer and commercialization. Foreign individuals, firms, R&D centers engaged in consulting activities, and technical services related to technology transfer and technological development are exempt from corporate income tax.
Fiscal incentives given to various technology-development zones	Establishing economic zones, new and high-tech industrial zones (HTIZs), and economic and technological development zones is one of the key measures the Chinese government has adopted in facilitating acquisition of new and advanced technologies, promoting technological innovation, promoting the commercialization of science and technology results, and enhancing China's industrial competitiveness. From the early 1980s, China began establishing special economic zones and, since the 1990s, high-tech industrial development zones. In 1991, China approved 21 national HTIZs, and by 2005, the total number countrywide had risen to 150, of which 53 are at the national level. These HTIZs have nursed 39,000 high-tech firms employing 4.5 million people. The total turnover of firms reached Y 2.7 trillion in 2004, an increase of 31% over the previous year. The per capita profit was Y 33,000, per capita tax yield was Y 29,000, and the per capita foreign earnings were Y 157,320 (US$19,000). In the national HTIZs, a series of investor-friendly policies and measures have been introduced. These measures include tax reduction and exemption policies.
Fiscal incentives related to income tax	The Chinese government offers various tax holiday schemes to different types of firms. Income tax incentives are as follows: • Foreign-invested enterprises can enjoy the preferential treatment of income tax exemption in the first 2 years after making profits and an income tax reduction (by half) in the following 3 years. • Foreign-invested high-tech enterprises can enjoy income tax exemption in the first 2 years after making profits and an income tax reduction (by half) in the following 6 years. • Sino-foreign joint ventures can enjoy income tax exemption in the first 2 years after making profits. • Other firms are eligible for income tax exemption in the first 2 years when starting productive operation. • Domestic firms in HTIZs are eligible for preferential treatment but with limits in terms of types of business activities (income earned from technology transfer or activities related to technology transfer, such as technical consulting service and training). A ceiling is imposed on how much they can benefit from income tax exemption (less than Y 300,000). • The income tax rate is set at 15% in these zones, which is much lower than the normal rate for those located outside the zones. Firms whose export share is above 70% of their annual production can enjoy further income tax reduction (10%).

144

Other incentives are as follows:

- *Turnover tax.* Foreign enterprises and foreign-invested enterprises are also exempt from the business tax on technology transfer.
- *Tariff and import duties.* Tariff and import-stage VAT exemptions have been granted to foreign-invested enterprises for their importation of equipment and technologies that are listed in the "Catalog of Encouragement."
- *Accelerated depreciation.* New and high-tech firms are granted accelerated depreciation for equipment and instruments (since 1991; see China's State Council Document [1991] No. 12).

Scholarships for students studying in science and engineering fields abroad

The Chinese government has created an Overseas Study Fund to sponsor Chinese students and scholars to pursue their studies or training overseas. In 2004, the fund sponsored 3,630 people for advanced studies or research programs overseas. In line with China's development priorities, the fund identified seven disciplines or academic fields as its sponsorship priorities for 2004:

- Telecommunications and information technology
- High and new technology in agricultural science
- Life sciences and population health
- Material science and new materials
- Energy and environment
- Engineering science
- Applied social science and subjects related to World Trade Organization issues

Incentives given to attract overseas Chinese back

The *Chunhui* program has sponsored 8,000 Chinese scholars with PhDs obtained overseas to come back to carry out short-term work. The Yangtze River Fellowship program awarded 537 overseas Chinese scholars professional appointments in Chinese universities for curriculum building and teaching and for joint academic research.

Fiscal incentives to attract the establishment of R&D centers by MNCs

The fiscal incentives offered include the following:

- Exemption from import duties and import-related VAT for imports of equipment, devices, and spare parts for R&D purposes (1997).
- Tariff and import-related VAT exemption for acquiring imported new and advanced technologies. Foreign-funded R&D centers receive the same fiscal benefits as foreign-funded high-tech firms and enjoy the same fiscal preferential treatments (November 2004).
- Exemption from corporate income tax for revenue earned through the delivery of consulting or other technical services related to transfers of technology and technical development activities (1999).
- Reduction in income tax payment for those R&D centers whose expenditures on R&D increased more than 10% annually.

Source: Yusuf, Wang, and Nabeshima 2009.

interviews conducted for this study indicates that neither industry nor research entities are pressing for additional fiscal or financial incentives.

What this book proposes is a partial redirection of Shanghai's development strategy based on the findings and views presented in earlier chapters and factoring in Shanghai's industrial assets and capabilities. The intention is, paraphrasing Paul Romer (1993), to introduce better recipes and not just to engage in more cooking. This strategy would

- emphasize a balanced development of manufacturing and services to maintain the share of manufacturing in municipal output in the 25 to 30 percent range over the longer term.
- prioritize activities with reference to longer-term profitability, local links, and value added as well as scope for incremental innovation and export prospects.
- encourage process innovation (over the medium term) by leading firms in the principal industries, rather than radical product innovation in new high-tech areas where newcomers often take the lead, not infrequently with the help of large firms.
- promote tertiary education and health care, as well as cultivate strong links between these service industries and other industries.
- focus on the quality of workers and entrepreneurs to prepare them to contribute more actively to innovation.
- create a culturally rich, aesthetically pleasing, and efficient urban environment that will attract and retain high-value-adding economic activities and an increasingly affluent and educated workforce.

For the purposes of growth that is fueled by productivity and innovation, Shanghai needs to pursue a two-pronged approach. One prong would rely on fiscal, land-use, skill-deepening, and innovation policies to sustain those industries that have sound long-term profitability by virtue of accumulated tacit knowledge, product customization and differentiation, multiple links, research intensity, potential for innovation, and high entry barriers, although as in 2009, such industries may go through cyclical downturns. Several of the industries are likely to produce complex capital goods,[18] components, and processed materials. Others at the research-intensive end of the spectrum might trace their technological lineage to the life sciences and

---

[18]The existence of equipment manufacturers is vital to the semiconductor industry. Technological leadership in integrated circuit (IC) production requires continuous refinement and miniaturization, which calls for capacity in equipment development. Dependence on imports of advanced production equipment is a handicap. Competitiveness in a fast-moving field requires control over production, which is why the localization of such manufacturing capacity is so important. As Heng (2008: 186) notes, "TSMC and UMC of Taiwan, never purchase manufacturing equipment from foreign companies because they believe that their IC development program would be restricted if foreign companies controlled all the needed technologies."

nanoscience or to the IT sector, or they might be engaged in developing advanced materials, and their competitive strength will depend on their ties with research centers. What matters is not only an industry's research intensity but also its profitability and the capacity to sustain profitability through a variety of measures, among which innovation in several areas could play a prominent role (Porter 2008b). Industries can be research intensive but may struggle to generate a pipeline of products and to achieve profitability (biotechnology is an example). In that case, it is far from obvious that such industries deserve priority over less technologically glamorous industries that are reliably profitable. The drugs introduced by the biopharmaceutical firms (or firms producing advanced materials) take 10 to 15 years to reach the market; development costs as much as drugs introduced by pharmaceutical companies—that is, US\$800 million to US\$1 billion; and biotechnology has made new and effective drugs no easier to discover (see Bernstein 2008; Goozner 2005; Pisano 2006). What discoveries (which have spawned new subdisciplines) and new techniques have uncovered are new layers of complexity requiring interdisciplinary effort but without any shortcuts. Small doses of venture capital, though sufficient for chip design, Web-based technologies, and software, are no more than drops in the bucket for biopharmaceutical firms. The U.S. experience cautions against putting too much store in high-tech industries, because since 2000, employment in the computer and electronics subsectors has stagnated and the Web-based and media industries have generated little new employment. Other high-tech stars, such as biotechnology, have yielded new products, but breakthrough discoveries have been rare. Nanotechnology has considerable promise, but again, the commercial successes of nanotech research have been modest and slow to materialize even though U.S. researchers and companies are in the forefront (Mandel 2008; Pilkington and others 2009).

A balanced portfolio of manufacturing industries for Shanghai would assign the highest weights to the machinery, electronic components, and processing industries (assuming that the pollution they cause can be contained through regulation and technological advances and that, through careful design of production facilities, as in Singapore, the land area used can be kept to a minimum). The portfolio would assign lower weights initially to the research-intensive life sciences and nanoscience, which have abundant potential but are slow to generate highly profitable products commanding global markets. Supporting these industries through research and doses of venture capital makes good strategic sense and safeguards future options. Nevertheless, a realistic appraisal of their contribution to the local economy is needed to ensure that they do not divert an excessive amount of capital and research talent from the backbone sectors.

China and Shanghai have demonstrated a strong and growing comparative advantage in manufactures (see table 6.5). China has a comparative advantage in more than one-third of the commodities that it exports.[19] Following the past examples of

---

[19]By comparison, Malaysia has a comparative advantage in 16 percent of the products that it exports.

Table 6.5 Exports of China and the Share of Commodities in Which China Has a Comparative Advantage

	1995	2000	2006/07
Number of commodities exported by China	766	763	763
Number of commodities in which China has a comparative advantage	274	279	278
Share in which China has a comparative advantage (%)	35.8	36.6	36.4

Source: Authors' calculations.
Note: At least one country exported about 780 products each year.

Figure 6.1 Product Space for China, 2000–04

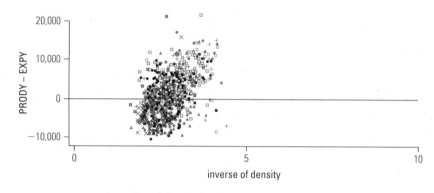

- electronic and electrical products
- automotive products
- engineering
- other low-technology products
- other resource-based products
- other high-technology products
- process industry
- textiles, garments and footwear
- agro-based products
- primary products

Source: Authors' calculations.

Germany, Japan, and the Republic of Korea, China can deepen and extend this comparative advantage into higher-value-adding and knowledge-intensive products, thereby increasing its export shares in the more profitable segments of the international market for manufactures.[20] Figure 6.1 shows the product space for China. Product spaces, a concept pioneered by Hausmann and Klinger (2006), assume that each commodity produced gives rise to different opportunities for future diversification. That is, some products offer easy and multiple diversification paths to other related products while others do not. In general, primary and resource-based products do not lead to many opportunities for diversification. In contrast, manufactured goods, such as electronics, generate skills and assets that are similar to those required for the

---

[20]However, Chinese manufacturers still lack core technologies for major manufactures such as color televisions and mobile phones and need to license these technologies from foreign suppliers. Moreover, many SOEs that have acquired foreign designs and technology do not have the engineering expertise to exploit them fully (Cao 2008).

Table 6.6   Selected "Upscale" Commodities with Highest Density in China, 2000–04

Product name	Standard Industrial Trade Classification code	Density	Technology class	PRODY–EXPY
Other sound recorders and other sound reproducing apparatus	7638	0.537294	MT3	4,765.33
Television receivers, monochrome	7612	0.524965	HT1	5,388.19
Optical instruments and apparatus	8710	0.483351	HT2	10,039.76
Peripheral units, including control and adapting units	7525	0.478158	HT1	5,142.37
Microphones, loudspeakers, and amplifiers	7642	0.472566	HT1	1,301.51
Printed circuits and parts thereof	7722	0.468498	MT3	2,855.42

Source: Authors' calculations.
Note: HT1 = electronic and electrical products; HT2 = other high-technology products; MT3 = engineering products. Technology classification is based on Sanjaya Lall (2000).

production of other manufactured commodities, and hence such products are classified as high value. The x axis is the inverse of the density (that is, closer to the origin indicates higher density), and the y axis measures the difference between PRODY (a weighted average of the GDP per capita of countries exporting that product is calculated to assign a value that is a proxy for quality) and EXPY (which is calculated as a weighted sum of PRODY, signifying the sophistication of the export basket of a country). A positive number means "upgrading" in the sense of exporting more sophisticated commodities relative to the overall export basket). The commodities that are in the area of high density are mostly higher-valued commodities such as engineering and high-technology goods (see table 6.6).[21]

With the global downturn in economic activity that began in 2008, firms in the industrial countries are abandoning certain types of manufacturing activity, as is the case with many *mittelstand* companies in Germany.[22] This trend is opening up lucrative niches in the global marketplace.[23] Chinese firms can occupy these niches. Furthermore, many firms are in crisis, which represents an opportunity for Chinese firms to acquire needed technology (codified and tacit), intellectual property, brand names, and market access.[24] The government can facilitate this

---

[21]The discussion in this section focuses on "upscale" goods, that is, ones for which PRODY and EXPY are both positive.

[22]In 2003, Chinese firms acquired 278 small and medium-size German firms (Zeng and Williamson 2007).

[23]The United States is the leader in only five product categories: computer hardware, software, biotech, aerospace, and entertainment (Wien 2008).

[24]Samsung was unable to develop or acquire the necessary semiconductor technology until the U.S. firm Micron Technology was in financial distress and willing to make the technology available (Nabeshima 2004).

Table 6.7   Export Similarity with OECD, 1972–2001

	1972	1981	1991	2001
Asia	0.16	0.20	0.26	0.27
China	0.09	0.28	0.55	0.75
Latin America	0.22	0.22	0.31	0.34

Source: Schott 2006.

Note: Asia excludes China. The export similarity is calculated as the overlap of export commodities to the United States from OECD and China (and other regions), with 0 being no overlap and 1 being complete overlap.

process by improving access to financing; however, the ultimate outcomes will depend on the initiatives of the firms themselves, the receptivity to such takeovers in the OECD countries, and the capacity of Chinese firms to absorb technology—and in some cases foreign firms. Chinese firms that will spearhead this process are more likely to succeed with manufactures (and services associated with manufactures) than with services, because they already have a head start and have an export product mix comparable to that of advanced countries (see table 6.7).[25] Among Chinese cities, Shanghai, with its well-developed industrial capabilities, can emerge as a leading global producer and exporter of advanced technology and high-end manufactures. This is not to deny the contributions that services and the export of services can make to Shanghai's economy. They can be vital complements.[26] However, even impersonal services are inherently less export intensive,[27] and East Asian and international experiences suggest that acquiring an international brand name in services and a sizable global market share is harder and takes longer because of entry barriers and competition from entrenched providers that have accumulated vital intangible capital.

Manufacturing employs 32.5 percent of Shanghai's workforce—a high percentage. Many of these jobs are for skilled, middle-age workers who are relatively well paid. The availability of employment on such a scale buttresses Shanghai's

---

[25] Even though China exports a similar bundle of goods, substantial quality differences may exist within each commodity. For instance, average unit values of Japanese exports are 2.9 times those of China, suggesting that Japanese exports are of higher quality (Fontagne, Gaulier, and Zignago 2008).

[26] In fact, as incomes rise, so does the share of the services industry. Because of its larger share, the growth in services, especially of productivity, would be desirable. However, reliance on the services sector alone is unlikely to enable a city (or a country) to achieve growth rates in the 6 to 8 percent range, although cities such as Bangalore and Hyderabad in India have done remarkably well since the mid-1990s with the help of IT services and IT-enabled services.

[27] Export of services to other parts of China is likely to become a growing business for firms in Shanghai, depending, of course, on the competitiveness of Shanghai-based suppliers.

prosperity, but it does more than that. Capital- and skill-intensive manufacturing activities also affect the income distribution in the urban area, helping to provide the crucial middle layer of income earners, who are the vanguard of China's consuming class and whose growth is also a way of checking income inequality. Manufacturing is an urban balance wheel, maintaining growth with equity and the urban economic diversity that is at the root of urbanization economies. If growth in China is to depend more on domestic consumption, then an expanding middle class in "consumer" cities such as Shanghai needs to sustain the conditions conducive to the spread of middle-class earners.

Input-output (I-O) data for China show that capital- and knowledge-intensive manufacturing activities give rise to a multiplicity of backward and forward links, which support a vast number of suppliers of products and services. From the I-O tables, one can see that transportation equipment manufacturing, to take one example, is linked to and sustains a wide spectrum of activities, several of which contribute to innovation and technological progress. The cumulative contribution of the activities associated with the transportation equipment subsector to growth, for example, is highly significant. Manufacturing is also strongly linked to the logistics-transport sector, which is a key industry in Shanghai (see table 3.2).[28] Manufacturing and logistics are mutually reinforcing and together constitute the principal growth pole of Shanghai's economy. In 2006, of 100 million ton-equivalent units of containers handled in China, Shanghai's ports handled 21 million (Wright 2007a), increasing to 28 million in 2008 (Lan 2009). With one of the busiest ports in China and a new deep-sea port, Shanghai offers domestic logistics firms opportunities to develop intermodal capabilities and become world-class players by absorbing business from southern ports, such as Singapore, which have less scope for expansion because land is in short supply.[29,30]

---

[28]Shipbuilding is now a booming industry in the Yangtze River Delta with sound long-term prospects.

[29]Unlike some other industries, the logistics industry is still rather fragmented. The top 10 logistics firms accounted for less than 40 percent of the global share in 2006 (Ward 2007). This fragmentation provides some opportunities for a new firm to enter the global market because multinational corporations are now looking for logistics firms that can operate globally. One such firm, Shanghai International Port Group, has acquired terminals in Belgium as a first step to becoming a global container operator (Wright 2007b). In addition, a strong logistics sector can stimulate financial and insurance transactions, as was the case in London and New York.

[30]The logistics sector is an important source of earnings and employment in cities such as Miami and Los Angeles. For instance, the Miami International Airport directly and indirectly has created nearly a quarter of a million jobs for the Miami-Dade County area, and its annual economic effect in 2006, through tourism, international banking, and trade, was estimated at US$19 billion. The ports of Long Beach and Los Angeles directly employ 280,000 workers and indirectly support the employment of another 900,000 in southern California (Pearlstein 2009).

The supplier networks that are at the heart of the transportation, engineering, and electronics industries are a significant source of value-adding and technological advances. Very likely, the survival of suppliers, many of which are small and medium-size firms that cocreate components and modules with the final assemblers and provide just-in-time services, will determine the future of these industries in Shanghai. Safeguarding the health of the supply chain has always been a consideration, but in a downturn, it takes on added significance because smaller firms servicing narrow markets are more vulnerable to demand shocks. With market demand shrinking and credit becoming harder to obtain, specialized component suppliers struggle to survive, and the weaker ones will close their doors.[31] Assisting the majority to weather the recession and also strengthening the foundations of the parts manufacturing industry call for three types of measures: (a) implementing credit (including trade financing) programs catering to firms that are critical nodes in the supply chain and ones with substantial technological capabilities; (b) encouraging consolidation of small firms with overlapping product lines into more viable units;[32] and (c) providing industrial extension, financial, and labor training services to small firms to bolster their productivity and widen revenue margins.

Proposals for Beijing

A profusion of tall buildings aside, Beijing could not be more different from Shanghai. It is a city with a storied past. As the capital of the Yuan dynasty, it was known as Dadu (great capital). When the first Ming emperor made the city his capital, it was renamed Beiping (the North pacified). From the early days, the city has marched to the beat of a different drummer.[33] An inland city in the drier,

---

[31]In 2008, about 300,000 factories ceased operation. They were often abandoned by the owners, leaving creditors and workers unpaid (Roberts 2009).

[32]In December 2008, the Chinese government relaxed the financing rule to allow firms to borrow from banks for the merger and acquisition of firms in the same line of business (in the past, the funding had to come from retained earnings or from issuing more stocks or bonds). This easing of the rule has led some of the cash-rich SOEs to acquire weaker rivals, whether they are state-owned, privately held, or located abroad, especially in strategic industries such as steel and automotives. For instance, Baosteel acquired Ningbo Steel and Baotou Steel with the help of a loan ("China: Pace of Mergers" 2009). The Chinese government is also planning to reduce the number of automotive makers from 14 to 10 by 2011 through mergers (Hille 2009). At the same time, however, the Chinese government is restricting merger and acquisition activities—especially those by foreign firms—through the antimonopoly law that became effective on August 1, 2008 (Tucker and Waldmeir 2008). Although the Ministry of Commerce approved InBev's acquisition of Anheuser-Busch, it restricted InBev from further increasing its share in Tsingtao Brewery and Zhujiang Brewery and prohibited the company from buying shares of two other Chinese breweries (Tucker 2008). The Ministry of Commerce prevented Coca-Cola from acquiring Huiyuan Juice, a leading juice maker in China (Tucker, Smith, and Anderlini 2009).

[33]Barme (2008) provides a brief history.

northern part of China with a less populous and less affluent hinterland, Beijing's geographic coordinates are less advantageous than those of Shanghai. Beijing's development will be constrained by possibly worsening water shortages,[34] and its exposure to cold northerly winds and dust storms detracts from its livability. The presence of the central government, with its armada of ministries, institutes, and regulatory agencies, is a plus because it is a source of economic stability and eases Beijing's access to resources. But its presence also means that the functioning of the city is subject to two layers of scrutiny and control—from the municipal authorities and from the central government—and subject to the expectations of both entities. Beijing presents China's "official" face to the world—a considerable responsibility at a time when China is consolidating its position as the world's second-ranked economic nation. Becoming the showcase for China's modernity, economic vitality, and technological prowess has implications for the spatial and architectural characteristics of the city and its economic options. The latter are of concern for this discussion.

Close to 80 percent of Beijing's GDP is derived from services; this figure is likely to creep upward as more services are crowded in by the advantages of agglomerating in the capital city of a centralized economy. Proximity of ministries and regulatory agencies is generally advantageous to businesses, and such proximity is doubly advantageous in China. Hence, Beijing will remain the headquarters capital of China, and a concentration of headquarters attracts myriad providers of business and consulting, personal, janitorial, and retail services. The presence of China's financial regulators in Beijing will ensure a substantial agglomeration of banks and other institutions. This cluster could be the nucleus of a thriving services economy. However, if the experience of other cities with a dominant financial sector is a guide, such an agglomeration of business services will not deliver rapid growth to the Beijing economy, just as it will not to Shanghai. It could help sustain moderate 2 to 3 percent growth in conjunction with the government sector. Expanding at a faster clip calls for additional engines of growth. Here, Beijing's vast and growing research apparatus can play a role. As noted in chapter 5, Beijing's strength relative to Shanghai and to every other city in China derives from three principal sources. First, by spending 6 percent of GDP on R&D and by expanding tertiary education, Beijing is adding to technological capacity and slowly beginning to show evidence of innovation capabilities that can nourish creative and IT industries. The MNCs that have established research facilities are also contributing to technological deepening.

Second, the city is arguably the leading center for the IT industry and one of the leading centers of research in life sciences, nanotechnology, optoelectronics,

---

[34]China is the most water-stressed country in East Asia. Rainfall in the north averages 200 to 400 millimeters per year, and per capita availability is only 762 cubic meters per person (World Bank 2009a; Yusuf and Nabeshima 2006a).

and advanced materials. If the R&D projects under way prove to be consistently fruitful, and if the Beijing municipality takes steps to ensure that certain kinds of manufacturing continue to enjoy access to land and facilities in the suburbs, these fields could help eventually create a dynamic economic system with some activities at the cutting edge of technology in a high-wage urban environment. A high-tech manufacturing sector that has a 16 to 20 percent share of GDP, averages a 10 percent growth rate, and exports a high percentage of its output can contribute a solid 2 percent of growth to the city's bottom line and enable Beijing to balance its trade accounts.

The IT industry enjoys a host of synergies with the creative industries, including multimedia, software, publishing, and advertising services. The interplay and networking of R&D, high-tech manufacturing, and creative industries, were it to be fruitfully realized through incentive and market-coordinating policies, could provide the urban economy with 4 to 5 percent annual growth and a steady supply of well-paid jobs. With the momentum delivered by these three subsectors, Beijing could aim for growth rates in the 8 to 9 percent range over at least a decade.

The third source of strength—and one that would be intrinsic to a growth strategy leveraging R&D, high-tech manufacturing, and creative industries—is the presence of an ecosystem of science parks; incubators;[35] providers of patient capital; and supporting legal, consulting, and accounting services. Such an ecosystem can induce and sustain a network of small and medium-size firms. Such firms are proliferating in Zhongguancun and other parts of Beijing. Returnees from overseas, a source of entrepreneurial dynamism, have started some of them. However, these firms need time to mature and enhance technological capabilities. As of now, few are notably innovative, and even fewer are conducting research or introducing products or services at the frontiers of their respective technologies.

Whereas the way forward for the manufacturing sector in Shanghai is to strengthen and build on its broad base of capital goods and components industries and to intensify the local technological content, the growth strategy for Beijing warrants an approach that ensures the development of high-tech manufacturing and creative industries within the Beijing city region. This approach

---

[35]Incubators can breed innovative start-ups with the help of risk capital, space, IT tools, advanced connectivity, market research, mentoring, and networking services and by brokering relationships between clients and investors. They can also advocate policy and legal reforms advantageous for start-ups and build regional networks among incubators to share ideas and business models. However, there is no single business model for incubators: each incubator must tailor its design and business model with reference to objectives, resources, and circumstances. Some of the more dynamic incubators continually push the frontiers by adapting the mix of services, including virtual incubation services. Chile's Access-Nova has built a network of angel investors to assist incubators while CIE-TEC in Costa Rica has mobilized additional resources through a partnership with a local bank.

already derives significant impetus from the government's spending on and incentives for R&D as well as the government's support for technology development. Ongoing efforts to augment the supply of venture capital and angel financing need to be supplemented by measures that will improve the quality of the mentoring and guidance packaged with this capital. This improvement is more a matter of time and the volume of deal flow than of anything else. The financing industry needs to build experience and gain in maturity.

Encouraging key universities to focus on raising the quality of their basic research and giving more attention to the practical relevance of the training they provide in technical skills and in entrepreneurship would help stimulate the entry of firms and innovation.

Perhaps to an even greater degree than in Shanghai, the local and central governments will need to tailor land development, zoning, affordable housing, and incentive policies for the Beijing urban region that enable manufacturing activities to thrive and to grow.[36] As has been the case in New York, London, and Tokyo, municipal policies aggressively championing services and commercial and residential real estate would quickly drive most manufacturing out of the Beijing urban region, leaving only the research infrastructure behind. In all likelihood, cutting-edge research in the life sciences, in advanced materials, and in nanotechnology, for example, might not translate into new starts in the Beijing region but elsewhere in China or the world. This conundrum is similar to what New York faces: it supports plenty of research, but other places capture the fruits of this research.[37] The upshot for Beijing—as for New York—could be less growth from highly productive manufacturing and more reliance on the more circumscribed growth potential inherent in services.

Unlike Shanghai, Beijing has little choice but to depend on services for the greater part of its growth. Through suitable actions taken now, it could continue to derive a significant share of its growth from manufacturing, maintain urbanization economies at a higher level, and continue to reap greater benefits in the form of productivity, innovation, and options for diversifying.

Rethinking the Role of Finance and Business Services

Although the share of services is bound to increase because of trends in demand and in relative prices, it is desirable that over the foreseeable future services should complement and not massively displace industry in both Shanghai and Beijing.

---

[36] An innovative city creatively juxtaposes hard and soft infrastructure to assemble a critical mass of participants and to provoke ideas and inventions. Landry (2008: 133) describes the infrastructures in the following terms: "Los Angeles is an interesting example of the fusion of popular culture and technological creativity which has resulted in the world's preeminent movie making industry."

[37] California has consistently been the foremost producer of invention patents in the United States since 1985, with New York ranked second through 1995 and third after Texas since.

The experience of Germany and Japan suggests that even though services have greatly enlarged their share of GDP, the prosperity of these countries and their positions in the world of trade continue to rest on their advanced manufacturing industries.[38] The high productivity of these industries supports numerous service activities (which have far lower value added and which have failed over almost two decades to catch up with equivalent activities in the United States), and it enables Germany and Japan to maintain favorable trade balances. In contrast, the relative decline of manufacturing is partly to blame for the trade deficit that the United States confronts and will need to narrow. Furthermore, balancing the portfolio of producer services with manufacturing industries minimizes the damage inflicted by shocks affecting particular activities and can—with appropriate coordination through market forces aided by public agencies and industrial associations—give rise to many more growth-promoting links.

The international experience with the development of major clusters of financial and business services is mixed at best. From a national perspective, financial development is definitely a plus, although efficiency might be more important than the sheer size of the sector when it comes to channeling resources to manufacturing firms (Bao and Yang 2009).[39] In the megacities, financial development is particularly helpful for SMEs, which depend on relations and exchange of information with local providers of financing to initiate riskier technology-intensive projects. Larger firms find it much easier to raise financing from a variety of sources (Guiso, Sapienza, and Zingales 2002). Financial development that increases the institutional stake and leverage of insurance companies, pension funds, and others in publicly listed corporate entities could, in a competitive global environment, encourage innovation and improve corporate governance (Aghion, Van Reenen, and Zingales 2009).[40] It is also associated with stronger economic performance. Whether finance and business services can be an effective growth engine for megacities is less obvious. Only London and New York can be classified as major world-class finance-cum-services centers. They are trailed by Hong Kong, China, and by Singapore (neither a megacity on the scale of Shanghai and Tokyo). Cities such as Paris, Frankfurt, Zurich, and São Paulo do not make the cut. The scale, diversity, and export of

---

[38]This reliance is also the cause of much economic grief because of the global recession in 2009.

[39]According to two extensive surveys of the literature, financial development can be growth enhancing, but the relationship can be nonlinear, and the pace of growth apparently does not differ between bank-based and financial market-based models of development (Ang 2008; Levine 2004). It is still an open question which model is more susceptible to crises and, to put this point differently, more amenable to effective regulation.

[40]However, examining the growth experience of Japan; the Republic of Korea; and Taiwan, China, W.-C. Liu and Hsu (2006) find that financial development under globalization produced mixed outcomes. Especially, capital outflow from these economies negatively affected their growth.

services from these secondary regional centers are much more limited. Finance and business services are the drivers of growth in London, New York, and—to some degree—Tokyo, but in each case, these drivers have generated only quite modest rates of growth for the city as a whole, and a small segment of the workforce has reaped much of the gains in income and wealth.[41] Higher growth in other cities with a services orientation depends on the push provided by alternative sources of growth, such as manufacturing and logistics.

Research on the effects of financial deepening suggests that short-term financial objectives can crowd out longer-term real investment through two different channels. The first channel is the crowding out of real investment by an increase in the investment in financial assets (Crotty 2005). Many nonfinancial firms have invested in financial assets and financial subsidiaries in recent years, to the point that they hold as many financial assets as physical assets, and significant amounts of profits are derived from those financial assets (Orhangazi 2008).[42] Short-term focus is the second channel. Increasing numbers of managers have adopted the "portfolio view" of the firm, with emphasis on the deployment of a firm's assets for the sake of short-run returns.[43] This changing viewpoint stems from several institutional developments relating to corporate governance, such as the increasing use of stock options as a part of the compensation package, more emphasis on the shareholder value[44] rather than on the long-term viability of firms, and the impatience of investors. These two channels together have encouraged firms to meet "the short term objectives of financial markets rather than . . . the long term growth of the firm" (Orhangazi 2008: 870). Management emphasizes the distribution of revenues to raise the company's stock prices and thereby enlarge the value of stock options (Orhangazi 2008: 869).[45] When "financial markets undervalue long term investments, then managers will undervalue them too as their activities are judged and rewarded by the performance of the company's assets" (Orhangazi 2008: 871).[46]

---

[41]The increasing share of profits in GDP in the United States and of the incomes earned by the highest-paid fifth of income earners can be traced in large part to the financialization of the economy.

[42]As early as in 1965, Tobin (1965) recognized that financial and real investments by firms can be substitutes—especially when the returns from financial investments are higher than those from real investments.

[43]This view changed the corporate strategy from "retain and reinvest" to "downsize and distribute" (Lazonick and O'Sullivan 2000).

[44]See, for instance, Grossman and Hart (1999) on the origin of shareholder value.

[45]Buying back stocks is one of the strategies often used to increase share prices. It again diminishes the resources available for real investment (Grullon and Michaely 2002; Lazonick and O'Sullivan 2000).

[46]Jack Welch, the former chief executive officer of General Electric, made headlines in March 2009 when he claimed, "[S]hareholder value is the dumbest idea in the world! It is not a strategy; it needs to be an outcome" (Büschemann 2009).

The financial crisis that started in 2008 has suspended a question over the value added by financial innovations[47]—and the longer-term contribution of finance to urban development. It has underlined again the difficulties in regulating increasingly sophisticated activities and the powerful vested interests they create so that serious financial shocks that have painful consequences for the real sector can be avoided. Regulating these activities has proven exceedingly problematic, with each regulatory measure spurring a frenzy of regulatory (and tax) arbitrage, masquerading as innovation, that partially negates efforts at control.[48] The financial crisis of 2008 to 2009 also raised questions about the longer-term stability of an economy overly dependent on consumption as the main driver of growth. Such stability is particularly questionable when the consumption is substantially facilitated by financial innovation and financial depth that make consumer credit more widely available at attractive rates and have the unfortunate side effects of burdening consumers with debt[49] and giving rise to real estate and other asset bubbles. Furthermore, when the authorities worldwide are unwilling to check such bubbles in time because of a reluctance to rein in booms, they only add fuel to the fire.

Not only cities such as London and New York, but also some of the regional financial centers, are discovering the risks of excessive (fiscal) reliance on the handsomely compensated top-tier employees of financial and affiliated business services. Moreover, the longer-term shape and pace of financial development are less clear, given the seriousness of the 2008 to 2009 crisis and the doubts it has cast on the economic gains to be derived from the current financial instruments, practices, and forms of organization—as well as the concerns it has aroused regarding the political power accumulated by the financial sector and the inability of regulators to effectively vet financial innovations and check the excesses of financial institutions (S. Johnson 2009).

Undoubtedly, finance and business services will retain a major role in urban economies, but for cities that have attained the current level of per capita income of Beijing and Shanghai and that share their growth aspirations, reconsidering the importance attached to the financial sector and associated business services may be desirable in future growth strategy. Financial centers across the East Asian region are aggressively searching for new financial niches that will support continuing expansion of the sector, but new opportunities are less than abundant. Singapore (where the financial sector already encompasses 11 percent of GDP),

---

[47]See Yusuf (2009b) for a review of recent financial innovations and their adoption by Chinese entities.

[48]In the opinion of Willem Buiter (2009), "Most of the new instruments and institutions were motivated purely by regulatory and tax arbitrage, domestic and crossborder. . . . Even the genuine innovations were, however, often abused and became socially damaging."

[49]These consumers are all too frequently lower-income people, whose average incomes have risen little, if at all, in the United Kingdom and the United States over a decade.

for example, hopes to continue to benefit from managing the wealth of high net worth individuals, whose numbers have risen in line with inequality.

From the perspective of rapid growth sustained by innovation, it might be desirable to groom a suite of tradable producer services, selecting those that directly or indirectly support a range of manufacturing-related activities. In addition to finance, tertiary education, health care, and engineering services may be well suited to Shanghai's strategic objectives and the creative industries to those of Beijing.

Inducing Innovation: Demand Pull and Supply Push

Innovation capability arises from a matrix of elements with no clear rules for combining them. Increased spending on research is only one ingredient—doubtless, an important one, but far from being enough. The quality and experience of researchers and the availability of state-of-the-art facilities and equipment noted earlier are a second element. The deliberate creation of spaces—science parks and incubators—to nurture activities that could quicken the technological change is a third. Institutions protecting intellectual property (IP) rights and incentive mechanisms for firms and researchers to innovate through monetary and other rewards are a fourth.[50] Regulations and standards that induce firms to develop and introduce new technologies are a fifth factor. For example, environmental regulations supported by publicly financed R&D have promoted innovation in a number of fields as well as the diffusion of technology.[51] A culture of inquiry—one that assigns a special significance to individuals who innovate—is a sixth factor. Last but not least is an urban environment that is conducive to the pursuit, exchange, and refining of new ideas and that actively promotes commercialization of innovations. Policy makers in the two Chinese megacities are working on all these registers; however, tangible evidence of innovativeness is materializing slowly as experienced researchers, intermediaries, and venture capitalists aggregate into critical masses and an innovation culture gels within rapidly evolving urban environments. Typically, a strong desire exists to hurry the process along without having a clear roadmap, which leaves considerable room for experimentation.

---

[50]In this regard, China may want to consider centralizing the appeal process to a single specialized IP court to facilitate the further development of the IP market. Experience in the United States has shown that the establishment of such an IP court has led to a reduction in the time it takes to reach settlements and judgments at the lower courts. The establishment of a single appeals court has clarified the scope and the extent of IP protection, providing much more certainty to trial outcomes, where otherwise judgments can range widely, depending on the jurisdiction of the court (Galasso and Schankerman 2008).

[51]See Popp, Newell, and Jaffe (2009) for a comprehensive survey of the findings on environmental regulation and its technological spillovers.

Governments' efforts to encourage innovation

One avenue to an innovative manufacturing sector that both Beijing and Shanghai are actively pursuing is the establishment of science parks. Each city has a number of parks that offer tax and financial benefits. These incentives can include incubators providing space, services, and seed money; extension services; multiple special funds for different categories of firms; bonuses and prizes for inventors;[52] subsidies for patenting; and scholarships and grants for researchers—not to mention tax holidays and depreciation allowances for R&D spending and high-tech firms. The success of science parks is predicated on many factors—location, social and urban amenities, and connectivity being among the most important. But in addition, the competence of the park's administrators in providing and managing infrastructure and a joint effort by public and private stakeholders to minimize transaction costs for occupants and maximize external links can be significant assets. Furthermore, a few big name anchor tenants can be a major draw, as can access to nearby business and financial services. The questions not being asked insistently enough by municipal policy makers are whether these parks are producing the desired results, suitably defined by measurable indicators of firm performance; which incentives are most effective and deserve to be expanded; and which incentives should be wound down.[53] Absent such a disentangling and assessment of the incentive regime in Shanghai, determining whether existing measures are yielding good returns and indicating how these returns might be augmented is difficult, especially given the prevailing economic circumstances. Casual empiricism suggests that the incentives to induce innovation are expensive, and thus far the returns

---

[52]Awarding prizes to stimulate innovation is not new. In 1714, the British government offered a prize for the development of a navigational device to improve the safety of long-distance voyages. The French government offered a prize for food preservation, which resulted in the development of canned food with long shelf lives. Although no winner emerged, the 1858 Bréant Prize stimulated research in infectious disease (Bays and Jansen 2009). How prizes should be designed so as to maximize the social utility of an innovation has brought forth a number of proposals. Kremer and Williams (2009) maintain that the prize ought not to be given for meeting ex ante specifications but should be awarded following piloting that demonstrates the marketability of the innovation.

[53]Tax exemption credits and rebates as a means of stimulating R&D spending have been most extensively analyzed in the United States. The results tend to be mixed, although on balance, tax credits show some results. A study of nine OECD countries found that a dollar's tax expenditure increased private spending on research by one dollar over the longer term. This finding suggests that tax incentives, as distinct from direct public spending on R&D, are superior if the private sector is more efficient at allocating resources for research or if private research produces more spillovers (B. Hall 2001; Yusuf, Wang, and Nabeshima 2009). In sum, the limited empirical evidence on the role of tax policy does not make a strong case for such incentives (N. Bloom, Griffith, and Van Reenen 2002; Klemm 2009; Yusuf, Wang, and Nabeshima 2009).

have been meager. For example:

- In principle, science parks can lead to productivity gains from idea spillovers through agglomeration, can reduce the wasteful duplication of research, and can induce older firms to sustain their patenting efforts. Successful parks also promote networking[54] and cocreation of innovations by linked firms (Gerlach, Rønde, and Stahl 2009; Martin, Mayer, and Mayneris 2008; Squicciarini 2008).[55] A study of new technology-based firms in Hsinchu Science Industrial Park showed that the elasticity of R&D with respect to outputs was greater for firms in the park than for firms outside it.[56] The study also found that park-based firms invested more efficiently in R&D (Yang, Motohashi, and Chen 2009). Measuring the success of the parks in Beijing and Shanghai with respect to specific metrics of survival and growth, return on assets (tangible and intangible), networking, productivity, and innovative performance requires detailed research supported by abundant data. What emerges from the interviews conducted is that science parks periodically change their objectives and are more preoccupied with attracting firms and maximizing exports than with technological advancement. The links between firms in Zhangjiang Park[57] and universities are relatively weak, in part because most universities are some distance away in Puxi and only the Shanghai Chinese Medicine University is adjacent to the park. Firms in Beijing's Zhongguancun Science and Technology Park also do not regularly interact with universities (J. Wang and Tong 2005). Interfirm collaboration is quite limited in science parks in both cities, with Chinese-owned firms being more skeptical than foreign-invested firms and firms run by individuals with overseas training or experience. Chinese-owned firms prefer to do most of their R&D in-house for fear of losing IP. Competitive

---

[54]A famous example of industrial networking is the one that led to the emergence of the PC and laptop manufacturing industry in Taiwan, China. In 1982, the Electronic Research and Service Organization (ERSO) of the Industrial Technology Research Institute launched a research project that developed a PC compatible with the IBM PC and licensed Microsoft's operating system. It then transferred this technology to local firms through an industrial alliance with local firms, including Acer. With continuing support from ERSO, the imposition of local content rules, and the provision of financial subsidies, which eased the entry of hundreds of new firms, exports of PCs from Taiwan, China, rose. By the early 1990s, they accounted for 95 percent of PCs exported worldwide (Amsden and Chu 2003; Mathews and Cho 2000).

[55]Martin, Mayer, and Mayneris (2008) note that in France productivity gains follow a U shape and decline as concentration raises congestion costs.

[56]The authors of the study, Yang, Motohashi, and Chen (2009: 81), maintain that output elasticity is a more appropriate measure than patent elasticity, because the ultimate objective of firms is to increase profits, and they will do this by suitably allocating their R&D spending to promote process and product innovations.

[57]Shanghai Zhangjiang Hi-Tech Park, located in Pudong New Area, was established in 1992. It occupies an area of 25 square kilometers. The park is separated into four different zones: Technical Innovation Zone, Hi-Tech Industry Zone, Scientific Research and Education Zone, and Residential Zone (Su and Hung 2009).

pressures and suspicion appear to override the advantages of collaboration. Cao (2004: 660, 667) observed that science parks such as Zhongguancun and Zhangjiang have been slow to evolve innovative entities because of (a) a shortage of experienced technologists and managers with language skills, especially in SMEs but also in larger enterprises; (b) "a tendency to copy technology rather than to invent it"; and (c) heavy government custodial oversight with a stress on "conspicuous statistics"—that is, the growth rate, the number of firms, and the value of exports—rather than on the quality of the growth.[58] The quality of skills, of products, and of technological progress is a recurrent concern in the literature on technology development in China (Zhao, Watanabe, and Griffy-Brown 2009).

- The quality of innovation being supported by incubators is difficult to gauge, and without a thorough evaluation of the selection criteria of factors influencing the survival of firms at the incubator stage and of the performance of graduates from incubators, it is impossible to say which programs are working and why.

- Developing networked clusters of firms in industrial parks is one way of building innovation capabilities and creating a base of suppliers that attract large MNCs and partner with foreign firms in building competitive strength.[59] Such networked clusters have yet to emerge in the leading parks, and neither the interviews conducted for this book nor the published research suggests that they have begun to germinate. A related concern is that few experienced engineers and technicians are leaving MNCs to start their own firms.

The increased funding for R&D, together with the financial and performance-related inducements to patent and to write papers in scientific journals, is leading to a surge in output. The worth of this output—in particular the longer-term commercial value of the findings—is uncertain, however.[60] Too many researchers might be

---

[58]See also Xue (2006a) on the limited R&D capacity in enterprises.

[59]Such clusters of specialized engineering firms were responsible for the emergence of Detroit as the center of auto manufacturing in the United States in the early 20th century. Other clusters account for the reputation of the textile-, ceramic-, and furniture-based industrial districts in Italy and of the electronic clusters in Silicon Valley and Hsinchu Park. Clusters are also advantageous because they provide fertile soil for the emergence of new firms (Quigley 2008).

[60]Spending on R&D and other elements of an innovation ecosystem can yield significant returns over the longer term, but as Lane (2009) observes, the number of success stories is few. Investments by the United States during the 1970s and 1980s were responsible for three-quarters of productivity growth in the post-1995 period through the expansion of the information technology and communication sector, its spillovers, and the life sciences. But massive investments in Japan and in Sweden, for example, have not produced equivalent productivity and employment outcomes. Lane (2009: 1273–74) writes, "We do not understand the mechanisms through which investment in R&D and their immediate products (knowledge and technology) interact with other aspects of societies and economies ... [and econometric techniques do not easily allow us] to encompass the non-linear and complex nature of value creation in the knowledge economy. Innovation is non-linear because the demand side and the supply side of ideas are inextricably intertwined."

engaged in inconsequential research. Quantity may be trumping quality. Leading researchers in the United States worry that the US$21 billion earmarked for research and scientific infrastructure as part of the stimulus package approved by the U.S. Congress in February 2009 will increase the rents earned by researchers (because the bulk of R&D spending is on salaries) but yield meager commercially consequential results that affect U.S. productivity and growth ("Science Wins $21 Billion" 2009). Technology development is a gradual process, and it is more likely to benefit from a slower increase in spending that is in line with the growth of absorptive capacity and that can be credibly sustained over a long period (Goolsbee 1998; Rotman 2009).[61]

Vision group

Given how little time has elapsed since research in China took off, starting in the late 1990s, another decade may be needed before the accumulating knowledge capital and technological capacity begin to yield a harvest of innovations. In the meantime, Chinese firms might most usefully upgrade their technological game by increasing their familiarity with best practices and determining how to close in on the technological frontier. For this purpose, a desirable step now might be the creation of a "vision group" by each municipality to screen and synthesize the new knowledge about how the leading Chinese and foreign MNCs operating in China are pursuing innovation. Such a vision group might arguably be more effective than additional monetary incentives for R&D because it could help bridge knowledge gaps.[62] The group could help identify and systematize the constellation of factors contributing to firm-level productivity and innovation in the Yangtze Basin area and make these findings widely known so that other firms could benchmark themselves. An important contribution of such a vision group would be to tailor the lessons for specific categories of firms in the Beijing and Shanghai urban regions, taking into account their characteristics and the conditions they face. A "Manufacturing Vision Group" was formed in the United States in 1988, and its investigation of new projects in several innovative companies brought to light a wealth of relevant clues about how some companies create the conditions for serial innovation (Bowen and others 1994).

Successful innovative firms

The municipal authorities in Beijing and Shanghai and the national government are providing leadership, incentives, and resources, but accelerating the development of the innovation system will depend on the business sector. Even as innovation is

---

[61]A waste of research funding is more likely when budgets are rising steeply because the capacity to do good research takes time to catch up (Goolsbee 1998; Rotman 2009).

[62]The notion of developing a vision for urban industry can generate "momentum for change. Visioning opens space between current reality and expectations and so stimulates creative responses. A core element for success is to develop a widespread culture of institutionalized leadership to promote continued self improvement" (Landry 2008: 146).

pushed by increased spending on inputs, it must be pulled by demand and the search for profitable opportunities if it is to be successful in the marketplace. Demand from the business sector, from the government, and from consumers is essential to realizing innovations that must meet the market test.[63] It is difficult for governments using public sector entities and "push" mechanisms alone to bring into existence an innovation system that delivers results. In most respects, the business sector is the part of the urban economy that is already primed to innovate. It has the organization, the exposure to new technologies, and the experience with absorbing, assimilating, and adapting technologies. It has the strongest incentives to innovate and to carefully select from among options, and it benefits immediately from successful innovation. Moreover, many firms are already engaged in R&D and have the infrastructure and teams in place. Firms conducting some R&D are more likely to establish research links with universities. Their support can be invaluable for government initiatives to improve the quality of tertiary education, to strengthen the research capabilities of universities, and to develop a local research culture.

Process innovation by firms provides the preconditions for building an innovation system, because these new processes can be integrated more readily into the operations of a firm and because the returns accrue quickly. Once process innovation, which is generally incremental, gathers momentum and its utility is widely perceived, R&D gains stronger adherence both within and beyond the firm and becomes better integrated into the operations of an entire industry. Thus, encouraging firms to pursue process and product innovations so that it becomes a mainstream activity and generates the demand for R&D is a key task for government policy. Table 6.8 lists the range of available instruments being deployed in China, which is reinforcing their use with exhortations to firms to pursue innovation. International experience underscores the role firms must play. Policies that seek to augment the supply of research in universities and public research institutions with the help of public financing may raise the supply of scientific findings, but they will produce few tangible economic results. Businesses must be convinced of both the utility of innovating and the value of routinizing innovation.

One striking finding from the research on leading international firms is that only a weak relationship seems to exist between the level of R&D spending and the metrics used to measure the success of firms. Increasing R&D can raise the number of patents, but patents do not readily translate into desired business outcomes such as profitability and market share. In fact, excessive spending can be dysfunctional if it throws up barriers to innovation by making scientists into constituents who become wedded to the status quo (Jaruzelski, Dehoff, and Bordia 2005). The most successful innovative companies are ones that can extract the maximum

---

[63]One famous example from the United Kingdom and the United States is the nurturing, testing, and widespread use of jet engines, made possible by their incorporation into aircraft purchased by the military in the two countries.

Table 6.8   Summary of Technology Policy Tools

Direct government funding of R&D	Direct or indirect support for commercialization and production; indirect support for development	Support for learning and diffusion of knowledge and technology
• R&D contracts with private firms (fully funded or cost shared) • R&D contracts and grants with universities • Intramural R&D conducted in government laboratories • R&D contracts with industry-led consortia or collaborations among two or more of the actors listed above	• Patent protection • R&D tax credits • Tax credits or production subsidies for firms to bring new technologies to market • Tax credits or rebates for purchasers of new technologies • Government procurement • Demonstration projects	• Education and training for technicians, engineers, and scientists; business decision makers; and consumers • Codification and diffusion of technical knowledge (screening, interpretation, and validation of R&D results; support for databases) • Technical standard setting • Technology and industrial extension services • Publicity, persuasion, and consumer information (including awards and media campaigns)

Source: Alic, Mowery, and Rubin 2003.

innovation from a moderate R&D budget. These companies share a number of characteristics:

- They have an innovation culture deliberately cultivated and constantly reinforced by top management and an innovation strategy fully aligned with corporate strategy.

- The innovation strategy is comprehensive and keyed to long-run competitiveness and the avoidance of frequent restructuring and changes of direction.[64] It embraces not only products but also process innovation, innovations in marketing, associated services, and the business model of the firm itself. A study of innovative firms by Hargadon and Sutton (2000: 158) found that serial innovators had perfected a "knowledge brokering cycle made up of four intertwined work practices: capturing good ideas, keeping ideas alive, imagining new uses for old ideas, and putting promising concepts to the test." Some research suggests that the firms with the most innovative business models—and not the ones with the innovative products—achieved the highest stock market returns and growth of revenues (Hagel, Brown, and Davison 2008; Jana 2008).

---

[64]The Hay Group finds that companies that have consistent and stable strategies and can avoid paroxysms of restructurings have a better chance of forging and sustaining a reputation for performance ("World's Most Admired Companies" 2009). The experience of General Motors highlights the limited utility of frequent restructurings that leave the firm culture and the fundamental strategic orientation untouched.

- Successful innovators adopt an open and collaborative approach to innovation, recognizing that they cannot excel in more than a few areas of research and need to canvass ideas from a variety of sources.[65]
- The focus of the research efforts and the quality of leadership are critical to success, as is the closeness of interaction between the research wing of the firm and the production and marketing departments.
- Successful innovators tended to have a flatter and nimbler managerial structure and effective procedures for vetting research proposals, tracking progress, and screening out failures (Lynch 2007). These companies also have well-articulated procedures for developing and commercializing products.
- In industrializing countries, the successful innovators leverage their knowledge of the local market to innovate by customizing products. They also innovate in the distribution of products.

Innovative SOEs

One of the issues confronting Shanghai and, to a lesser degree, Beijing is that large companies do most of the applied research and innovation.[66] Such companies are responsible for most of the incremental process and product innovation, and through their own efforts and the marketing of innovations by others, they achieve commercial success for radical advances.[67] Large firms often do not give rise to breakthrough innovations, for reasons delineated by Christensen and Raynor (2003); nevertheless, their development and marketing inputs frequently determine the success of disruptive innovations.[68] Some research by Zucker and

---

[65]Open innovation systems that emphasize tools such as alliances, licensing, consortia and innovation exchanges, and joint ventures assume that innovation is a cumulative process that requires melding a number of different and intersecting technologies. Tetra Pak concluded that it had to draw on the expertise of a number of other companies before it could develop a paperboard container that could be sterilized and was lightweight, rectangular, and easy to hold and pour. Similarly, Cargill managed to perfect a new family of corn-based plastics only when it teamed up with Dow Chemical (Rigby and Zook 2002). During World War II, the large-scale production of penicillin became a reality after U.S. agricultural scientists and technicians who knew a lot about culturing molds became involved.

[66]Huawei Technologies, Datang Telecom Technology, and Zhongxing Telecom lead the way, each devoting about 10 percent of sales revenue to R&D (Cao 2008).

[67]Baumol (2004: 4) notes that "technical progress requires both breakthrough ideas and a protracted follow-up process of cumulative incremental improvement of those breakthroughs with the combined incremental contribution of this second phase often exceeding that of the first." Baumol (2004: 10) continues, "In today's economy, many rival firms use innovation as their main battle weapon with which they protect themselves from competitors. . . . The result is precisely analogous to an arms race."

[68]The spread of electricity and the internal combustion engine was expedited by takeovers that consolidated production in a few large firms that could reap scale advantages and sustain technological advance.

Darby (2007) also shows that notwithstanding the drawbacks of industrial concentration and oligopolistic producers, consumers derive larger welfare gains from the innovativeness of large oligopolistic firms. Most of the bigger firms in the Chinese megacities are wholly or partially state owned, and they dominate both traditional and high-tech subsectors. Hence, in the medium term and perhaps over the longer run as well, SOEs need to take the lead in innovating, which has not been their strength thus far (Muller and Sternberg 2008: 236–37). In fact, for the urban innovation system to find its stride, no substitute exists for the initiative and leadership that large firms with transnational strategies can provide. Government incentives and purchasing policies can encourage innovation,[69] universities and research institutions can assist, and incubators and science parks can nurture new ideas, but SOEs that seek to compete and earn profits on the basis of innovation must provide a good part of the impetus—the demand for innovation—and some of them need to become the innovation hothouses of China. Many more SOEs must be induced to become as dynamic and competitive as China's corporate icons, such as Huawei, Lenovo, ZTE, Shanghai Automotive Industry Corporation, China International Marine Containers, and Wanxiang.[70] A further round of ownership and governance reforms will need to be complemented by changes in management and organization. These changes include trimming the dead weight of diffuse (and sometimes geographically dispersed) unprofitable activities that distract management and aligning incentives in support of profitable innovation. The quality of management and board of director monitoring of management will directly influence the productivity and innovativeness of SOEs.[71] Repeatedly, research findings show that the productivity of firms, their capacity to innovate, the returns on innovation, and their harnessing of IT to enhance competitiveness are correlated with management (N. Bloom, Sadun, and Van Reenen 2007). Augmenting the talent in the managerial ranks of the SOEs is inseparable from other measures to raise long-term performance.[72] Large Chinese firms will have to lead Shanghai and China to an innovative economy that is profitable and sustainable. If the global recession and a slowing of growth in China lead to an industrial shakeout and reduced capacity, then research suggests that well-established older firms that pursue competition strategies

---

[69]For instance, Shanghai has the first maglev trains operated commercially in the world. Future railroad development could be based on this technology (especially for a newer high-speed train system), and as the leader, firms in Shanghai can accumulate tacit knowledge concerning this technology and evolve as global players.

[70]Some evidence suggests that older SOEs are taking a more active interest in upgrading their production capabilities and in innovating (Girma, Gong, and Görg 2009).

[71]For instance, Yusuf, Nabeshima, and Perkins (2005) find that managers circulate among SOEs and reformed SOEs. Reformed SOEs with managers from former SOEs did not see their performance improve.

[72]Better management practices can also lead to more efficient use of resources (N. Bloom and others 2008).

based on innovation are more likely to survive and prosper (Klepper and Simons 2005; Y. Li, Liu, and Ren 2007).

Much like international production networking, the networking of the innovation process is becoming an important source of competitive advantage. This process is exemplified by the example of the iPod, which brought together in one imaginative and extraordinarily successful package innovations in a number of discrete technologies. The revolutionary feature of this product was the skillful yoking of innovative energies of many firms and the use of electronics production networks to locate the manufacture of components first in Taiwan, China, and later in China (Sener and Zhao 2009).[73] It is a lesson for Chinese MNCs, and one firm from Anhui, Chery, has begun applying it in developing cars by integrating design and technology bought from specialist providers worldwide. For innovative firms, acquiring skills to seek and integrate innovation from diverse sources is becoming vital. In-house innovation and in-house production capacity should be seen as only some of the assets a company can draw on. No less significant are the assets to be harnessed from other sources. Winning innovation contests will demand that globally oriented firms look beyond their own walls, think of the innovation possibility set in a far more expansive way, and begin planning their international networking and acquisitions accordingly.

Sustaining firms' R&D operations

Firms can react to a recession by slashing their R&D expenditures in an effort to improve short-term results. In recessions, firms worry about two kinds of failure, "missing the boat" (missing a great opportunity) or "sinking the boat" (bankruptcy) (Dickson and Giglierano 1986). They worry more about the failure of a firm than about the missed opportunity. However, this focus can prove short-sighted: companies that sustain their efforts to innovate improve their chances of bouncing back and increasing their market share. This was the experience of U.S. companies following the recession of 1990 and 1991. Some important innovations have been introduced during recessions, to the advantage of the producing firms. For example, Texas Instruments launched the transistor in 1954, and in 2001, Apple's iPod followed an increase in the company's R&D spending by 42 percent between 1999 and 2002. This learning has induced many MNCs to

---

[73]From the cost breakdown of the video iPod, Apple is estimated to have made a gross profit of about US$80 per unit (from the retail price of US$299). Chinese firms were responsible for assembling all these parts into a complete iPod. However, the value added in China was only about US$4 (Dedrick, Kraemer, and Linden 2008). In 2006, more than 41,000 workers were associated with the production of the iPod. Of this total, China's share was 30 percent, although its share of total wages was 2.4 percent, because most of the workers were engaged in assembly. In contrast, the majority of workers in Japan, Korea, and the United States were classified as professionals and earned significantly higher wages (Linden, Dedrick, and Kraemer 2009).

protect their R&D efforts from the recession that began in 2008. Companies such as Intel, Microsoft, Cisco, and Texas Instruments raised their R&D between 2007 and 2008. Procter & Gamble is increasing its spending on new engineering and manufacturing technologies, and other companies are resisting pressures to cut back (Edwards and Burrows 2009; "How Procter & Gamble" 2009; Scheck and Glader 2009). However, if slower growth persists through 2010, R&D might succumb to a sense of uncertainty, and more companies will be induced to scale back (N. Bloom 2007). Minimizing such cutbacks among firms in China may require going beyond the fiscal incentives currently extended to firms and offering targeted subsidies time limited for one to two years to firms in the technology-intensive subsectors. This strategy would offset the uncertainty firms face and enable them to husband valuable intangible intellectual capital that takes years to accumulate.

In addition, a significant expansion of the municipal governments' extension and product development services to small and medium-size enterprises may be desirable. Such services can provide a means of transferring valuable technical and problem-solving skills to industry; they can also be vehicles for absorbing a large number of temporarily unemployed skilled and technical workers and channeling their expertise into value-adding activities. Such a program could be modeled on the Fraunhofer Institutes in Germany or the Advanced Technology Program (ATP) introduced by the National Institute for Standards and Technology in the United States.[74] It would confer three additional benefits: (a) it would increase the skill intensity of the small and medium-size enterprise sector and encourage R&D activity in firms that rarely engage in research, (b) it would give university graduates an opportunity to acquire practical experience and provide job opportunities (Bramwell and Wolfe 2008; Lundvall 2007), and (c) it would partially neutralize the disincentive effects of the economic downturn for students contemplating a future in science and engineering or in R&D.

Health Care as an Urban Growth Pole

A health care industry that has links to manufacturing industries such as the pharmaceutical industry, diagnostic equipment manufacturers, and manufacturers of implants and high-tech electronic instruments and other IT services

---

[74]Darby, Zucker, and Wang (2003: 5–6) explain the advantages of the ATP as follows: "It has a goal of encouraging collaboration among firms and between firms and universities and other organizations in the U.S. innovation system. ATP encourages the formation of JVs [joint ventures], providing potentially higher award levels and more years of funding, and encourages JV members to establish governance structures for internal management of JVs. . . . ATP in effect opens up boundaries where the ATP project impinges, encouraging joint governance and reasonable access by all JV members of intellectual property created within the JV. . . . The firms not only have more financial resources through ATP funding but also have changed social relationships. These relationships provide intellectual capital and social contacts that add value through learning processes."

Figure 6.2 Components of the Boston Life Sciences Cluster

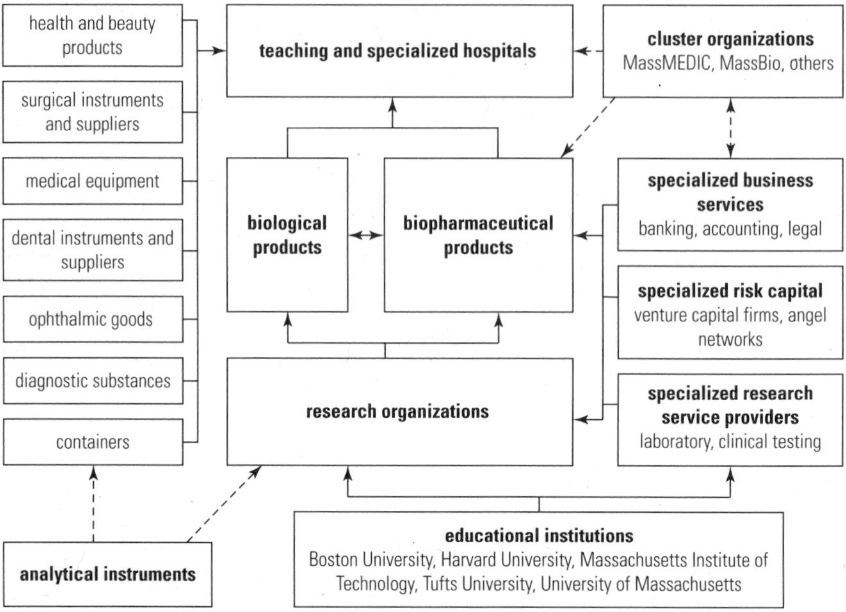

Source: Porter 2008a.

providers[75] can be a source of local employment, substantial value added, innovation at many levels, and exports of services and complex manufactures. In addition, a health care industry provides direct social benefits to the population of the municipality. A competitive health care industry in conjunction with tertiary education and high-tech manufacturing subsectors could create an economic powerhouse with long-run growth potential (see figure 6.2).[76]

With an aging population, Shanghai can anticipate strong demand for elder care and chronic diseases in particular. This kind of demand can be used to reshape the health care system in Shanghai so that care providers are linked to and benefit from university-based research on new drugs, traditional medicine, bioengineering, bioinformatics, robotics, and imaging technologies, to name just a few of the research fields that are helping to enhance the quality of medical

---

[75]The technological revolution that is sweeping the medical sector as a result of the confluence of biology, information, engineering, and material technologies is described in "Medicine Goes Digital" (2009).

[76]Porter and Teisberg (2006) discuss the competition strategies for health care providers and programs that could enlarge the benefits for users. See also West and Miller (2009), who examine some of the constraints on wider use of digital technologies in medicine.

care.[77] Health care, much like telecommunications, is also increasingly a capital-intensive service that relies on an array of diagnostic and imaging devices,[78] implants, instrumentation, and IT equipment. Many of these are high-value, knowledge-intensive manufactures that are growth areas for Shanghai's electronics, new materials, precision engineering, pharmaceutical, and biotechnology industries.[79] Because each of these fields attracts new starts, they look to venture capitalists for early-stage and mezzanine financing.

With the help of suitable incentives, health care can become the core of a flourishing cluster comprising university hospitals, high-tech manufacturing firms, research centers, and providers of risk capital as well as other services. Experience from the United States suggests that such a cluster may not form spontaneously but may require incentives from the government,[80] coupled with coordination among a variety of producers and providers of health services, insurance companies, and agencies responsible for standard setting, certification, and regulation. Businesses in New York have difficulty in obtaining long-term leases from landlords, whose sights are frequently fixed on the possibility of converting their land to residential uses if prices rise. More surprisingly, obtaining venture financing in New York is far from

---

[77]Fudan University created its own medical center by merging with Shanghai Medical University in 2000. Shanghai Jiao Tong University also established a medical school and merged it with Shanghai No. 2 Medical University in 2005.

[78]Improvements can be made in a number of areas. One promising area is miniaturization of magnetic resonance imaging (MRI). Researchers so far have been able to miniaturize a nuclear magnetic resonance device, which is quite similar to MRI (Blümich 2008).

[79]The development of the biotechnology industry started with the "863" plan in 1986, and the industry was given a high priority in the Torch program in 1988. The drive to develop biotechnology in Shanghai started in 1996, when agreement was reached among the Ministry of Science and Technology, the Ministry of Health, the Chinese Academy of Science, the State Food and Drug Administration, and the Shanghai Municipal Government to build the National Shanghai Biotechnology and Pharmaceutical Industry Base (NSBPIB) in the Shanghai Zhangjian Hi-Tech Park (ZJHP). NSBPIB influenced existing biotechnology-pharmaceutical entities, such as the Chinese Human Genome Center, the Institute of Materia Medica, and the Shanghai Chinese Medical University, to move into the park. More than 8,000 biotech-related researchers work in the park, and the government is actively courting returnees to add to the local human capital base. In 2003, there were 50 biotech companies founded by the returnees in ZJHP, accounting for 10 percent of all start-ups in the park (Su and Hung 2009). However, the biotechnology industry faces an uncertain future (Pisano 2006).

[80]New biotech start-ups in ZJHP depend heavily on government funding through the Shanghai Commission of Science and Technology, Shanghai Venture Capital, and the Ministry of Science and Technology. In addition, tax incentives are given to R&D institutions in Shanghai. They are exempt from business tax if they engage in technology transfer, technology development, technological consultation, and technical services to biotech firms (Su and Hung 2009).

easy, and high-tech industries have had a hard time taking root even though the city's many universities are centers of research in the life sciences, for example, and produce thousands of graduates with the skills needed by a biopharmaceuticals cluster. This example brings out the difficulty of reviving complex manufacturing activities in a city that has deindustrialized and come to depend on services.

The point to be emphasized here is that the gains for the city in terms of growth and employment can be greatly magnified if the links from health care to manufacturing and university-based research can be realized within the geographic confines of the city. Medical-manufacturing-research clusters have great promise and can become prolific exporters of state-of-the-art medical services as well as complex high-tech and profitable products.

Quality of Education and Tertiary Education as a Leading Sector

Premier Wen Jiabao has observed that China must "cultivate large numbers of innovative talents [through] a free environment to enable [students] to develop creative thinking and critical thinking. . . . To raise a question or to discover a problem is more important than solving a problem" (cited in interview by Xin and Stone 2008). The competitiveness of industry and services in the two megacities, the capacity to innovate, and the pace of diversification into new activities will be a function most directly of the quality of education. Those individuals with more education of better quality have a higher probability of starting a technology-intensive business, hiring skilled workers, and engaging in innovation.[81] Workers who have a solid grounding in the sciences and in engineering and have good analytic problem-solving and teamworking capabilities require less remedial training once they join a firm and can more fruitfully contribute to incremental process innovations, which are frequently the lifeblood of competitiveness. Interviews with firms in Shanghai suggest that one of the major hurdles they face relates to the workforce.[82] University graduates enter the job market with a grounding in theory but with little practical knowledge and few analytical skills. This problem is experienced in many countries and addressed perhaps most comprehensively by Singapore.[83] Employers ascribe

---

[81]Entrepreneurial performance is associated with the quality of formal schooling (Berry and Glaeser 2005; Glaeser 2007; van der Sluis, van Praag, and Vijverberg 2008).

[82]Lack of industry experience, a "big picture mindset," creativity, and the ability to "think outside the box" were some of the weaknesses noted. Firms also did not cite education and training as the distinguishing feature of graduates from the best schools. Nor did they comment on readiness to work long hours (Wadhwa and others 2007; authors' interviews with firm representatives).

[83]Singapore established its first vocational institution in 1964. By 1972, it had nine institutions, training more than 4,000 students a year. As the economic structure became more skill intensive, so did the general education and skill level of vocational education. The Institute of Technical Education caters mainly to those who are not academically inclined and equips them with necessary technical skills in close collaboration with

(*continued on next page*)

it to continuing reliance on rote learning and on training to take tests; to the knowledge and pedagogical techniques of many of the teaching staff, which could be seriously outdated; and to the low quality of textbooks, the limited attention given to practical training and interaction with potential employers, and the obsolescence of lab and testing equipment that is available to the students. The massive expansion in tertiary enrollment has exacerbated all these factors. Together they combine to constrain the productivity, innovativeness, and entrepreneurial capacity of the workforce, which is the single most important asset of both Beijing and Shanghai.

Some suggestions from Europe for improving the performance of universities are of relevance to Shanghai and Beijing. These suggestions are performance criteria that include both the quality of graduates and graduation rates, diversified and shorter diploma courses that give students more choice and the option of deciding when to stop, and greater autonomy for universities (Boarini and Martins 2008). The emphasis of tertiary education policies supporting innovation ought not to be limited to enhancing science, technology, engineering, and mathematics skills but should seek to produce graduates who are versatile, with "unique skills and a penchant for sustaining their excellence through career-long self-education" (Flanagan 2006).[84] In a world where technology is continually evolving, such an attribute would be of enduring value.

The importance of creating and fully using the research potential of Chinese universities cannot be minimized. This task calls for attention to the design of institutions and a focus on the quality of teaching and research so as to build a tradition of scientific excellence. It can entail autonomy in hiring a staff, in determining salaries and incentive mechanisms, and in managing budgets. It can depend on the capacity to compete for first-rate talent from across the nation and around the world. It is strongly influenced by the visionary leadership of key university administrators. A comparison between American and European universities reveals starkly how these factors influence the quality of university faculty and the value of the research conducted.[85]

(*continued from previous page*)

industries and with the help of the latest equipment, some of it donated by industry. Singaporean experience shows that good vocational education costs 50 percent more per year than general schooling (Law 2009). However, the Singaporean experience with vocational education has proven hard to replicate in Korea and Indonesia, for example, partly because parents continue to prefer general to vocational education and partly because—as in Indonesia—returns to vocational education are lower even though the cost per public school student is 28 percent higher (Newhouse and Suryadarma 2009).

[84]See also World Bank (2008a) on the thinking with regard to tertiary education policies.

[85]When he was president of Harvard University, Larry Summers (2004: 72) observed that the success of the leading American universities derived from their "abiding commitment to the authority of ideas rather than the idea of authority," to their "commitment to seeking truth through contrasting positions," to "the idea of skeptical inquiry," and to vigorous competition "for the best students, the best young faculty, and the allegiance of donors."

Table 6.9 Number of Highly Cited Researchers, 1980–99

Discipline	United States	EU17	EU17 without United Kingdom
Agricultural sciences	113	84	64
Biology and biochemistry	138	40	29
Chemistry	143	72	51
Clinical medicine	161	36	17
Computer science	226	45	35
Ecology-environment	192	73	48
Economics-business	263	24	11
Engineering	138	32	24
Geosciences	219	70	43
Immunology	201	81	66
Materials sciences	159	50	33
Mathematics	221	75	53
Microbiology	159	71	49
Molecular biology and genetics	197	63	47
Neuroscience	182	73	39
Pharmacology	93	121	73
Physics	148	74	59
Plant and animal science	147	100	59
Psychology-psychiatry	228	23	5
Social sciences, general	295	11	3
Space sciences	206	74	45
Total	3,829	1,292	853

Source: Bauwens, Mion, and Thisse 2008.
Note: The EU17 are the 15 states that composed the European Union prior to the expansion of May 1, 2004, plus nonmembers Norway and Switzerland.

By identifying the top 250 most highly cited researchers in each of 21 scientific disciplines, Bauwens, Mion, and Thisse (2008) were able to show that American universities accounted for two-thirds of the total from 1981 to 1999 and European universities for only 22 percent (see table 6.9). Two other findings are also notable. First, universities in the United States have a significant edge over European universities in every field except pharmacology. Second, the top 25 institutions with the most highly cited researchers accounted for 30 percent of the total, and all but 3 were in the United States. Clearly, American universities are contributing to inventiveness, and they are able to do so because they have built up a durable tradition based on the excellence of both teaching and research as well as other institutional differences.[86] For instance, Aghion (2009: 23) observes that

> both Anglo-American and Scandinavian countries (plus Switzerland) perform relatively well, whereas continental countries (particularly France, Italy, and Spain) perform relatively poorly. Interestingly, unlike their Anglo-American counterparts, Swiss or Swedish universities are mostly public, charge low tuitions, and are not very selective when accepting applicants at the undergraduate level. However, good performance always relies on high budgets per student combined with budget and hiring autonomy. . . . The main findings are that (i) higher autonomy is more growth-enhancing or patent-enhancing in states that are closer to the technological frontier, and (ii) autonomy and spending are complementary in generating higher growth or higher patenting in the state.

Incentives and encouragement to university faculty to conduct applied research with the potential of yielding commercial outcomes need to be carefully calibrated to not divert attention and resources from the core mission of the leading research universities. First, Chinese universities, many of which have expanded enrollment, need to ensure the quality of their teaching and research by building up the caliber and experience of their faculties.[87] Equipping students with up-to-date theoretical knowledge and soft skills that employers value must be the principal objective of the university.[88] Strengthening the capacity to conduct basic research to generate new knowledge, which the private sector does little of, is a second major objective requiring investment in graduate and postdoctoral programs. For this, universities need a faculty with the requisite skills to lead and manage significant research projects, a well-equipped laboratory infrastructure, and leadership at the apex of the university as well as at department level. The evolution of the field of biotechnology vividly illustrates the contributions of fundamental research in several seemingly unrelated fields conducted over a period of many years. Biotechnology owes its current eminence to breakthroughs in theoretical biology, in imaging techniques arising from advances in high-energy physics, and in computing technologies. Many of these advances were the results of university-based research financed by the U.S. government through the National Science Foundation and the National Institutes of Health. According to Lawlor (2003: 30), "It is the long-term nurturing of the broad basic science base that has produced the U.S. competitive edge in biotechnology [with the help] of a non-centralized government funded but largely university performed basic research."

---

[86]This finding does not mean that all these researchers are Americans. The data are based on the addresses of the institutions with which the researchers are affiliated.

[87]Salmi (2009) describes the attributes of world-class universities. See also Altbach (2003) and Levin, Jeong, and Ou (2006).

[88]Simon and Cao (2009) also note insufficient soft skills among graduates and cite the need for creativity and a willingness to take risks, which are intrinsic to entrepreneurship.

Applied research and its commercialization through licensing, consulting, and start-ups can be a third objective; however, it should not detract from the first two. In fact, the success of university entrepreneurship depends on the university's reputation in providing high-quality education in important research fields. Very few universities in the United States—perhaps no more than five—derive a significant income from licensing of research findings and royalties. Most do not even manage to cover the operating expenses of their technology licensing offices from the commercialization of research. The equity stakes universities acquire in start-ups are modest and have frequently proven to be worthless (Lerner 2005).[89] Start-ups in fields directly linked to basic and upstream applied research in universities, such as biopharmaceuticals and nanotechnology, can be a benefit, but the risks are high and the payoff is uncertain (Feldman 2003).[90] Moreover, as indicated by Miner and others (2001: 140–41), "Efforts [by the university] to stimulate new ventures may generate short-term prosperity but may ultimately harm the university. For example, . . . incentives [could] lead productive faculty who previously generated streams of inventions to leave the university to create new firms. Over time, this process could ultimately destroy the university's underlying capacity to generate new knowledge and could leave the university with the faculty members least likely to produce sustained inventions." Even the premier research universities in Beijing and Shanghai must first augment their core functions of providing world-class training and conducting world-class research before embarking on technological entrepreneurship.[91] The first two are vital for the longer-term success and technological evolution of their respective economies and to the crafting of an intellectual climate conducive to innovation. Technological entrepreneurship can become a minor source of revenue for a few research universities and a conduit for knowledge transfer from the leading institutions, but only after they have built up strong research programs. Although universities in both cities are engaging in research in photonics, nanotechnology, new materials, and biotechnology, some years may pass before they can contribute significantly to advances in knowledge. Simon and Cao (2009: 99–100) observe that a small fraction of Chinese researchers have master's-level or doctoral qualifications, and the overall quality improvements have not been significant even after factoring in returnees from abroad, whose numbers did not exceed 10 percent at independent R&D

---

[89]University venture funds in the United States have a poor track record, and few have reached maturity (Lerner 2005).

[90]Chinese universities are also discovering the downside of start-ups and distancing themselves from direct ownership and responsibilities (Zhou 2008).

[91]China's effort to develop world-class universities is spearheaded by the National 211 Project introduced in 1997 (Sigurdson 2008). On the importance of basic research, see Zhu and Xu (2008).

institutions.[92] This observation is reflected in the citations garnered by Chinese publications in scientific journals, which have remained at about the 13th place. Moreover, the research conducted in Chinese laboratories falls well short of cutting edge, because quality and creativity still lag and because the kind of scientific leadership required to catapult Chinese research into the front ranks is quite sparse. This situation is apparent from the performance of researchers in the field of biology, which has received a substantial volume of resources. According to Simon and Cao (2009: 318), only about 500 biologists in China can be classified as "productive"; that is, they each published at least eight papers in a journal with an impact factor of at least two, including at least one in a journal with an impact factor of five. Likewise, although China is investing heavily in research on nanotechnology, the number of specialists in the several disciplines that contribute to nanotechnology is very small, which also affects the training of new researchers.

A global recession that is forcing leading universities around the world to retrench some of their research endeavors and to look for partners presents an opportunity to launch two or three broad-ranging blue-sky research projects composed of cross-national teams with researchers in Chinese megacities codirecting the activities and playing a significant role. The research should be of long-term consequence, with spillovers for other areas, and the subject matter could be drawn from the physical or social sciences. The advantages of such research at this point are first to engage a sizable number of researchers in challenging, high-level, collaborative endeavors with potentially large payoffs. Second, through collaboration, such research will build much-needed experience and analytical skills among young researchers, thereby helping to raise the quality of teaching and research in universities. By staying focused and building up their research capital and teaching capabilities, some universities will raise the human capital coefficients of the Beijing and Shanghai urban regions, better service the needs of industry for skills, and begin building fruitful links with industry.

By strengthening tertiary education and promoting university research, both Beijing and Shanghai can greatly enlarge the benefits to the growing knowledge-intensive segments of their economies. Furthermore, it could make the university sector attractive as a service provider for foreign students, some of whom would supplement the local talent pool, and for foreign companies wanting to enter research partnerships or to outsource their research. Through a variety of channels, the education sector can boost growth in the megacities and build resilience against shocks affecting individual industries.

---

[92]Of the 1.39 million Chinese who went abroad to study between 1978 and 2008, only 28 percent have returned, and they tend to be ranked lower in terms of quality, achievements, and caliber. Hence, future progress in deepening the innovation systems in Beijing and Shanghai will depend in part on attracting the more able members of the diaspora ("China: Returnees" 2009).

An Innovative City

Throughout the world, most innovation is occurring in a few large cities, and a lot hangs on what kind of people live in the city and visit the city; how they interact, float, and exchange ideas; and how they perceive opportunities for fulfilling their ambitions. Large cities have the edge over smaller ones in terms of employment opportunities and avenues for pursuing entrepreneurial options. Those open cities that attract many visitors and migrants from within the country and abroad are doubly advantaged by the influx and circulation of diverse ideas and talent. As E. L. Glaeser (2009: 50) notes, "Attracting and retaining skilled people is a critical task for local governments." Moreover, the experience of the United States and of European countries suggests that consumer amenities—theaters, galleries, museums, bars and restaurants, public spaces, and green spaces—in conjunction with public services are the most effective means of building the skilled workforce that is invaluable under any set of circumstances but especially when industrial change is in the offing. Phillips (2008: 731) presciently observes, "Most cities are the longest running examples of large open source projects. Cities were open source long before Linux." Cities that steadily augment the quality of the sociocultural environment, cultural diversity, amenities, and physical aesthetics are triply advantaged because talented and discriminating knowledge workers gravitate to the city, and some may choose to live there. Cities can also instill the culture of inquiry and interest in sciences by actively promoting science-oriented conferences, fairs, and exhibitions.

Beijing and Shanghai enjoy the advantages of size, and they are magnets for migrants and visitors from overseas. Moreover, they are cities in the throes of change, and they have the luxury few older cities enjoy of creating sociocultural environments and urban aesthetics that will buttress the productive innovation system each is eager to create (see, for example, Florida 2005, 2008).[93]

In China and in many other middle-income countries, insufficient attention to forward-looking urban planning that is tuned to the imperatives of global warming is leading, in one major city after another, to single-function zones, emphasis on automobile mobility, urban sprawl (and dormitory suburbs), wide boulevards designed for vehicles, hundreds of residential tower blocks with negligible recreational amenities, shopping malls, gated communities, and segregation by income groups—with the poor concentrated in squalid, decaying

---

[93] A continuing adjustment of the *hukou* (household registration) system might be needed to ensure the flow of high-quality human capital from elsewhere in China and from abroad. See C. C. Fan (2008) for current issues surrounding the *hukou* system. Shanghai's fourth reform of the system, announced in February 2009, took another step toward easing the constraints on obtaining resident status.

ghettos often (but not always) on the periphery of the city. Instead, the dynamic global city of tomorrow[94] needs (a) to be compact so as to facilitate energy-frugal public transportation,[95] encourage a healthier lifestyle that promotes walking and bicycling, and reduce emissions of greenhouse gases and other pollutants;[96] (b) to be industrially balanced; (c) to be well connected nationally and with international urban nodes; and (d) to house numerous mixed-use neighborhoods teeming with street life (such neighborhoods maximize use of land and infrastructure and minimize criminal activity)[97] and cultural and recreational amenities that enhance the quality of urban living.[98] Together these can make the urban experience, in Richard Sennett's words, "a source of mutual strength rather than a source of mutual estrangement and 'civic bitterness'" (Burdett and Sudjic 2008). Leading global cities have only some of these attributes.[99] Many are struggling to make density more appealing and to redesign and reengineer the city so as to usher in a "greener" lifestyle because these attributes, among others, will determine whether they can retain a skilled labor force and initiate a cycle generating a succession of knowledge-intensive industries integral to the urban dynamic.

---

[94] According to the Nobel laureate Paul Krugman (2009), the city that in his view most closely resembles what a future city ought to be is Hong Kong, China. In his opinion, "Hong Kong, with its incredible cluster of tall buildings stacked up the slope of a mountain, is the way the future was supposed to look. The future—the way I learned it from science-fiction movies—was supposed to be Manhattan squared: vertical, modernistic, art decoish."

[95] Many believe that the current demand for oil is not sustainable in the future. As a result, the price of oil will continue to rise, although the price dipped in 2008 because of the global recession. In a world where oil (and other energy sources) are scarce, cities need to be compact to reduce the use of automobiles and to be more energy frugal (Rubin 2009).

[96] William Whyte's (2009) study of street life, conducted in the 1980s and still of relevance, underscored the importance of carefully designing public spaces and street furniture. The renewed emphasis on the role of the bicycle brings back memories of a time when Chinese streets were crowded with bicycles only.

[97] The philosopher Alain de Botton (2009: 52) remarks that "urban planners always lose sight of the benefits of chaos. . . . [C]ities laid out on apparently rational grounds, where different specialized facilities—houses, shopping centers, offices—are separated from one another across a vast terrain connected by motorways deprive their inhabitants of the pleasures of incidental discoveries and presuppose that we march from place to place with a sense of unflagging purpose."

[98] Surveys of life satisfactions in China identify unemployment and pollution as two main sources of unhappiness among its urban residents (Appleton and Song 2008). The housing prices across cities in China are influenced by pollution. Housing prices in cities with less air pollution are higher than in those with more severe air pollution (S. Zheng, Kahn, and Liu 2009).

[99] For example, the griminess of London and its decaying infrastructure are undermining the city's appeal.

Table 6.10 Selected Regional Science and Innovation-Related Strategies Adopted in the United Kingdom

Number	Strategy
1	Grow and maintain world-class infrastructure for the academic and industry base.
2	Develop, attract, and retain high-quality people.
3	Close the R&D funding gap between the private and public sectors.
4	Promote the image of the region as a vibrant hotbed of scientific endeavor.
5	Create a culture for "open" innovation.
6	Attract and retain people of the highest caliber to work in the region's universities, businesses, and public authorities.
7	Create a region where the knowledge base, businesses, and the political community work in enhanced harmony to deliver sustainable economic growth through innovation.

Source: OECD 2008.

In response to the declining economic vigor of some once-thriving urban centers (such as Detroit), a number of OECD countries have embarked on regional innovation strategies, defined visions, passed innovation laws, established innovation funds (OECD 2008), tested and mainstreamed ideas, and created institutions. Often, pressures released by the decline of existing industries catalyzed these strategies (OECD 2008). Local efforts attempt bottom-up approaches aimed at making city regions innovative through spatial planning for facilities (such as science parks and incubators), cluster networking support, and special programs with higher education institutions (see table 6.10).

In their haste to modernize, China's megacities run the risk of losing sight of the mistakes made by others and of insufficiently emphasizing objectives whose importance is only now being perceived:[100] compactness, low greenhouse gas[101] emissions and resilience in the face of climate change being among the most

---

[100]Planning, designing, and cross-linking of public spaces are frequently ignored to the detriment of the urban environment. Cities such as Barcelona and Munich have enriched the urban milieu by making public spaces an integral part of their planning efforts (Landry 2008).

[101]With buildings consuming 30 to 40 percent of the energy used in cities, close attention to the site layout, building design, observance of codes, type of materials used, and technology of heating and cooling will be vital (Glicksman, Norford, and Greden 2001). Most buildings in China fall short of desirable standards of construction quality and insulation. This problem suggests that mechanisms for enforcing standards, codes, and bylaws through effective judicial processes might deserve attention. That progress is in the air is suggested by a comment from the chief executive officer of Nokia that Beijing provided his company with one of the most environmentally friendly buildings in the world ("Ask the Boss" 2009: 86).

important.[102] "Urban deserts" do not breed innovation.[103] And cities that are resistant to in-migration and diversity quickly lose dynamism and entrepreneurial vigor, which in time can result in declining growth.

Many cities are aspiring to be "creative"; few will succeed. Landry (2008: 244) lists several attributes of a creatively viable and vital city. They include "critical mass [of talent]; diversity; accessibility; linkage and synergy; competiveness; and organizational capacity." For Beijing and Shanghai to emerge as trendsetters in China and in the world, they must attract innovative companies and provide a crucible for testing and selecting concepts and products. Both cities will need to compete for a cosmopolitan creative class because they can offer choices and are rich in opportunities.[104]

The transition to a creative central place in the global economy demands committed local leadership and action at three levels: the visual, the intellectual, and the strategic. Physically, Shanghai, for instance, needs to strike a happy balance between local distinctiveness and enduring and vital global chic. In Puxi, Shanghai has the physical space for achieving this goal through inspired efforts to build dynamic neighborhoods fused by a well-planned transportation infrastructure.

Intellectual leadership will derive from the excellence of universities and think tanks; their physical presence in the heart of the city feeds and stirs piquancy into the sophistication of urban culture. In cities such as London, Philadelphia, and New York, the location and the quality of the universities have added immeasurably to the richness of the discourse. This requirement means avoiding a narrow focus on technology development by key universities and engaging more broadly and expansively with the sciences as well as the arts. In both Beijing and Shanghai, the convening of seminars, workshops, and science festivals catering to a general audience would further the process of engagement between the creative class and the general urban population, thereby enabling the culture of creativity to strike deeper roots.[105] Writing on the celebration of science in New York, Lawrence

---

[102]Leman (2009) describes the challenges Shanghai faces from heat waves, storms, and rising sea levels. See also Newman, Beatley, and Boyer (2009) on making cities resilient.

[103]Since 1993, Shanghai has experienced a massive construction wave—so much that the municipal government has needed to print a new map of the city every three months (H. Lu 2004).

[104]Jean-Claude Biver, chief executive officer of Hublot, speaks for most businesspeople when he maintains that a city must address the "quality of environment, quality of the air, quality of the traffic, good communication, a strong and effective university, good recruitment possibilities, important artistic activities, and good connections" ("Ask the Boss" 2009: 86).

[105]Shenzhen began hosting an International High-Tech Achievements Fair in the fall of 1999, and Beijing convenes an International High-Tech Industries week in May each year (P. Fan and Watanabe 2006: 314).

Krauss (2008: 643) observes that "what all of these science festivals have done is to let people indulge their natural inner fascination with the world around us in a context that is neither intimidating nor culturally remote, as a university lecture hall too often seems."

The grand visual characteristics of Beijing need to be followed up by audacious strategic initiatives that mobilize its increasingly formidable intellectual assets by crafting a network culture at the neighborhood level, put Beijing on the map, and enable it to begin influencing the international tempo of innovation—and not only through the scale of its construction activities.

The global cities of today are all reinventing themselves or rethinking their development strategies to sustain or enhance their economic prospects and to attract the skilled workforce needed for new industries. Many global cities have become monosectoral service-based economies without any emerging leading subsectors. To survive, these cities will need to reverse decades of shortsighted decision making, zoning,[106] land development, and transportation policies and to prepare for a harsher economic environment made more challenging by an aging workforce, rising energy and resource costs, and a changing climate.[107] These cities are not the models for future global cities, but they do offer lessons on the desirable industrial structures and capabilities that have been described.

Concluding Observations

This study's findings lead to the following five broad policy messages on medium- to long-term growth strategy:

- Maintain and upgrade the manufacturing base in key areas, more so in the case of Shanghai than of Beijing.
- Augment the research capital of the city by focusing universities on teaching and basic research that will deepen knowledge.
- Develop service industries, such as education and health, that have spillovers for manufacturing.
- Attend to the cultural and social amenities of the city so that it attracts and holds knowledge workers.
- Continuously evaluate current incentive policies to incrementally improve and weed out those that are not yielding results and that tax municipal implementation capacity and drain resources.

---

[106]For example, floor area ratio rules might need to be periodically adjusted and minimum ratios introduced along with maximum ones (Joshi and Kono 2009).

[107]Coastal cities will need to prepare for rising sea levels by minimizing land subsidies associated with the pumping of groundwater, by building dikes and pumping facilities, and by using natural passive defenses such as wetlands and mangrove forests (Day and others 2007; UN-HABITAT 2008).

In addition to longer-term objectives, development strategy needs to address near-term objectives. First, industries that will be the drivers of future growth, especially those dependent on the initiative and energies of smaller firms, should be given the support needed to weather the recession that began in 2008 and the incentives to consolidate and improve competitiveness by accumulating knowledge capital. In this context, Chinese firms might step up their efforts to acquire equipment, tacit knowledge, and IP from technologically advanced foreign firms that are going out of business.

Second, an economic slowdown is the time to accelerate the exit from declining labor-intensive industries and to reallocate those land and human resources to other uses with a higher payoff. In particular, this effort will require retraining workers made redundant by sunsetting industries. Freeing and transferring resources will stimulate productivity in addition to reducing the excess capacity in a number of light-manufacturing industries. It will also lessen urban sprawl.

How the two cities can weigh and assimilate the suggestions presented in this book will depend on a careful assessment of longer-term challenges and of the efficacy of policies currently in place. Such an assessment should be a part of the future research agenda.

References

Abu-Lughod, Janet L. 1999. *New York, Chicago, Los Angeles: America's Global Cities.* Minneapolis: University of Minnesota Press.

Adams, James D., and Roger J. Clemmons. 2008. "The Origins of Industrial Scientific Discoveries." NBER Working Paper 13823, National Bureau of Economic Research, Cambridge, MA.

Aghion, Philippe. 2009. "Growth and Education." Commission on Growth and Development Working Paper 56, World Bank, Washington, DC.

Aghion, Philippe, John Van Reenen, and Luigi Zingales. 2009. "Innovation and Institutional Ownership." CEPR Discussion Paper 7195, Centre for Economic Policy Research, London.

Aitken, Brian J., Gordon H. Hanson, and Ann E. Harrison. 1997. "Spillovers, Foreign Investment, and Export Behavior." *Journal of International Economics* 43 (1–2): 103–32.

Aitken, Brian J., and Ann E. Harrison. 1999. "Do Domestic Firms Benefit from Direct Foreign Investment? Evidence from Venezuela." *American Economic Review* 89 (3): 605–18.

Alic, John A., David C. Mowery, and Edward S. Rubin. 2003. "U.S. Technology and Innovation Policies: Lessons for Climate Change." Pew Center on Global Climate Change, Arlington, VA.

Allen, Franklin, Rajesh Chakrabarti, Sankar De, Jun Qian, and Meijun Qian. 2007. "The Financial System Capacities of China and India." Working Paper, University of Pennsylvania, Philadelphia.

Altbach, Philip G. 2003. "The Costs and Benefits of World-Class Universities." *International Higher Education* 33 (Fall). http://www.bc.edu/bc_org/avp/soe/cihe/newsletter/News33/text003.htm.

Amsden, Alice H., and Wan-Wen Chu. 2003. *Beyond Late Development: Taiwan's Upgrading Policies.* Cambridge, MA: MIT Press.

Ang, James B. 2008. "A Survey of Recent Developments in the Literature of Finance and Growth." *Journal of Economic Surveys* 22 (3): 536–76.

Appleseed. 2003. *Engines of Economic Growth: The Economic Impact of Boston's Eight Research Universities on the Metropolitan Boston Area.* Boston, MA: Appleseed.

Appleton, Simon, and Lina Song. 2008. "Life Satisfaction in Urban China: Components and Determinants." *World Development* 36 (11): 2325–40.

Aral, Sinan, Erik Brynjolfsson, and Marshall Van Alstyne. 2007. "Information, Technology, and Information Worker Productivity." NBER Working Paper 13172, National Bureau of Economic Research, Cambridge, MA.

Arnold, Martin. 2009. "U.K. Government under Fire on Venture Capital." 2009. *Financial Times*, September 2.

"Ask the Boss." 2009. *Monocle* 3 (25). Winkontent: London.

Au, Chung-Chung, and J. Vernon Henderson. 2006a. "Are Chinese Cities Too Small?" *Review of Economic Studies* 73 (2): 549–76.

———. 2006b. "How Immigration Restrictions Limit Agglomeration and Productivity in China." *Journal of Development Economics* 80 (2): 350–88.

Auerswald, Philip, and Lewis Branscomb. 2003. "Spin-Offs and Start-Ups: The Role of the Entrepreneur in Technology-Based Innovation." In *The Emergence of Entrepreneurship Policy: Governance, Start-Ups, and Growth in the Knowledge Economy*, ed. David M. Hart, 61–91. Cambridge, U.K.: Cambridge University Press.

———. 2008. "Research and Innovation in a Networked World." *Technology in Society* 30 (3–4): 339–47.

Avnimelech, Gil, Martin Kenney, and Morris Teubal. 2004. "Building Venture Capital Industries: Understanding the U.S. and Israeli Experience." BRIE Working Paper 160, Berkeley Roundtable on the International Economy, University of California, Berkeley. http://repositories.cdlib.org/brie/BRIEWP160.

Bair, Jennifer. 2009. *Frontiers of Community Chain Research.* Stanford, CA: Stanford University Press.

Bairoch, Paul. 1991. *Cities and Economic Development: From the Dawn of History to the Present.* Chicago: University of Chicago Press.

Baldwin, Richard, and Simon Evenett. 2008. "Restoring the G20's Credibility on Trade: Plan B and the WTO Trade Talks." VoxEU.org. http://www.voxeu.org/index.php?q=node/2692.

Bao, Qun, and Jiayu Yang. 2009. "Is Financial Development Another Source of Comparative Advantage? Evidence from China." *China and World Economy* 17 (2): 15–34.

Barme, Geremie R. 2008. *The Forbidden City.* Cambridge, MA: Harvard University Press.

Barrios, Salvador, Luisito Bertinelli, and Eric Strobl. 2006. "Coagglomeration and Spillovers." *Regional Science and Urban Economics* 36 (4): 467–81.

Baumol, William J. 1967. "Macroeconomics of Unbalanced Growth: The Anatomy of Urban Crisis." *American Economic Review* 57 (3): 419–20.

———. 2004. "Education for Innovation: Entrepreneurial Breakthroughs vs. Corporate Incremental Improvements." NBER Working Paper 10578, National Bureau of Economic Research, Cambridge, MA.

Baumol, William J., and William G. Bowen. 1966. *Performing Arts: The Economic Dilemma.* New York: Twentieth Century Fund.

Bauwens, Luc, Giordana Mion, and Jacques-François Thisse. 2008. "The Resistible Decline of European Science." CEPR Discussion Paper 6625, Centre for Economic Policy Research, London.

Bays, Jonathan, and Paul Jansen. 2009. "Prizes: A Winning Strategy for Innovation." *What Matters*, July 7. http://whatmatters.mckinseydigital.com/innovation/prizes-a-winning-strategy-for-innovation.

Begg, Iain. 1999. "Cities and Competitiveness." *Urban Studies* 36 (5–6): 795–809.

Beijing Municipal Statistics Bureau and Beijing General Team of Investigation under the National Bureau of Statistics. 1996. *Beijing Statistical Yearbook 1996*. Beijing: China Statistics Press.

———. 2001. *Beijing Statistical Yearbook 2001*. Beijing: China Statistics Press.

———. 2002. *Beijing Statistical Yearbook 2002*. Beijing: China Statistics Press.

———. 2003. *Beijing Statistical Yearbook 2003*. Beijing: China Statistics Press.

———. 2004. *Beijing Statistical Yearbook 2004*. Beijing: China Statistics Press.

———. 2005. *Beijing Statistical Yearbook 2005*. Beijing: China Statistics Press.

———. 2006. *Beijing Statistical Yearbook 2006*. Beijing: China Statistics Press.

———. 2007. *Beijing Statistical Yearbook 2007*. Beijing: China Statistics Press.

———. 2008. *Beijing Statistical Yearbook 2008*. Beijing: China Statistics Press.

Bernstein, Amy. 2008. "Gary Pisano: The Thought Leader—Interview." Strategy+Business. http://www.strategy-business.com/press/16635507/07210.

Berry, Christopher, and Edward L. Glaeser. 2005. "The Divergence of Human Capital Levels across Cities." NBER Working Paper 11617, National Bureau of Economic Research, Cambridge, MA.

Bers, John A., John P. Dismukes, Lawrence K. Miller, and Aleksey Dubrovensky. 2009. "Accelerated Radical Innovation: Theory and Application." *Technological Forecasting and Social Change* 76 (1): 165–77.

Bettencourt, Luís M. A., José Lobo, and Deborah Strumsky. 2007. "Invention in the City: Increasing Returns to Patenting as a Scaling Function of Metropolitan Size." *Research Policy* 36 (1): 107–20.

Bi, Xiaoning. 2009. "Regulator Rolls Out Norms for GEB." *China Daily*, April 1.

Bin, Guo. 2008. "Technology Acquisition Channels and Industry Performance: An Industry-Level Analysis of Chinese Large- and Medium-Size Manufacturing Enterprises." *Research Policy* 37 (2): 194–209.

Blalock, Garrick, and Paul J. Gertler. 2008. "Welfare Gains from Foreign Direct Investment through Technology Transfer to Local Suppliers." *Journal of International Economics* 74 (2): 402–21.

Blomström, Magnus, and Fredrik Sjöholm. 1999. "Technology Transfer and Spillovers: Does Local Participation with Multinationals Matter?" *European Economic Review* 43 (4–6): 915–23.

Bloom, David E., and Jeffrey G. Williamson. 1998. "Demographic Transition and Economic Miracles in Emerging Asia." *World Bank Economic Review* 12 (3): 419–55.

Bloom, Nicholas. 2007. "Uncertainty and the Dynamics of R&D." NBER Working Paper 12841, National Bureau of Economic Research, Cambridge, MA.

Bloom, Nicholas, Christos Genakos, Ralf Martin, and Raffaella Sadun. 2008. "Modern Management: Good for the Environment or Just Hot Air?" NBER Working Paper 14394, National Bureau of Economic Research, Cambridge, MA.

Bloom, Nicholas, Rachel Griffith, and John Van Reenen. 2002. "Do R&D Tax Credits Work? Evidence from a Panel of Countries 1979–1997." *Journal of Public Economics* 85 (1): 1–31.

Bloom, Nicholas, Raffaella Sadun, and John Van Reenen. 2007. "Americans Do IT Better: U.S. Multinationals and the Productivity Miracle." CEPR Discussion Paper 6291, Centre for Economic Policy Research, London.

Blümich, Bernhard. 2008. "The Incredible Shrinking Scanner: MRI-Like Machine Becomes Portable." *Scientific American* (November): 92–98.

Boarini, Romina, and Joaquim Oliveira Martins. 2008. "How Do Policies Influence the Investment in Higher Education?" VoxEU.org. http://www.voxeu.org/index.php?q=node/1690.

Boozer, Michael, Gustav Ranis, Frances Stewart, and Tavneet Suri. 2003. "Paths to Success: The Relationship between Human Development and Economic Growth." Discussion Paper 874, Economic Growth Center, Yale University, New Haven, CT.

Bosworth, Barry P., and Susan M. Collins. 2007. "Accounting for Growth: Comparing China and India." NBER Working Paper 12943, National Bureau of Economic Research, Cambridge, MA.

Bowen, H. Kent, Kim B. Clark, Charles A. Holloway, and Steven C. Wheelwright. 1994. "Regaining the Lead in Manufacturing." *Harvard Business Review* 72 (5): 121–30.

Bradsher, Keith. 2009. "China Vies to Be World's Leader in Electric Cars." *New York Times*, April 1.

Bramwell, Allison, and David A. Wolfe. 2008. "Universities and Regional Economic Development: The Entrepreneurial University of Waterloo." *Research Policy* 37 (8): 1175–87.

Brandt, Loren, and Thomas Rawski. 2008. *China's Great Economic Transformation*. New York: Cambridge University Press.

Branscomb, Lewis. 2008. "Research Alone Is Not Enough." *Science* 321 (5891): 915–16.

Bresnahan, Timothy, Alfonso Gambardella, Annalee Saxenian, and Scott Wallsten. 2001. "'Old Economy' Inputs for 'New Economy' Outcomes: Cluster Formation in the New Silicon Valley." SIEPR Discussion Paper 00-043, Stanford Institute for Economic Policy Research, Stanford, CA.

Brule, Tyler. 2009. "The City of Your Dreams." *Financial Times*, June 12.

Brülhart, Marius, and Federica Sbergami. 2009. "Agglomeration and Growth: Cross-Country Evidence." *Journal of Urban Economics* 65 (1): 48–63.

Brynjolfsson, Erik, and Lorin M. Hitt. 2003. "Computing Productivity: Firm-Level Evidence." *Review of Economics and Statistics* 85 (4): 793–808.

Brynjolfsson, Erik, and Adam Saunders. 2009. *Wired for Innovation: How Information Technology Is Reshaping the Economy*. Cambridge, MA: MIT Press.

Buenstorf, Guido, and Steven Klepper. 2009. "Heritage and Agglomeration: The Akron Tyre Cluster Revisited." *Economic Journal* 119 (537): 705–33.

Buiter, Willem. 2009. "Harmful Financial Innovation." *Financial Times*, July 1. http://blogs. ft.com/maverecon/2009/07/harmful-financial-innovation/.

Burdett, Ricky, and Deyan Sudjic. 2008. *The Endless City*. London: Phaidon Press.

Büschemann, Karl-Heinz. 2009. "The 'Dumbest Idea in the World.'" *Atlantic Times*, April. http://www.atlantic-times.com/archive_detail.php?recordID=1716.

Bwalya, Samuel Mulenga. 2006. "Foreign Direct Investment and Technology Spillovers: Evidence from Panel Data Analysis of Manufacturing Firms in Zambia." *Journal of Development Economics* 81 (2): 514–26.

Campante, Filipe, and Edward L. Glaeser. 2009. "Yet Another Tale of Two Cities: Buenos Aires and Chicago." NBER Working Paper 15104, National Bureau of Economic Research, Cambridge, MA.

Cao, Cong. 2004. "Zhongguancun and China's High-Tech Parks in Transition: Growing Pains or Premature Senility?" *Asian Survey* 44 (5): 647–68.

———. 2008. "Technological Development Challenges in Chinese Industry." In *China's Science and Technology Sector and the Forces of Globalisation*, ed. Elspeth Thomson and Jon Sigurdson, 1–30. Singapore: World Scientific Publishing.

Carlino, Gerald A., Satyajit Chatterjee, and Robert M. Hunt. 2007. "Urban Density and the Rate of Invention." *Journal of Urban Economics* 61 (3): 389–419.

Carter, Colin A., Funing Zhong, and Fang Cai. 1996. *China's Ongoing Agricultural Reform*. San Francisco, CA: 1990 Institute.

Cassis, Youssef, and Éric Bussière. 2005. *London and Paris as International Financial Centres in the Twentieth Century*. Oxford, U.K.: Oxford University Press.

Castaldi, Carolina. 2009. "The Relative Weight of Manufacturing and Services in Europe: An Innovation Perspective." *Technological Forecasting and Social Change* 76 (6): 709–22.

Castellani, Davide, and Antonello Zanfei. 2003. "Technology Gaps, Absorptive Capacity, and the Impact of Inward Investments on Productivity of European Firms." *Economics of Innovation and New Technology* 12 (6): 1.

Castells, Manuel. 1998. "Why the Megacities Focus? Megacities in the New World Disorder." Publication MCP-018, Mega-Cities Project, New York. http://www. megacitiesproject.org/publications_pdf_mcp018intro.pdf.

CBRE Consulting. 2008. *A Study of the Economic Impact and Benefits of UC San Diego*. San Francisco, CA: CBRE Consulting.

Charette, Robert N. 2009. "This Car Runs on Code." *IEEE Spectrum*, February. http://www. spectrum.ieee.org/feb09/7649.

Chen, Henry, Paul Gompers, Anna Kovner, and Josh Lerner. 2009. "Buy Local? The Geography of Successful and Unsuccessful Venture Capital Expansion." NBER Working Paper 15102, National Bureau of Economic Research, Cambridge, MA.

Chen, Kun, and Martin Kenney. 2007. "Universities/Research Institutes and Regional Innovation Systems: The Cases of Beijing and Shenzhen." *World Development* 35 (6): 1056–74.

Chen, Yun-Chung. 2008. "Why Do Multinational Corporations Locate Their Advanced R&D Centres in Beijing?" *Journal of Development Studies* 44 (5): 622–44.

Cheung, Kui-Yin, and Ping Lin. 2004. "Spillover Effects of FDI on Innovation in China: Evidence from the Provincial Data." *China Economic Review* 15 (1): 25–44.

Chi, Wei. 2008. "The Role of Human Capital in China's Economic Development: Review and New Evidence." *China Economic Review* 19 (3): 421–36.

"China: Foreign R&D Gives Economy a Boost." 2008. *Oxford Analytica*, February 7.

"China: GEM Will Finally Take Off, but Cautiously." 2009. *Oxford Analytica*, April 22.

"China: Pace of Mergers and Acquisitions Will Increase." 2009. *Oxford Analytica*, March 16.

"China: Returnees Are Critical in Innovation Push." 2009. *Oxford Analytica*, July 1.

"China to Establish Stock Market for Growth Enterprises." 2008. Xinhua News Agency, March 5.

Christensen, Clayton M., and Michael E. Raynor. 2003. *The Innovators' Solution*. Boston: Harvard Business School Press.

Coe, David T., and Elhanan Helpman. 1995. "International R&D Spillovers." *European Economic Review* 39 (5): 859–87.

Coe, David T., Elhanan Helpman, and Alexander W. Hoffmaister. 1997. "North-South R&D Spillovers." *Economic Journal* 107 (440): 134–49.

Coe, Neil M., Peter Dicken, and Martin Hess. 2008. "Global Production Networks: Realizing the Potential." *Journal of Economic Geography* 8 (3): 271–95.

Cohen, Wesley M., and Daniel A. Levinthal. 1990. "Absorptive Capacity: A New Perspective on Learning and Innovation." *Administrative Science Quarterly* 35 (1): 128–52.

Comin, Diego, and Bart Hobijn. 2004. "Cross-Country Technology Adoption: Making the Theories Face the Facts." *Journal of Monetary Economics* 51 (1): 39–83.

Comin, Diego, Bart Hobijn, and Emilie Rovito. 2008. "Technology Usage Lags." *Journal of Economic Growth* 13 (4): 237–56.

Commission on Growth and Development. 2008. *The Growth Report: Strategies for Sustained Growth and Inclusive Development*. Washington, DC: World Bank.

Cooke, Philip, Carla Laurentis, Franz Tödtling, and Michaela Trippl. 2007. *Regional Knowledge Economies: Markets, Clusters, and Innovation*. Northampton, MA: Edward Elgar.

Crafts, Nicholas, and Gianni Toniolo. 2008. "European Economic Growth, 1950–2005: An Overview." CEPR Discussion Paper 6863, Centre for Economic Policy Research, London.

Crahan, Margaret E., and Alberto Vourvoulias-Bush, eds. 1997. *The City and the World: New York's Global Future*. New York: Council on Foreign Relations.

Crotty, James. 2005. "The Neoliberal Paradox: The Impact of Destructive Product Market Competition and 'Modern' Financial Markets on Nonfinancial Corporation Performance in the Neoliberal Era." In *Financialization and the World Economy*, ed. Gerald A. Epstein, 77–110. Northampton, MA: Edward Elgar Publishing.

Darby, Michael, Lynne Zucker, and Andrew Wang. 2003. "Universities, Joint Ventures, and Success in the Advanced Technology Program." NBER Working Paper 9463, National Bureau of Economic Research, Cambridge, MA.

Day, John W. Jr., Donald F. Boesch, Ellis J. Clairain, G. Paul Kemp, Shirley B. Laska, William J. Mitsch, Kenneth Orth, Hassan Mashriqui, Denise J. Reed, Leonard Shabman, Charles A. Simenstad, Bill J. Streever, Robert R. Twilley, Chester C. Watson, John T. Wells, and Dennis F. Whigham. 2007. "Restoration of the Mississippi Delta: Lessons from Hurricanes Katrina and Rita." *Science* 315 (5819): 1679–84.

de Botton, Alain. 2009. "Vive le Flâneur!" *Monocle* 3 (25). Winkontent: London.

Dedrick, Jason, Kenneth L. Kraemer, and Greg Linden. 2008. "Who Profits from Innovation in Global Value Chains? A Study of the iPod and Notebook PCs." Personal Computing Industry Center, University of California, Irvine.

Deichmann, Uwe, Kai Kaiser, Somik Lall, and Zmarak Shalizi. 2005. "Agglomeration, Transport, and Regional Development in Indonesia." Policy Research Working Paper 3477, World Bank, Washington, DC.

Deng, Haiyan, John Haltiwanger, Robert McGuckin, Jianyi Xu, Yaodong Liu, and Yuqi Liu. 2007. "The Contribution of Restructuring and Reallocation to China's Productivity and Growth." Economics Program Working Paper 07-04, Conference Board, New York.

Dertouzos, Michael L., Richard K. Lester, and Robert M. Solow. 1989. *Made in America: Regaining the Productive Edge.* Cambridge, MA: MIT Press.

Devas, Nick, and Carole Rakodi. 1993. *Managing Fast Growing Cities: New Approaches to Urban Planning and Management in the Developing World.* Harlow, Essex, England: Longman Scientific & Technical.

DeWoskin, Ken. 2008. "Can China Attract the World's Capital?" *Far Eastern Economic Review,* October 3. http://www.feer.com/economics/2008/october/can-china-attract-the-worlds-capital1.

Dickson, Peter R., and Joseph J. Giglierano. 1986. "Missing the Boat and Sinking the Boat: A Conceptual Model of Entrepreneurial Risk." *Journal of Marketing* 50 (1): 58–70.

Dollar, David, and Shang-Jin Wei. 2007. "Das (Wasted) Kapital: Firm Ownership and Investment Efficiency in China." IMF Working Paper 07/9, International Monetary Fund, Washington, DC.

Drennan, Matthew P. 2002. *The Information Economy and American Cities.* Baltimore, MD: Johns Hopkins University Press.

Drofiak, Alex, and Elizabeth Garnsey. 2009. "The Cambridge High Tech Cluster: Resilience and Response to Cyclical Trends." Centre for Technology Management Working Paper 2009/01, University of Cambridge, Cambridge, U.K.

Duke, Mike, Deborah Andrews, and Timothy Anderson. 2009. "The Feasibility of Long Range Battery Electric Cars in New Zealand." *Energy Policy* 37 (9): 3455–62.

Durlauf, Steven N., Paul A. Johnson, and Jonathan R. W. Temple. 2005. "Growth Econometrics." In *Handbook of Economic Growth,* vol. 1A, ed. Philippe Aghion and Steven N. Durlauf, 554–678. Amsterdam: North-Holland.

Dyer, Geoff. 2008. "Beijing Hesitates at the Global Threshold." *Financial Times,* November 24.

Easterly, William. 2006. "Reliving the 1950s: The Big Push, Poverty Traps, and Takeoffs in Economic Development." *Journal of Economic Growth* 11 (4): 289–318.

Easterly, William, Michael Kremer, Lant Pritchett, and Lawrence H. Summers. 1993. "Good Policy or Good Luck? Country Growth Performance and Temporary Shocks." *Journal of Monetary Economics* 32 (3): 459–83.

Eaton, Jonathan, and Samuel Kortum. 1999. "International Technology Diffusion: Theory and Measurement." *International Economic Review* 40 (3): 537–70.

———. 2001. "Trade in Capital Goods." *European Economic Review* 45 (7): 1195–235.

Edwards, Cliff, and Peter Burrows. 2009. "Intel Tries to Invest Its Way out of a Rut." *BusinessWeek,* April 23.

Eichengreen, Barry, and Poonam Gupta. 2009. "The Two Waves of Service Sector Growth." NBER Working Paper 14968, National Bureau of Economic Research, Cambridge, MA.

Eichengreen, Barry, and Kevin H. O'Rourke. 2009. "A Tale of Two Depressions." VoxEU.org. http://www.voxeu.org/index.php?q=node/3421.

Eichengreen, Barry, and David Leblang. 2008. "Democracy and Globalization." *Economics and Politics* 20 (3): 289–334.

European Commission. 2002. "University Spin-Outs in Europe: Overview and Good Practice." Innovation Paper 21, Office for Official Publications of the European Communities, Luxembourg.

Fan, C. Cindy. 2008. "Migration, Hukou, and the City." In *China Urbanizes: Consequences, Strategies, and Policies*, ed. Shahid Yusuf and Tony Saich, 65–89. Washington, DC: World Bank.

Fan, Peilei, and Chihiro Watanabe. 2006. "Promoting Industrial Development through Technology Policy: Lessons from Japan and China." *Technology in Society* 28 (3): 303–20.

Feenstra, Robert C., and Gary C. Hamilton. 2006. *Emergent Economies, Divergent Paths: Economic Organization and International Trade in South Korea and Taiwan*. New York: Cambridge University Press.

Feldman, Maryann P. 2003. "Entrepreneurship and American Research Universities: Evolution in Technology Transfer." In *The Emergence of Entrepreneurship Policy: Governance, Start-Ups, and Growth in the U.S. Knowledge Economy*, ed. David M. Hart, 92–112. Cambridge, U.K.: Cambridge University Press.

Flanagan, James L. 2006. "U.S. Competitiveness and the Profession of Engineering." *IEEE–USA Today's Engineer Online* (November). http://www.todaysengineer.org/2006/nov/competitiveness.asp.

Florida, Richard. 2002. *The Rise of the Creative Class and How It's Transforming Work, Leisure, and Everyday Life*. New York: Basic Books.

———. 2005. *Cities and the Creative Class*. London: Routledge.

———. 2008. *Who's Your City? How the Creative Economy Is Making Where to Live the Most Important Decision of Your Life*. New York: Basic Books.

———. 2009. "Talentopolis." *What Matters*, July 7. http://whatmatters.mckinseydigital.com/innovation/talentopolis?pg=2.

Fontagne, Lionel, Guillaume Gaulier, and Soledad Zignago. 2008. "Specialization across Varieties and North-South Competition." *Economic Policy* 23 (53): 51–91.

Ford, Larry R. 2008. "World Cities and Global Change: Observations on Monumentality in Urban Design." *Eurasian Geography of Economics* 49 (3): 237–62.

Foster, Richard N., and Sarah Kaplan. 2001. *Creative Destruction: Why Companies That Are Built to Last Underperform the Market—and How to Successfully Transform Them*. New York: Broadway Business.

Freeman, Lance. 2008. "Should We Use Zoning to Preserve Manufacturing?" Planetizen. http://www.planetizen.com/node/34999.

Freund, Caroline. 2009. "Demystifying the Collapse in Trade." VoxEU.org. http://www.voxeu.org/index.php?q=node/3731.

"Friends and Rivals." 2007. *Economist*, September 15.

Fujita, Kuniko. 2003. "Neo-industrial Tokyo: Urban Development and Globalisation in Japan's State-Centred Developmental Capitalism." *Urban Studies* 40 (2): 249–81.

Fujita, Kuniko, and Richard Child Hill. 2005. "Innovative Tokyo." Policy Research Working Paper 3507, World Bank, Washington, DC.

Fujita, Masahisa, and Jacques-François Thisse. 2002. *Economics of Agglomeration: Cities, Industrial Location, and Regional Growth.* New York: Cambridge University Press.

Fukuda, Kayano, and Chihiro Watanabe. 2008. "Japanese and U.S. Perspectives on the National Innovation Ecosystem." *Technology in Society* 30 (1): 49–63.

Fung, Victor K., William K. Fung, and Yoram Wind. 2008. *Competing in a Flat World: Building Enterprises for a Borderless World.* Upper Saddle River, NJ: Pearson Education.

Galasso, Alberto, and Mark Schankerman. 2008. "Patent Thickets and the Market for Innovation: Evidence from Settlement of Patent Disputes." CEPR Discussion Paper 6946, Centre for Economic Policy Research, London.

Galbraith, James K., and J. Travis Hale. 2009. "The Evolution of Economic Inequality in the United States, 1969–2007: Evidence from Data on Inter-industrial Earnings and Inter-regional Incomes." UTIP Working Paper 57, University of Texas Inequality Project, University of Texas, Austin.

Gallagher, Michael, Abrar Hasan, Mary Canning, Howard Newby, Lichia Saner-Yiu, and Ian Whitman. 2009. *OECD Reviews of Tertiary Education: China.* Paris: Organisation for Economic Co-operation and Development. http://browse.oecdbookshop.org/oecd/pdfs/browseit/9109031E.PDF.

Gallagher, Sims Kelly. 2006. "Limits to Leapfrogging in Energy Technologies? Evidence from the Chinese Automobile Industry." *Energy Policy* 34 (4): 383–94.

Gan, Lin. 2003. "Globalization of the Automobile Industry in China: Dynamics and Barriers in Greening of the Road Transportation." *Energy Policy* 31 (6): 537–51.

Gao, Jian, and Gary H. Jefferson. 2007. "Science and Technology Take-Off in China? Sources of Rising R&D Intensity." *Asia Pacific Business Review* 13 (3): 357–71.

Ge, Ying. 2009. "Globalization and Industry Agglomeration in China." *World Development* 37 (3): 550–59.

Gerlach, Heiko, Thomas Rønde, and Konrad Stahl. 2009. "Labor Pooling in R&D Intensive Industries." *Journal of Urban Economics* 65 (1): 99–111.

Girma, Sourafel. 2005. "Absorptive Capacity and Productivity Spillovers from FDI: A Threshold Regression Analysis." *Oxford Bulletin of Economics and Statistics* 67 (3): 281–306.

Girma, Sourafel, and Yundan Gong. 2008. "FDI, Linkages, and the Efficiency of State-Owned Enterprises in China." *Journal of Development Studies* 44 (5): 728–49.

Girma, Sourafel, Yundan Gong, and Holger Görg. 2006. "Can You Teach Old Dragons New Tricks? FDI and Innovation Activity in Chinese State-Owned Enterprises." CEPR Discussion Paper 5838, Centre for Economic Policy and Research, London.

———. 2009. "What Determines Innovation Activity in Chinese State-Owned Enterprises? The Role of Foreign Direct Investment." *World Development* 37 (4): 866–73.

Girma, Sourafel, and Holger Görg. 2007. "The Role of the Efficiency Gap for Spillovers from FDI: Evidence from the U.K. Electronics and Engineering Sectors." *Open Economies Review* 18 (2): 215–32.

Girma, Sourafel, and Katharine Wakelin. 2007. "Local Productivity Spillovers from Foreign Direct Investment in the U.K. Electronics Industry." *Regional Science and Urban Economics* 37 (3): 399–412.

Gittelman, Michelle. 2006. "National Institutions, Public-Private Knowledge Flows, and Innovation Performance: A Comparative Study of the Biotechnology Industry in the U.S. and France." *Research Policy* 35 (7): 1052–68.

Glaeser, Edward L. 2005a. "Reinventing Boston: 1640–2003." *Journal of Economic Geography* 5 (2): 119–53.

———. 2005b. "Urban Colossus: Why Is New York America's Largest City?" NBER Working Paper 11398, National Bureau of Economic Research, Cambridge, MA.

———. 2007. "Entrepreneurship and the City." NBER Working Paper 13551, National Bureau of Economic Research, Cambridge, MA.

———. 2009. "Growth: The Death and Life of Cities." In *Making Cities Work: Prospects and Policies for Urban America*, ed. Robert P. Inman, 22–62. Princeton, NJ: Princeton University Press.

Glaeser, Edward L., Joseph Gyourko, and Raven Saks. 2005. "Why Is Manhattan So Expensive? Regulation and the Rise in Housing Prices." *Journal of Law and Economics* 48 (2): 331–69.

Glaeser, Edward L., and William R. Kerr. 2008. "Local Industrial Conditions and Entrepreneurship: How Much of the Spatial Distribution Can We Explain?" NBER Working Paper 14407, National Bureau of Economic Research, Cambridge, MA.

Glaeser, Edward L., and Janet E. Kohlhase. 2003. "Cities, Regions, and Decline of Transport Costs." Harvard Institute of Economic Research Discussion Paper 2014, Harvard University, Cambridge, MA.

Glaeser, Edward L., and Matthew Resseger. 2009. "The Complementarity between Cities and Skills." NBER Working Paper 15103, National Bureau of Economic Research, Cambridge, MA.

Glaeser, Edward L., Matthew Resseger, and Kristina Tobio. 2008. "Urban Inequality." NBER Working Paper 14419, National Bureau of Economic Research, Cambridge, MA.

Glicksman, Leon R., Leslie K. Norford, and Lara V. Greden. 2001. "Energy Conservation in Chinese Residential Buildings: Progress and Opportunities in Design and Policy." *Annual Review of Energy and the Environment* 26 (1): 83–115.

Goldberg, Itzhak, Lee Branstetter, John Gabriel Goddard, and Smita Kuriakose. 2008. "Globalization and Technology Absorption in Europe and Central Asia." World Bank Working Paper 150, World Bank, Washington, DC.

Goolsbee, Austan. 1998. "Does Government R&D Policy Mainly Benefit Scientists and Engineers?" *American Economic Review* 88 (2): 298–302.

Goozner, Merrill. 2005. *The $800 Million Pill: The Truth behind the Cost of New Drugs.* Berkeley: University of California Press.

Görg, Holger, and Eric A. Strobl. 2001. "Multinational Companies and Productivity Spillovers: A Meta-analysis." *Economic Journal* 111 (475): 723–39.

Gregory, Neil, Stanley Nollen, and Stoyan Tenev. 2009. *New Industries from New Places: The Emergence of Hardware and Software Industries in China and India.* Palo Alto, CA: Stanford University Press.

Griffith, Rachel, Stephen J. Redding, and Helen Simpson. 2002. "Productivity Convergence and Foreign Ownership at the Establishment Level." IFS Working Paper 22, Institute for Fiscal Studies, London.

Griffith, Rachel, Stephen J. Redding, and John Van Reenen. 2004. "Mapping the Two Faces of R&D: Productivity Growth in a Panel of OECD Industries." *Review of Economics and Statistics* 86 (4): 883–95.

Griliches, Zvi. 2000. *R&D, Education, and Productivity.* Cambridge, MA: Harvard University Press.

Grossman, Sanford J., and Oliver D. Hart. 1999. "Corporate Financial Structure and Managerial Incentives." In *Corporate Governance*, vol. 2, ed. Kevin Keasey, Steve Thompson, and Mike Wright, 211–41. Cheltenham, U.K.: Edward Elgar.

Grullon, Gustavo, and Roni Michaely. 2002. "Dividends, Share Repurchases, and the Substitution Hypothesis." *Journal of Finance* 57 (4): 1649–84.

Guiso, Luigi, Paola Sapienza, and Luigi Zingales. 2002. "Does Local Financial Development Matter?" NBER Working Paper 8923, National Bureau of Economic Research, Cambridge, MA.

Haddad, Mona, and Ann Harrison. 1993. "Are There Positive Spillovers from Direct Foreign Investment? Evidence from Panel Data for Morocco." *Journal of Development Economics* 42 (1): 51–74.

Hagel, John III, John Seely Brown, and Lang Davison. 2008. "Shaping Strategy in a World of Constant Disruption." *Harvard Business Review* (October): 81–89.

Hall, Bronwyn. 2001. "The Economics of Tax Credits." Presented at the Tax Policy Institute Conference on the R&D Tax Credit, Washington, DC, February 15.

Hall, Bronwyn, Francesca Lotti, and Jacques Mairesse. 2008. "Innovation and Productivity in SMEs: Empirical Evidence for Italy." NBER Working Paper 14594, National Bureau of Economic Research, Cambridge, MA.

Hall, Bronwyn, and Jacques Mairesse. 2006. "Empirical Studies of Innovation in the Knowledge Driven Economy." NBER Working Paper 12320, National Bureau of Economic Research, Cambridge, MA.

Hall, Peter. 1998. *Cities in Civilization.* New York: Pantheon.

Hall, Robert E., and Charles I. Jones. 1999. "Why Do Some Countries Produce So Much More per Worker Than Others?" *Quarterly Journal of Economics* 114 (1): 83–116.

Hamilton, Gary G., and Gary Gereffi. 2008. "Global Commodity Chains, Market Makers, and the Rise of Demand-Responsive Economies." In *Frontiers of Commodity Chain Research*, ed. Jennifer Bair, 136–61. Stanford, CA: Stanford University Press.

Han, Sun Sheng. 2000. "Shanghai between State and Market in Urban Transformation." *Urban Studies* 37 (11): 2091–112.

Hargadon, Andrew, and Robert I. Sutton. 2000. "Building an Innovation Factory." *Harvard Business Review* 78 (3): 157–66.

Harney, Alexandra. 2008. *The China Price: The True Cost of Chinese Competitive Advantage.* New York: Penguin Group.

Hausmann, Ricardo, and Bailey Klinger. 2006. "Structural Transformation and Patterns of Comparative Advantage in the Product Space." Center for International Development, Harvard University, Cambridge, MA.

He, Jianwu, and Louis Kuijs. 2007. "Rebalancing China's Economy: Modeling a Policy Package." China Research Paper 7, World Bank, Beijing.

Hellman, Thomas, Laura Lindsey, and Manju Puri. 2004. "Building Relationships Early: Banks in Venture Capital." NBER Working Paper 10535, National Bureau of Economic Research, Cambridge, MA.

Henderson, J. Vernon. 2004. "Issues Concerning Urbanization in China." Prepared for the 11th Five-Year Plan of China, World Bank, Washington, DC.

Heng, Michael Siam-Heng. 2008. "Development of China's Semiconductor Industry: Prospects and Problems." In *China's Science and Technology Sector and the Forces of Globalization*, ed. Elspeth Thomson and Jon Sigurdson, 173–90. Singapore: World Scientific Publishing.

Hicks, Diana, and Deepak Hegde. 2005. "Highly Innovative Small Firms in the Markets for Technology." *Research Policy* 34 (5): 703–16.

Hille, Kathrin. 2009. "Beijing Drives Car and Steel Mergers Message." *Financial Times*, March 23.

Hirukawa, Masayuki, and Masako Ueda. 2008a. "Venture Capital and Industrial 'Innovation.'" CEPR Discussion Paper 7089, Centre for Economic Policy Research, London.

———. 2008b. "Venture Capital and Innovation: Which Is First?" CEPR Discussion Paper 7090, Centre for Economic Policy Research, London.

Hohenberg, Paul, and Lynn Lees. 1995. *The Making of Urban Europe, 1000–1994*. Cambridge, MA: Harvard University Press.

Holz, Carsten A. 2008. "China's Economic Growth 1978–2025: What We Know Today about China's Economic Growth Tomorrow." *World Development* 36 (10): 1665–91.

"How Procter & Gamble Plans to Clean Up." 2009. *BusinessWeek*, April 2.

Hu, Albert Guangzhou. 2008. "What Do They Patent in China, and Why?" In *Greater China's Quest for Innovation*, ed. Henry S. Rowen, Marguerite Gong Hancock, and William F. Miller, 255–68. Stanford, CA: Walter H. Shorenstein Asia-Pacific Research Center.

Hu, Albert Guangzhou, and Gary H. Jefferson. 2006. "A Great Wall of Patents: What Is behind China's Recent Patent Explosion?" National University of Singapore, Singapore.

———. 2008. "Science and Technology in China." In *China's Great Economic Transformation*, ed. Loren Brandt and Thomas G. Rawski, 286–336. New York: Cambridge University Press.

Hu, Mei Chih, and John A. Mathews. 2008. "China's National Innovative Capacity." *Research Policy* 37 (9): 1465–79.

Hu, Ping. 2007. "Research on Regional Inequalities of Industrial Structure and Its Contribution to Economic Growth in Yangzi River Delta." *E-Journal of China Urban Studies* 2 (3): 132–38.

Huang, Jikun, Keijiro Otsuka, and Scott Rozelle. 2008. "Agriculture in China's Development: Past Disappointments, Recent Successes, and Future Challenges." In *China's Great Economic Transformation*, ed. Loren Brandt and Thomas G. Rawski, 467–505. New York: Cambridge University Press.

Huang, Yasheng. 2005. *Selling China: Foreign Direct Investment during the Reform Era*. New York: Cambridge University Press.

———. 2008. *Capitalism with Chinese Characteristics: Entrepreneurship and the State*. Cambridge, U.K.: Cambridge University Press.

Huang, Yasheng, Tony Saich, and Edward S. Steinfeld, eds. 2005. *Financial Sector Reform in China*. Cambridge, MA: Harvard University Press.

Hufbauer, Gary, and Sherry Stephenson. 2009. "Trade Policy in a Time of Crisis: Suggestions for Developing Countries." CEPR Policy Insight 33, Centre for Economic Policy Research, London.

Hummels, David, Jun Ishii, and Kei-Mu Yi. 2001. "The Nature and Growth of Vertical Specialization in World Trade." *Journal of International Economics* 54 (1): 75–96.

Indergaard, Mich. 2004. *Silicon Alley: The Rise and Fall of a New Media District*. New York: Routledge.

Jaffe, Adam B. 1986. "Technological Opportunity and Spillovers of R&D: Evidence from Firms' Patents, Profits, and Market Value." *American Economic Review* 76 (5): 984–1001.

Jana, Reena. 2008. "Innovation: The Biggest Bang for the Buck." *BusinessWeek*, September 22.

Jaruzelski, Barry, and Kevin Dehoff. 2007a. "The Booz Allen Hamilton Global Innovation 1000: The Customer Connection." *Strategy+Business* 49: 1–16.

———. 2007b. "The Customer Connection: The Global Innovation 1000." Strategy+Business. http://www.strategy-business.com/resiliencereport/resilience/rr00053?pg=all.

Jaruzelski, Barry, Kevin Dehoff, and Rakesh Bordia. 2005. "The Booz Allen Hamilton Global Innovation 1000: Money Isn't Everything." *Strategy+Business* 41: 1–14.

———. 2006. "The Booz Allen Hamilton Global Innovation 1000: Smart Spenders." *Strategy+Business* 45: 46–61.

Javorcik, Beata Smarzynska. 2004. "Does Foreign Direct Investment Increase the Productivity of Domestic Firms? In Search of Spillovers through Backward Linkages." *American Economic Review* 94 (3): 605–27.

Javorcik, Beata Smarzynska, and Mariana Spatareanu. 2005. "Disentangling FDI Spillover Effects: What Do Firm Perceptions Tell Us?" In *Does Foreign Direct Investment Promote Development?*, ed. Theodore H. Moran, Edward M. Graham, and Magnus Blomström, 45–71. Washington, DC: Peterson Institute for International Economics and Center for Global Development.

———. 2008. "To Share or Not to Share: Does Local Participation Matter for Spillovers from Foreign Direct Investment?" *Journal of Development Economics* 85 (1–2): 194–217.

Johnes, Jill, and Li Yu. 2008. "Measuring the Research Performance of Chinese Higher Education Institutions Using Data Envelopment Analysis." *China Economic Review* 19 (4): 679–96.

Johnson, Elmer W. 2001. *Chicago Metropolis 2020: The Chicago Plan for the Twenty-First Century*. Chicago: University of Chicago Press.

Johnson, Simon. 2009. "The Quiet Coup." *Atlantic*, May.

Jorgenson, Dale W., Mun S. Ho, Jon D. Samuels, and Kevin J. Stiroh. 2007. "Industry Origins of the American Productivity Resurgence." Harvard University, Cambridge, MA.

Joshi, Kirti Kusum, and Tatsuhito Kono. 2009. "Optimization of Floor Area Ratio Regulation in a Growing City." *Regional Science and Urban Economics* 39 (4): 502–11.

Kay, John. 2009. "Wind Down the Market in Five-Legged Dogs." *Financial Times*, January 21.

Keller, Wolfgang. 2002. "Geographic Localization of International Technology Diffusion." *American Economic Review* 92 (1): 120–42.

Kenney, Martin. 2008. "Lessons from the Development of Silicon Valley and Its Entrepreneurial Support Network for Japan and Kyushu." In *Growing Industrial Clusters in Asia: Serendipity and Science*, ed. Shahid Yusuf, Kaoru Nabeshima, and Shoichi Yamashita, 39–66. Washington, DC: World Bank.

Kenney, Martin, and Richard Florida. 2000. "Venture Capital in Silicon Valley: Fueling New Firm Formation." In *Understanding Silicon Valley: The Anatomy of an Entrepreneurial Region*, ed. Martin Kenney, 98–123. Stanford, CA: Stanford University Press.

Kenney, Martin, Kyonghee Han, and Shoko Tanaka. 2003. "The Globalization of Venture Capital: The Cases of Taiwan and Japan." In *Financial Systems, Corporate Investment in Innovation and Venture Capital*, ed. Anthony Bartzokas and Sunil Mani, 52–84. Cheltenham, U.K.: Edward Elgar.

———. 2004. "Venture Capital Industries." In *Global Change and East Asian Policy Initiatives*, ed. Shahid Yusuf, M. Anjum Altaf, and Kaoru Nabeshima, 391–428. New York: Oxford University Press.

Khanna, Tarun, and Krishna G. Palepu. 2006. "Emerging Giants: Building World-Class Companies in Developing Countries." *Harvard Business Review* 84 (10): 60–69.

Kleinberg, Robert. 1990. *China's Opening to the Outside World*. Boulder, CO: Westview Press.

Klemm, Alexander. 2009. "Causes, Benefits, and Risks of Business Tax Incentives." IMF Working Paper 09/21, International Monetary Fund, Washington, DC.

Klepper, Steven, and Kenneth L. Simons. 2005. "Industry Shakeouts and Technological Change." *International Journal of Industrial Organization* 23 (1–2): 23–43.

Kollmeyer, Christopher. 2009. "Explaining Deindustrialization: How Affluence, Productivity Growth, and Globalization Diminish Manufacturing Employment." *American Journal of Sociology* 114 (6): 1644–74.

Krauss, Lawrence M. 2008. "Celebrating Science as Culture." *Science* 321 (5889): 643.

Kremer, Michael, and Heidi Williams. 2009. "Incentivizing Innovation: Adding to the Toolkit." Harvard University, Cambridge, MA.

Krugman, Paul. 2009. "The Future Is Not What It Used to Be." 2009. *New York Times*, May 22.

Kugler, Maurice. 2006. "Spillovers from Foreign Direct Investment: Within or between Industries?" *Journal of Development Economics* 80 (2): 444–77.

Lai, Hongyi. 2006. *Reform and the Non-state Economy in China: The Political Economy of Liberalization Strategies*. New York: Palgrave Macmillan.

Lall, Sanjaya. 2000. "The Technological Structure and Performance of Developing Country Manufactured Exports, 1985–98." *Oxford Development Studies* 28 (3): 337–69.

Lall, Sanjaya, John Weiss, and Jinkang Zhang. 2006. "The 'Sophistication' of Exports: A New Trade Measure." *World Development* 34 (2): 222–37.

Lall, Somik V., Zmarak Shalizi, and Uwe Deichmann. 2004. "Agglomeration Economies and Productivity in Indian Industry." *American Economic Review* 73 (3): 643–73.

Lan, Xinzhen. 2009. "Rebranding Shanghai." *Beijing Review* 52 (19): 32–33.

Landry, Charles. 2008. *The Creative City: A Toolkit for Urban Innovators.* London: Earthscan.

Lane, Julia I. 2009. "Assessing the Impact of Science Funding." *Science* 324 (5932): 1273–75.

Law, Song Seng. 2009. "Vocational Technical Education and Economic Development: The Singapore Experience." ITE Paper 9, ITE Education Services, Singapore.

Lawlor, Michael. 2003. "Biotechnology and Government Funding." *Challenge* 46 (1): 15–37.

Lazonick, William, and Mary O'Sullivan. 2000. "Maximizing Shareholder Value: A New Ideology for Corporate Governance." *Economy and Society* 29 (1): 13–35.

Lee, Keun, and Byung-Yeon Kim. 2009. "Both Institutions and Policies Matter but Differently for Different Income Groups of Countries: Determinants of Long-Run Economic Growth Revisited." *World Development* 37 (3): 533–49.

Leman, Edward. 2009. "Adapting to Climate Change in Shanghai and the Yangtze Delta Region." Presented at the Fifth Urban Research Symposium 2009, Marseille, France, June 28–30.

Lenoir, Timothy, Nathan Rosenberg, Henry Rowen, Christophe Lécuyer, Jeannette Colyvas, and Brent Goldfarb. 2004. "Inventing the Entrepreneurial University: Stanford and the Co-evolution of Silicon Valley." Stanford University, Stanford, CA.

Lerner, Josh. 2005. "The University and the Start-Up: Lessons from the Past Two Decades." *Journal of Technology Transfer* 30 (1–2): 49–56.

Levin, Henry M., Dong Wook Jeong, and Dongshu Ou. 2006. "What Is a World Class University?" Presented at the 2006 Conference of the Comparative and International Education Society, Honolulu, HI, March 16.

Levine, Ross. 2004. "Finance and Growth: Theory and Evidence." NBER Working Paper 10766, National Bureau of Economic Research, Cambridge, MA.

Lewis, Robert. 2009. "Industrial Districts and Manufacturing Linkages: Chicago's Printing Industry, 1880–1950." *Economic History Review* 62 (2): 366–87.

Lewis, William. 2004. *The Power of Productivity.* Chicago: University of Chicago Press.

Li, Cao. 2004. "Population Peak May Hinder Development." *China Daily*, October 25.

Li, Jiatao, and Deborah R. Yue. 2005. "Managing Global Research and Development in China: Patterns of R&D Configuration and Evolution." *Technology Analysis and Strategic Management* 17 (3): 317–37.

Li, Po Chien, and Bou Wen Lin. 2006. "Building Global Logistics Competence with Chinese OEM Suppliers." *Technology in Society* 28 (3): 333–48.

Li, Shaomin, and Jun Xia. 2008. "The Role and Performance of State Firms and Non-state Firms in China's Economic Transition." *World Development* 36 (1): 39–54.

Li, Yuan, Yi Liu, and Feng Ren. 2007. "Product Innovation and Process Innovation in SOEs: Evidence from the Chinese Transition." *Journal of Technology Transfer* 32 (1–2): 63–85.

Liang, Feng. 2008. "Does Foreign Direct Investment Improve the Productivity of Domestic Firms? Technology Spillovers, Industry Linkages, and Firm Capabilities." Haas School of Business, University of California, Berkeley.

Lin, Justin Yifu, Fang Cai, and Zhou Li. 2003. *The China Miracle: Development Strategy and Economic Reform*. Hong Kong, China: Chinese University Press.

Linden, Greg, Jason Dedrick, and Kenneth L. Kraemer. 2009. "Innovation and Job Creation in a Global Economy: The Case of Apple's iPod." University of California, Irvine.

Liu, Fengchao, and Yutao Sun. 2009. "A Comparison of the Spatial Distribution of Innovative Activities in China and the U.S." *Technological Forecasting and Social Change* 76 (6): 797–805.

Liu, Nian Cai. 2007. "Research Universities in China: Differentiation, Classification, and Future World-Class Status." In *World Class Worldwide: Transforming Research Universities in Asia and Latin America*, ed. Philip G. Altbach and Jorge Balán, 54–69. Baltimore, MD: Johns Hopkins University Press.

Liu, Wan-Chun, and Chen-Min Hsu. 2006. "The Role of Financial Development in Economic Growth: The Experiences of Taiwan, Korea, and Japan." *Journal of Asian Economics* 17 (4): 667–90.

Lu, Ding, and Albert Guangzhou Hu. 2008. "China's Regional Variations in Patenting." In *China's Science and Technology Sector and the Forces of Globalization*, ed. Elspeth Thomson and Jon Sigurdson, 31–46. Singapore: World Scientific Publishing.

Lu, Hanchao. 1999. *Beyond the Neon Lights*. Berkeley, CA: University of California Press.

———. 2004. "Shanghai Rising: Resurgence of China's New York City?" In *Urban Transformation in China*, ed. Aimin Chen, Gordon G. Liu, and Kevin H. Zhang, Burlington, VT: Ashgate, 250–65.

Lu, Jiangyong, and Zhigang Tao. 2009. "Trends and Determinants of China's Industrial Agglomeration." *Journal of Urban Economics* 65 (2): 167–80.

Lu, Qiwen, and William Lazonick. 2001. "The Organization of Innovation in a Transitional Economy: Business and Government in Chinese Electronic Publishing." *Research Policy* 30 (1): 55–77.

Lundvall, Bengt-Åke. 2007. "Higher Education, Innovation, and Economic Development." Presented at the World Bank's Regional Bank Conference on Development Economics, Beijing, January 16–17.

Luthra, Shashank, Ramesh Mangaleswaran, and Asutosh Padhi. 2005. "When to Make India a Manufacturing Base." *McKinsey Quarterly* (September): 62–73.

Lynch, Lisa M. 2007. "Organizational Innovation and U.S. Productivity." VoxEU.org. http://www.voxeu.org/index.php?q=node/775.

MacFarquhar, Roderick, and John K. Fairbank. 1987. *The Cambridge History of China: The People's Republic, Part 1—The Emergence of Revolutionary China, 1949–1965*. Vol. 14. Cambridge, U.K.: Cambridge University Press.

Magtibay-Ramos, Nedelyn, Gemma Estrada, and Jesus Felipe. 2008. "An Input-Out Analysis of the Philippine BPO Industry." *Asian-Pacific Economic Literature* 22 (1): 41–56.

Maine, Elicia, and Elizabeth Garnsey. 2005. "Commercializing Generic Technology: The Case of Advanced Materials Ventures." Working Paper 2004/04, Centre for Technology Management, University of Cambridge, Cambridge, U.K.

Mandel, Michael. 2008. "Can America Invent Its Way Back?" *BusinessWeek*, September 22.

Markusen, Ann, and Vickie Gwiasda. 1994. "Multi-polarity and the Layering of Functions in World Cities: New York City's Struggle to Stay on Top." *International Journal of Urban and Regional Research* 18 (2): 167–93.

Martin, Philippe, Thierry Mayer, and Florian Mayneris. 2008. "Spatial Concentration and Firm-Level Productivity in France." CEPR Discussion Paper 6858, Centre for Economic Policy Research, London.

Mathews, John A., and Dong-Sung Cho. 2000. *Tiger Technology: The Creation of a Semiconductor Industry in East Asia.* Cambridge, U.K.: Cambridge University Press.

Mathieu, Azèle, and Bruno van Pottelsberghe. 2008. "A Note on the Drivers of R&D Intensity." CEPR Discussion Paper 6684, Centre for Economic Policy Research, London.

Mayer, Thierry, and Gianmarco Ottaviano. 2008. "The Happy Few: The Internationalisation of European Firms." *Intereconomics* 43 (3): 135–48.

"Medicine Goes Digital." 2009. *Economist,* April 16.

Mehra, Salil K., and Yanbei Meng. 2008. "Against Antitrust Functionalism: Reconsidering China's Antimonopoly Law." *Virginia Journal of International Law* 49 (2): 379–429.

Melo, Patricia C., Daniel J. Graham, and Robert B. Noland. 2009. "A Meta-analysis of Estimates of Urban Agglomeration Economies." *Regional Science and Urban Economics* 39 (3): 332–42.

Meyer, Marshall W., and Xiaohui Liu. 2004. "Managing Indefinite Boundaries: The Strategy and Structure of a Chinese Business Firm." *Management and Organization Review* 1 (1): 57–86.

Midler, Paul. 2009. *Poorly Made in China: An Insider's Account of the Tactics behind China's Production Game.* Hoboken, NJ: Wiley.

Milanovic, Branko. 2009. "Two Views on the Cause of the Global Crisis." YaleGlobal Online. http://yaleglobal.yale.edu/content/two-views-global-crisis.

Miner, Anne S., Dale T. Eesley, Michael Devaughn, and Thekla Rura-Polley. 2001. "The Magic Beanstalk Vision: Commercializing University Inventions and Research." In *The Entrepreneurship Dynamic: Origins of Entrepreneurship and the Evolution of Industries,* ed. Claudia Bird Schoonhoven and Elaine Romanelli, 109–46. Palo Alto, CA: Stanford University Press.

"Most College Students Still Await Offers." 2009. *China Daily,* March 20.

Motohashi, Kazuyuki. 2008. "IT, Enterprise Reform, and Productivity in Chinese Manufacturing Firms." *Journal of Asian Economics* 19 (4): 325–33.

Muller, Claudia, and Rolf Sternberg. 2008. "China's Return Migrants and Its Innovative Capacity." In *Greater China's Quest for Innovation,* ed. Henry S. Rowen, Marguerite Gong Hancock, and William F. Miller, 231–52. Stanford, CA: Walter H. Shorenstein Asia-Pacific Research Center.

Murphy, Kevin M., Andrei Schleifer, and Robert W. Vishny. 1989. "Increasing Returns, Durables, and Economic Fluctuations." NBER Working Paper 3014, National Bureau of Economic Research, Cambridge, MA.

Nabeshima, Kaoru. 2004. "Technology Transfer in East Asia: A Survey." In *Global Production Networking and Technological Change in East Asia,* ed. Shahid Yusuf, M. Anjum Altaf, and Kaoru Nabeshima, 395–434. New York: Oxford University Press.

National Bureau of Statistics of China. 1996. *China Statistical Yearbook 1996.* Beijing: China Statistics Press.

———. 2001. *China Statistical Yearbook 2001.* Beijing: China Statistics Press.

———. 2006. *2004 First National Economic Census.* Beijing: China Statistics Press.

———. 2007. *China Statistical Yearbook 2007.* Beijing: China Statistics Press.

———. 2008. *China Statistical Yearbook 2008.* Beijing: China Statistics Press.

National Bureau of Statistics of China and Ministry of Science and Technology. 1999. *China Statistical Yearbook on Science and Technology 1999.* Beijing: China Statistics Press.

———. 2000. *China Statistical Yearbook on Science and Technology 2000.* Beijing: China Statistics Press.

———. 2001. *China Statistical Yearbook on Science and Technology 2001.* Beijing: China Statistics Press.

———. 2002. *China Statistical Yearbook on Science and Technology 2002.* Beijing: China Statistics Press.

———. 2003. *China Statistical Yearbook on Science and Technology 2003.* Beijing: China Statistics Press.

———. 2004. *China Statistical Yearbook on Science and Technology 2004.* Beijing: China Statistics Press.

———. 2005. *China Statistical Yearbook on Science and Technology 2005.* Beijing: China Statistics Press.

———. 2006. *China Statistical Yearbook on Science and Technology 2006.* Beijing: China Statistics Press.

———. 2007. *China Statistical Yearbook on Science and Technology 2007.* Beijing: China Statistics Press.

Naughton, Barry. 2007. *The Chinese Economy: Transitions and Growth.* Cambridge, MA: MIT Press.

Needleman, Sarah E. 2009. "Doing the Math to Find the Good Jobs." *Wall Street Journal,* January 6.

New York City Department of City Planning. 2009. "About NYC Zoning." New York City Government, New York. http://www.nyc.gov/html/dcp/html/zone/zonehis.shtml.

Newhouse, David, and Daniel Suryadarma. 2009. "The Value of Vocational Education: High School Type and Labor Market Outcomes in Indonesia." Policy Research Working Paper 5035, World Bank, Washington, DC.

Newman, Peter, Timothy Beatley, and Heather Boyer. 2009. *Resilient Cities: Responding to Peak Oil and Climate Change.* Washington, DC: Island Press.

Ng, Ying Chu, and Sung-Ko Li. 2009. "Efficiency and Productivity Growth in Chinese Universities during the Post-reform Period." *China Economic Review* 20 (2): 183–92.

Nicolini, Marcella, and Laura Resmini. 2007. "Productivity Spillovers and Multinational Enterprises: In Search of a Spatial Dimension." DYNREG Working Paper 10, Economic and Social Research Institute, Dublin.

Nolan, Peter, Jin Zhang, and Chunhang Liu. 2008. "The Global Business Revolution, the Cascade Effect, and the Challenge for Firms from Developing Countries." *Cambridge Journal of Economics* 32 (1): 29–47.

Nordhaus, William D. 2008. "Baumol's Diseases: A Macroeconomic Perspective." *B.E. Journal of Macroeconomics* 8 (1): 1–37.

Obstfeld, Maurice, and Alan M. Taylor. 2003. "Globalization and Capital Markets." In *Globalization in Historical Perspective*, ed. Michael D. Bordo, Alan M. Taylor, and Jeffrey G. Williamson, 121–83. Cambridge, MA: National Bureau of Economic Research.

O'Cléireacáin, Carol. 1997. "The Private Economy and the Public Budget of New York City." In *The City and the World: New York's Global Future*, ed. Margaret E. Crahan and Alberto Vourvoulias-Bush, 22–38. New York: Council on Foreign Relations.

O'Flaherty, Brendan. 2005. *City Economics*. Cambridge, MA: Harvard University Press.

OECD (Organisation for Economic Co-operation and Development). 2008. *OECD Reviews of Regional Innovation: North of England, U.K.* Paris: OECD.

Office of the Third National Industrial Census. 1997. *The Data of the Third National Industrial Census of the People's Republic of China in 1995*. Beijing: China Statistics Press.

Oliner, Stephen D., and Daniel E. Sichel. 2000. "The Resurgence of Growth in the Late 1990s: Is Information Technology the Story?" *Journal of Economic Perspectives* 14 (4): 3–22.

Orhangazi, Özgür. 2008. "Financialisation and Capital Accumulation in the Non-financial Corporate Sector: A Theoretical and Empirical Investigation on the U.S. Economy: 1973–2003." *Cambridge Journal of Economics* 32 (6): 863–86.

Overman, Henry G., and Anthony J. Venables. 2005. "Cities in the Developing World." CEPR Discussion Paper 0695, Centre for Economic Policy Research, London.

Pan, Zuohong, and Fan Zhang. 2002. "Urban Productivity in China." *Urban Studies* 39 (12): 2267–81.

Parker, Simon. 2007. "Interview: Ken Livingstone." *Prospect Magazine* (133). http://www.prospectmagazine.co.uk/2007/04/interviewkenlivingstone/.

Patten, Lord. 2006. "Europe Pays the Price for Spending Less." *Nature* 441 (7094): 691–93.

Pearlstein, Steven. 2009. "California's Wipeout Economy." *Washington Post*, March 25.

Peri, Giovanni, and Dieter Urban. 2006. "Catching-Up to Foreign Technology? Evidence on the "Veblen-Gerschenkron" Effect of Foreign Investments." *Regional Science and Urban Economics* 36 (1): 72–98.

Perkins, Dwight H., and Shahid Yusuf. 1984. *Rural Development in China*. Baltimore, MD: Johns Hopkins Press.

Phillips, Fred. 2008. "Change in Socio-technical Systems: Researching the Multis, the Biggers, and the More Connecteds." *Technological Forecasting and Social Change* 75 (5): 721–34.

Pietrobelli, Carlo, and Federica Saliola. 2008. "Power Relationships along the Value Chain: Multinational Firms, Global Buyers, and Performance of Local Suppliers." *Cambridge Journal of Economics* 32 (6): 947–62.

Pilkington, Alan, Linda L. Lee, Casey K. Chan, and Seeram Ramakrishna. 2009. "Defining Key Inventors: A Comparison of Fuel Cell and Nanotechnology Industries." *Technological Forecasting and Social Change* 76 (1): 118–27.

Pisano, Gary P. 2006. "Can Science Be a Business? Lessons from Biotech." *Harvard Business Review* (October): 114–25.

Popp, David, Richard G. Newell, and Adam B. Jaffe. 2009. "Energy, the Environment, and Technological Change." NBER Working Paper 14832, National Bureau of Economic Research, Cambridge, MA.

Porter, Michael E. 2008a. "Clusters, Innovation, and Competitiveness: New Findings and Implications for Policy." Institute for Strategy and Competitiveness, Cambridge, MA.

———. 2008b. "The Five Competitive Forces That Shape Strategy." *Harvard Business Review* 86 (1): 78–93.

Porter, Michael E., and Elizabeth Olmsted Teisberg. 2006. *Redefining Health Care: Creating Value-Based Competition on Results.* Cambridge, MA: Harvard Business School Press.

Prahalad, C. K., and M. S. Krishnan. 2008. *The New Age of Innovation: Driving Cocreated Value through Global Networks.* New York: McGraw-Hill.

PricewaterhouseCoopers. 2007. "Largest City Economies in the World in 2005 and 2020." PricewaterhouseCoopers, New York.

Puri, Manju, and Rebecca Zarutskie. 2008. "On the Lifecycle Dynamics of Venture-Capital- and Non-Venture-Capital-Financed Firms." NBER Working Paper 14250, National Bureau of Economic Research, Cambridge, MA.

Quigley, John M. 2008. "Urbanization, Agglomeration, and Economic Development." Commission on Growth and Development Working Paper Series 19, World Bank, Washington, DC.

Quintás, María A., Xosé H. Vázquez, José M. Garcia, and Gloria Caballero. 2008. "Geographical Amplitude in the International Generation of Technology: Present Situation and Business Determinants." *Research Policy* 37 (8): 1371–81.

Racine, Jean-Louis, Itzhak Goldberg, John Gabriel Goddard, Smita Kurikose, and Natasha Kapil. 2009. "Restructuring of Research and Development Institutes in Europe and Central Asia." World Bank, Washington, DC.

Rauch, James E., and Vitor Trindade. 2002. "Ethnic Chinese Networks in International Trade." *Review of Economics and Statistics* 84 (1): 116–30.

Reader, John. 2006. *Cities.* New York: Grove Press.

"Red Flags." 2009. *Economist*, May 28.

Rigby, Darrell, and Chris Zook. 2002. "Open-Market Innovation." *Harvard Business Review* 80 (10): 80–89.

Roberts, Dexter. 2009. "As Factories Fail, So Does Business Law." *BusinessWeek*, April 2.

Rogers, Richard. 1997. *Cities for a Small Planet: Reith Lectures.* London: Faber & Faber.

Romer, Paul. 1993. "Ideas Gaps and Object Gaps in Economic Development." *Journal of Monetary Economics* 32 (3): 543–73.

Rongping, Mu, and Qu Wan. 2008. "The Development of Science and Technology in China: A Comparison with India and the United States." *Technology in Society* 30 (3–4): 319–29.

Rosen, Rae D., and Reagan Murray. 1997. "Opening Doors: Access to the Global Market for Financial Sectors." In *The City and the World: New York's Global Future*, ed. Margaret E. Crahan and Alberto Vourvoulias-Bush, 39–50. New York: Council on Foreign Relations.

Rosenberg, Nathan. 2003. "America's Entrepreneurial Universities." In *The Emergence of Entrepreneurship Policy: Governance, Start-Ups, and Growth in the U.S. Knowledge Economy*, ed. David M. Hart, 113–37. Cambridge, U.K.: Cambridge University Press.

Rosenstein-Rodan, Paul N. 1943. "Problems of Industrialization of Eastern and South-Eastern Europe." *Economic Journal* 53 (210–211): 202–11.

Rosenthal, Stuart S., and William C. Strange. 2004. "Evidence on the Nature and Sources of Agglomeration Economics." In *Handbook of Regional and Urban Economics*, ed. J. Vernon Henderson and Jacques-François Thisse, 2119–71. Amsterdam: North-Holland.

———. Forthcoming. "Small Establishments/Big Effects: Agglomeration, Industrial Organization and Entrepreneurship." In *The Economics of Agglomeration*, ed. Edward L. Glaeser. Chicago: University of Chicago Press.

Rotman, David. 2009. "Can Technology Save the Economy?" *Technology Review* 112 (3). http://www.technologyreview.com/biotech/22452/.

Rubin, Jeff. 2009. *Why Your World Is about to Get a Whole Lot Smaller: Oil and the End of Globalization*. New York: Random House.

Runiewicz-Wardyn, Malgorzata, ed. 2008. *Knowledge-Based Economy: As Factor of Competitiveness and Economic Growth*. Warsaw: Academic and Professional Press.

Saggi, Kamal. 2006. "Foreign Direct Investment, Linkages, and Technology Spillovers." In *Global Integration and Technology Transfer*, ed. Bernard Hoekman and Beata Smarzynska Javorcik, 51–65. Washington, DC: World Bank.

Sakakibara, Mariko. 1997. "Evaluating Government-Sponsored R&D Consortia in Japan: Who Benefits and How?" *Research Policy* 26 (4–5): 447–73.

———. 2001. "Cooperative Research and Development: Who Participates and in Which Industries Do Projects Take Place?" *Research Policy* 30 (7): 993–1018.

Sakakibara, Mariko, and Dong-Sung Cho. 2002. "Cooperative R&D in Japan and Korea: A Comparison of Industrial Policy." *Research Policy* 31 (5): 673–92.

Salmi, Jamil. 2009. *The Challenges of Establishing World-Class Universities*. Washington, DC: World Bank.

Sassen, Saskia. 1991. *The Global City: New York, London, Tokyo*. Princeton, NJ: Princeton University Press.

Schaede, Ulrike. 2008. *Choose and Focus: Japanese Business Strategies for the 21st Century*. Ithaca, NY: Cornell University Press.

Scheck, Justin, and Paul Glader. 2009. "R&D Spending Holds Steady in Slump." *Wall Street Journal*, April 6.

Schoar, Antoinette. 2009. "The Divide between Subsistence and Transformational Entrepreneurship." NBER Working Paper 14861, National Bureau of Economic Research, Cambridge, MA.

Schoors, Koen, and Bartoldus van der Tol. 2002. "Foreign Direct Investment Spillovers within and between Sectors: Evidence from Hungarian Data." Department of Economics Working Paper 157, Ghent University, Belgium.

Schott, Peter K. 2006. "The Relative Sophistication of Chinese Exports." NBER Working Paper 12173, National Bureau of Economic Research, Cambridge, MA.

"Science Wins $21 Billion Boost as Stimulus Package Becomes Law." 2009. *Science* 323 (5917): 992–93.

Scott, Allen J. 2001a. *Global City Regions*. Oxford, U.K.: Oxford University Press.

———. 2001b. "Globalization and the Rise of City-Regions." *European Planning Studies* 9 (7): 813–26.

Sener, Fuat, and Laixun Zhao. 2009. "Globalization, R&D, and the iPod Cycle." *Journal of International Economics* 77 (1): 101–8.

Sergeant, Harriet. 1998. *Shanghai.* London: John Murray.

Shanghai Municipal Statistics Bureau. 1994. *Shanghai Statistical Yearbook 1994.* Beijing: China Statistics Press.

———. 1995. *Shanghai Statistical Yearbook 1995.* Beijing: China Statistics Press.

———. 2001. *Shanghai Statistical Yearbook 2001.* Beijing: China Statistics Press.

———. 2002. *Shanghai Statistical Yearbook 2002.* Beijing: China Statistics Press.

———. 2007. *Shanghai Statistical Yearbook 2007.* Beijing: China Statistics Press.

———. 2008. *Shanghai Statistical Yearbook 2008.* Beijing: China Statistics Press.

Shanghai Science and Technology Commission. 2007. *Shanghai Science and Technology Yearbook 2007.* Shanghai, China: Shanghai Science and Technology Press.

Shanghai Venture Capital Association. 2008. *Shanghai Venture Capital Industry Investigation Report, 2007.* Shanghai, China: Shanghai Venture Capital Association.

"Shanghigh." 2009. *Financial Times,* April 3.

Sigurdson, Jon. 2005. *Technological Superpower China.* Northampton, MA: Edward Elgar.

———. 2008. "Ningbo and Dalian: Patterns of Science and Technology Development." In *China's Science and Technology Sector and the Forces of Globalization,* ed. Elspeth Thomson and Jon Sigurdson, 143–72. Singapore: World Scientific Publishing.

Simon, Denis Fred. 2007. "Whither Foreign R&D in China: Some Concluding Thoughts on Chinese Innovation." *Asia Pacific Business Review* 13 (3): 471–80.

Simon, Denis Fred, and Cong Cao. 2008. "China's Emerging Science and Technology Talent Pool: A Quantitative and Qualitative Assessment." In *Greater China's Quest for Innovation,* ed. Henry S. Rowen, Marguerite Gong Hancock, and William F. Miller, 181–96. Stanford, CA: Walter H. Shorenstein Asia-Pacific Research Center.

———. 2009. *China's Emerging Technological Edge.* New York: Cambridge University Press.

Smeets, Roger. 2008. "Collecting the Pieces of the FDI Knowledge Spillovers Puzzle." *World Bank Research Observer* 23 (2): 107–38.

Smilor, Raymond, Niall O'Donnell, Gregory Stein, and Robert Welborn. 2005. "The Research University and the Development of High Technology Centers in the U.S." Presented at the Conference on University Industry Linkages in Metropolitan Areas in Asia, Washington, DC, November 17.

Smitka, Michael J. 1991. *Subcontracting in the Japanese Automobile Industry.* New York: Columbia University Press.

Spear, Steven. 2008. *Chasing the Rabbit: How Market Leaders Outdistance the Competition and How Great Companies Can Catch Up and Win.* New York: McGraw-Hill.

Squicciarini, Mariagrazia. 2008. "Science Parks' Tenants versus Out-of-Park Firms: Who Innovates More? A Duration Model." *Journal of Technology Transfer* 33 (1): 45–71.

Statistical Research and Training Institute. 2002. *Japan Statistical Yearbook 2002.* Tokyo: Statistics Bureau, Ministry of Internal Affairs and Communication.

Stephan, Paula E. 2009. "The 'I's' Have It: Immigration and Innovation, the Perspective from Academe." National Bureau of Economic Research Conference on Research Innovation Policy and the Economy, Washington, DC.

Stewart, Thomas A., and Anand P. Raman. 2007. "Lessons from Toyota's Long Drive." *Harvard Business Review* 85 (7–8): 74–83.

Sturgeon, Timothy J. 2000. "How Silicon Valley Came to Be." In *Understanding Silicon Valley: Anatomy of an Entrepreneurial Region*, ed. Martin Kenney, 15–47. Stanford, CA: Stanford University Press.

Sturgeon, Timothy J., Johannes Van Biesebroeck, and Gary Gereffi. 2008. "Value Chains, Networks, and Clusters: Reframing the Global Automotive Industry." *Journal of Economic Geography* 8 (3): 297–321.

Su, Yu-Shan, and Ling-Chun Hung. 2009. "Spontaneous vs. Policy-Driven: The Origin and Evolution of the Biotechnology Cluster." *Technological Forecasting and Social Change* 76 (5): 608–19.

Subler, Jason. 2008. "China's Landmark Antimonopoly Law Finally Taking Effect." *International Herald Tribune*, July 31.

Summers, Lawrence H. 2004. "Why Universities Endure." *Harvard Magazine* 107 (2): 72.

Sun, Yifei, Debin Du, and Li Huang. 2006. "Foreign R&D in Developing Countries: Empirical Evidence from Shanghai, China." *China Review* 6 (1): 67–91.

Sun, Yifei, and Ke Wen. 2007a. "Country Relational Distance, Organizational Power, and R&D Managers: Understanding Environmental Challenges for Foreign R&D in China." *Asia Pacific Business Review* 13 (3): 425–49.

———. 2007b. "Uncertainties, Imitative Behaviours, and Foreign R&D Location: Explaining the Over-concentration of Foreign R&D in Beijing and Shanghai within China." *Asia Pacific Business Review* 13 (3): 405–24.

Tabeta, Shunsuke. 2009. "China Sees Opening in Electric Car Sector." *Nikkei Weekly*, June 15.

Tajima, Toshio, and Shinsuke Furuya, eds. 2008. *Offshore Development, Staffing Service, and Vocational Education in China's Software Industry*. Tokyo: Institute of Social Science, University of Tokyo.

Tobin, James. 1965. "Money and Economic Growth." *Econometrica* 33 (4): 671–84.

Tuan, Chyau, and Linda Fung-Yee Ng. 2007. "The Place of FDI in China's Regional Economic Development: Emergence of the Globalized Delta Economies." *Journal of Asian Economics* 18 (2): 348–64.

Tucker, Sundeep. 2008. "InBev Ruling Sparks Fears for M&A in China." *Financial Times*, December 1.

Tucker, Sundeep, Peter Smith, and Jamil Anderlini. 2009. "Beijing Scuppers $2.4bn Coke Move." *Financial Times*, March 19.

Tucker, Sundeep, and Patti Waldmeir. 2008. "Deals on Hold? Business Awaits the Impact of Asia's New Competition Regimes." *Financial Times*, July 29.

UNCTAD (United Nations Conference on Trade and Development). 2005. *World Investment Report 2005*. New York: United Nations.

UN-HABITAT (United Nations Human Settlements Programme). 2008. *State of the World Cities 2008/2009: Harmonious Cities*. London: UN-HABITAT.

"Urban Competitiveness." 2008. *Economist*, August 16.

U.S. Census Bureau. 2008. *Statistical Abstract of the United States: 2008*. Washington, DC: U.S. Department of Commerce, Bureau of the Census.

Vance, Ashlee. 2008. "Frontiers Expand for Super-Fast Computers." *International Herald Tribune*, April 19.

van der Sluis, Justin, Mirjam van Praag, and Wim Vijverberg. 2008. "Education and Entrepreneurship Selection and Performance: A Review of the Empirical Literature." *Journal of Economic Surveys* 22 (5): 795–841.

Venables, Anthony J., and Patricia Rice. 2005. "Spatial Determinants of Productivity: Analysis for the Regions of Great Britain." CEPR Discussion Paper 4527, Centre for Economic Policy Research, London.

Vernon, Raymond. 1979. "The Product Cycle Hypothesis in a New International Environment." *Oxford Bulletin of Economics and Statistics* 41 (4): 255–67.

Veugelers, Reinhilde. 2009. "A Lifeline for Europe's Young Radical Innovators." Bruegel Policy Brief 2009/01, Breugel, Brussels. http://www.bruegel.org/uploads/tx_btbbreugel/pb_2009-01_YICs.pdf.

Waldmeir, Patti. 2009. "Chinese Electric Car Group Speeds Up U.S. Plans." *Financial Times*, September 1.

Wadhwa, Vivek, Gary Gereffi, Ben Rising, and Ryan Ong. 2007. "Where the Engineers Are." *Issues in Science and Technology* 23 (3): 73–85.

Wang, Bing, and Jun Ma. 2007. "Collaborative R&D: Intellectual Property Rights between Tsinghua University and Multinational Companies." *Journal of Technology Transfer* 32 (4): 457–74.

Wang, Jici, and Xin Tong. 2005. "Sustaining Urban Growth through Innovative Capacity: Beijing and Shanghai in Comparison." Policy Research Working Paper 3545, World Bank, Washington, DC.

Wang, Ying. 2009. "More Teaching Jobs for Graduates." *China Daily*, March 20.

Ward, Andrew. 2007. "Where Winners Are Fast Rather Than Large." *Financial Times*, March 27.

Wei, Shang-Jin. 1993. "Open Door Policy and China's Rapid Growth: Evidence from City-Level Data." NBER Working Paper 4602, National Bureau of Economic Research, Cambridge, MA.

Wei, Yingqi, and Xiaming Liu. 2006. "Productivity Spillovers from R&D, Exports, and FDI in China's Manufacturing Sector." *Journal of International Business Studies* 37 (4): 544–57.

Wei, Yingqi, Xiaming Liu, and Chengang Wang. 2008. "Mutual Productivity Spillovers between Foreign and Local Firms in China." *Cambridge Journal of Economics* 32 (4): 609–31.

West, Darrell M., and Edward Alan Miller. 2009. *Digital Medicine: Health Care in the Internet Era*. Washington, DC: Brookings Institution Press.

Whyte, William H. 2009. *City: Rediscovering the Center*. Philadelphia: University of Pennsylvania Press.

Wien, Byron. 2008. "America's Decline Will Not Be Easily Reversed." *Financial Times*, August 11.

Wieser, Robert. 2005. "Research and Development Productivity and Spillovers: Empirical Evidence at the Firm Level." *Journal of Economic Surveys* 19 (4): 587–621.

Williamson, Peter, and Ming Zeng. 2009. "Value-for-Money Strategies for Recessionary Times." *Harvard Business Review* (March): 66–74.

World Bank. 2008a. *Accelerating Catch-Up: Tertiary Education for Growth in Sub-Saharan Africa*. Washington, DC: World Bank.

———. 2008b. "Mid-Term Evaluation of China's 11th Five Year Plan." World Bank, Washington, DC.

———. 2008c. *World Development Indicators 2008*. Washington, DC: World Bank.

———. 2009a. *Addressing China's Water Scarcity*. Washington, DC: World Bank.

———. 2009b. "China: Reducing Inequality and Promoting Lagging Region Development in Guangdong." World Bank, Washington, DC.

———. 2009c. *World Development Report 2009: Reshaping Economic Geography*. Washington, DC: World Bank.

World Bank Institute. 2007. *Building Knowledge Economies: Advanced Strategies for Development*. Washington, DC: World Bank.

"World's Most Admired Companies." 2009. *Fortune*, March 16.

"World's Most Innovative Companies, The." 2006. *BusinessWeek*, April 24.

Wright, Robert. 2007a. "A Failure to Keep Up with the Times." *Financial Times*, March 27.

———. 2007b. "A Very Solid Foundation from Which to Grow." *Financial Times*, March 27.

WTO (World Trade Organization). 2009. "WTO Sees 9% Global Trade Decline in 2009 as Recession Strikes." Press Release 554, WTO, Geneva.

Wu, Weiping. 2007. "Cultivating Research Universities and Industrial Linkages: The Case of Shanghai." *World Development* 35 (6): 1075–93.

Xin, Hao, and Dennis Normile. 2008. "Gunning for the Ivy League." *Science* 319 (5860): 148–51.

Xin, Hao, and Richard Stone. 2008. "Q&A: China's Scientist Premier." *Science* 322 (5900): 362–64.

Xu, Ang. 2008. "China Looks Abroad: Changing Directions in International Science." *Minerva* 46 (1): 37–51.

Xue, Lan. 2006a. "The Role of Universities in China's Economic Development: A National Innovation System Perspective." Presented at the Pan Asia Conference: Challenges of Economic Policy Reform in Asia, Stanford Center for International Development, Stanford, CA, June 1–3.

———. 2006b. "Universities in China's National Innovation System." Presented at the United Nations Educational, Scientific, and Cultural Organization's online Forum on Higher Education, Research, and Knowledge, November 27–30.

Yang, Chih-Hai, Kazuyuki Motohashi, and Jong-Rong Chen. 2009. "Are New Technology-Based Firms Located on Science Parks Really More Innovative? Evidence from Taiwan." *Research Policy* 38 (1): 77–85.

Yao, Yao, and Yuemin Ning. 2008. "An Analysis of the Developing Level and Spatial Differences of Manufacturing in the Yangtze River Delta." *E-Journal of China Urban Studies* 3 (2): 57–64.

Yatsko, Pamela. 2001. *New Shanghai: The Rocky Rebirth of China's Legendary City*. New York: John Wiley & Sons.

Yeandle, Mark, Jeremy Horne, Nick Danev, and Alexander Knapp. 2009. *The Global Financial Centres Index*. London: City of London.

Yusuf, Shahid. 2007. "Promise and Peril: Regional Development in China's Pearl River Delta and the Northeast." In *Development on the Ground: Clusters, Networks, and Regions in Emerging Economies*, ed. Allen J. Scott and Gioacchino Garofoli, 117–44. New York: Routledge.

———. 2009a. *Development Economics through the Decades: A Critical Look at 30 Years of the World Development Report*. Washington, DC: World Bank.

———. 2009b. "Financial Innovation and Economic Performance." In *Innovation for Development and the Role of Government: A Perspective from the East Asia and Pacific Region*, ed. Qimiao Fan, Kouqing Li, Douglas Zhihua Zeng, Yang Dong, and Runzhong Peng, 53–70. Washington, DC: World Bank.

———. 2009c. "From Creativity to Innovation." *Technology in Society* 31 (1): 1–8.

Yusuf, Shahid, M. Anjum Altaf, Barry Eichengreen, Sudarshan Gooptu, Kaoru Nabeshima, Charles Kenny, Dwight H. Perkins, and Marc Shotten. 2003. *Innovative East Asia: The Future of Growth*. New York: Oxford University Press.

Yusuf, Shahid, and Kaoru Nabeshima. 2006a. *China's Development Priorities*. Washington, DC: World Bank.

———. 2006b. *Postindustrial East Asian Cities*. Palo Alto, CA: Stanford University Press.

———. 2007. *How Universities Promote Economic Growth*. Washington, DC: World Bank.

Yusuf, Shahid, Kaoru Nabeshima, and Dwight H. Perkins. 2005. *Under New Ownership: Privatizing China's State-Owned Enterprises*. Stanford, CA: Stanford University Press.

———. 2007. "China and India Reshape Global Industrial Geography." In *Dancing with Giants: China, India, and the Global Economy*, ed. L. Alan Winters and Shahid Yusuf, 35–66. Washington, DC: World Bank.

Yusuf, Shahid, Shuilin Wang, and Kaoru Nabeshima. 2009. "Fiscal Policies for Innovation." In *Innovation for Development and the Role of Government: A Perspective from the East Asia and Pacific Region*, ed. Qimiao Fan, Kouqing Li, Douglas Zhihua Zeng, Yang Dong, and Runzhong Peng, 149–80. Washington, DC: World Bank.

Yusuf, Shahid, and Weiping Wu. 1997. *The Dynamics of Urban Growth in Three Chinese Cities*. Washington, DC: Oxford University Press.

Zeng, Ming, and Peter Williamson. 2007. *Dragons at Your Door: How Chinese Cost Innovation Is Disrupting Global Competition*. Cambridge, MA: Harvard Business School Press.

Zhang, Chunlin, Douglas Zhihua Zeng, William Peter Mako, and James Seward. 2009. *Promoting Enterprise-Led Innovation*. Washington, DC: World Bank.

Zhao, Jimin. 2006. "Whither the Car? China's Automobile Industry and Cleaner Vehicle Technologies." *Development and Change* 37 (1): 121–44.

Zhao, Weilin, Chihiro Watanabe, and Charla Griffy-Brown. 2009. "Competitive Advantage in an Industry Cluster: The Case of Dalian Software Park in China." *Technology in Society* 31 (2): 139–49.

Zheng, Jinghai, Arne Bigsten, and Angang Hu. 2009. "Can China's Growth Be Sustained? A Productivity Perspective." *Law, Finance, and Economic Growth in China* 37 (4): 874–88.

Zheng, Siqi, Matthew E. Kahn, and Hongyu Liu. 2009. "Towards a System of Open Cities in China: Home Prices, FDI Flows, and Air Quality in 35 Major Cities." NBER Working Paper 14751, National Bureau of Economic Research, Cambridge, MA.

Zhou, Yu. 2008. *The Inside Story of China's High-Tech Industry: Making Silicon Valley in Beijing.* New York: Rowman & Littlefield.

Zhu, Zuoyan, and Gong Xu. 2008. "Basic Research: Its Impact on China's Future." *Technology in Society* 30: 293–98.

Zucker, Lynne G., and Michael R. Darby. 2007. "Star Scientists, Innovation, and Regional and National Immigration." NBER Working Paper 13547, National Bureau of Economic Research, Cambridge, MA.

Index

Figures, notes, and tables are indicated by *f*, *n*, and *t*, respectively.